Wealth by Association

Wealth by Association

Global Prosperity Through Market Unification

John C. Edmunds and John E. Marthinsen

Westport, Connecticut
London

332.45
E24 w

Library of Congress Cataloging-in-Publication Data

Edmunds, John C., 1947–
    Wealth by association : global prosperity through market unification / John C. Edmunds and John E. Marthinsen
        p. cm.
    Includes bibliographical references and index.
    ISBN 1–56720–529–1 (alk. paper)
    1. Monetary unions. 2. Wealth. 3. Economic and Monetary Union. 4. International economic integration. I. Marthinsen, John E. II. Title.
    HG3894 E36 2003
    332.4′5—dc21   2002069696

British Library Cataloguing in Publication Data is available.

Library of Congress Catalog Card Number: 2002069696
ISBN: 1–56720–529–1

First published in 2003

Praeger Publishers, 88 Post Road West, Westport, CT 06881
An imprint of Greenwood Publishing Group, Inc.
www.praeger.com

Printed in the United States of America

The paper used in this book complies with the Permanent Paper Standard issued by the National Information Standards Organization (Z39.48–1984).

10   9   8   7   6   5   4   3   2   1

We dedicate this book to the visionaries who launched the economic convergence process that is currently in progress around the world. Above all, these futurists were able to see above and beyond a world that was handicapped by heavy protectionism, myopic nationalism, and costly, recurring wars, to one where peace, freedom of movement, rising living standards for all, and open borders prevailed.

At a more personal level, we dedicate this book to a few very special individuals who have taught us and provided inspiration to us in many profound and meaningful ways. To Craig Marthinsen, for his kindness, generosity, as well as personal and professional accomplishments; to Marc Lindenberg, for his tenacity, leadership, and professional accomplishments; and to Carol Hamilton for her determination and loyalty, we wish to express our sincerest thanks.

Finally, we wish to thank the William F. Glavin Center for Global Management, Babson College Board of Research, and Susan Chern for their support in formatting the final version of this paper so that it conformed to the publication guidelines of the Greenwood Publishing Group. This help was delivered quickly and professionally.

Contents

Contents

Exhibits and Tables

EXHIBITS

TABLES

Preface

The main theme of this book is that enormous wealth materializes when financial markets unify. The largest, most immediate, and most unexpected source of this newly created wealth is the gain in market values from reduced cross-border risk. We believe that, once a group of countries adopts a common currency, their union acts like a huge economic magnet that eventually draws in other nations and can bestow benefits on them (oftentimes before they formally join). By contrast, those countries that decide not to become members can suffer a penalty that becomes more expensive the longer they stay out of the union.

A subtheme of this book is that currency unification also increases the potential for growth in real gross domestic product (GDP)[1] and prosperity. The latent potential increase in world output and wealth that currency unification can unshackle is staggering. This book explores the potential increases in output for different countries and regions and also explains how the currency unification process can be an accelerant to increased real growth.

Our line of reasoning does not focus on the benefits of free trade in goods and services or the advantages of unrestricted capital flows. Instead, we argue that all assets quickly become more valuable when the array of exchange rate–related risks disappears. Among the most important risks that currency unification reduces or eliminates are foreign exchange uncertainty, inflation differentials, competitive devaluations, and protectionism in financial services.

The beneficial effect of reduced risk is the centerpiece of our analysis, and it will be developed fully by means of wide-ranging examples and illustrations, with the stages of unification laid out in sequence. We compute step-by-step the potential gains so the reader can understand both the source and size of value creation. Our analysis illustrates that a unification does not need to encompass a large number of countries initially to create value; it can start with a pair of countries and lead to the same beneficial result as a more ambitious scheme to unify many currencies all at once. A point in favor of the gradualist approach is that benefits accrue from the first stages onward. There is less need to align a constellation of complicated political agreements. The threshold requirements for a mutually advantageous union are low because of the multitude of possible bilateral or trilateral arrangements.

The exemplar of currency unification is the European Monetary Union (EMU). Direct gains from the EMU accrued suddenly, as if by magic, and *have already exceeded* $15 trillion. Gains of similar and greater magnitude are easily within reach by Asia and Latin America.

Prior to the European unification, experts debated what the gains would be, and some questioned whether there would be net gains at all. The debate concentrated on economic, political, and emotional issues. Among the most commonly cited economic disadvantages of a monetary union were the loss of monetary and, as seen recently with Ireland, fiscal autonomy, the abdication of exchange-rate policies, and the increased need to compete via productivity differences. Among the most commonly cited economic gains were cost reductions and increased competition that came from streamlining cash management systems, specialization, economies of scale, rationalization, mergers and acquisitions, the elimination of intra-EMU hedging costs, reduced transactions costs (that is, bid–ask spreads), and lower borrowing costs. As well, large potential benefits were to be derived from enhanced monetary policy credibility and broader capital markets.

Very few of the experts took into account what proved to be the biggest gain, by far, namely, the gains in the market values of both financial assets and real assets. Financial asset gains were plainly visible after European bond and share markets rallied. Gains in the values of real property, intellectual property, and human capital, though often not as evident, were also immense.

This book is aimed at a worldwide audience, because its analysis applies to all the major regional economies. The arguments are accessible to the general reader and do not require extensive knowledge of finance and economics. Readers interested in financial markets, currency regimes, and international affairs will find the book provocative and useful. Readers interested in investments, finance, international economics, international politics, and regional affairs will find relevant computations here that will show how key relationships are evolving.

Action recommendations for investors and policy makers form an important capstone to our analysis. We illustrate analytical methods that investors, including professional money managers, can use to estimate potential gains, and we lay out the steps they must take to profit from currency unification and describe how to determine when the timing is right to take action. We also describe how the collective efforts of investors to purchase assets before their prices rise will give a foretaste of the gains to come and will give market participants an early ratification that currency unification is the right policy.

NOTE

1. For the descriptive portion of this book, the terms GDP (gross domestic product) and GNP (gross national product) are used interchangeably, but the text is careful to distinguish between GDP and GNP for data cited from published sources. Typically, the difference between a nation's GDP and GNP is very small.

Chapter 1

Introduction

The Maastricht meeting held in December 1991, in the town of Maastricht in the Netherlands, did not get the advance fanfare that it merited. There had been countless earlier meetings of European heads of state and finance ministers. One more meeting hardly registered in the minds of European newspaper readers. The press was tossing around stories about a pie-in-the-sky plan to unify the European currencies, but readers were skeptical, because they had heard these ideas before. For many years, there had been one scheme after another to lock the European currencies into a straitjacket so that they would not fluctuate vis-à-vis one another and damage trade within the European Community (EC). These schemes all sought to fuse the exchange rates in Europe, like logs tied together to form a raft, which would then float versus the dollar and the yen.

Every one of these schemes had been announced with proper solemnity and pomp, and they were touted as the solution to the EC's currency instabilities. Some of the schemes had fetching names such as "the snake in the tunnel," but, in the end, each one failed in its own way, even if its goals had been modest. Currencies always broke out of their exchange rate couplings when things went awry, and they did so at the most damaging times, at moments glowing with an aura of high drama. The "lashes" that joined the currencies looked strong but always gave way when the stresses intensified. When that happened, the damage was real, because the day-to-day affairs of ordinary citizens were disrupted.

The abandonment of a currency union or withdrawal of a country from a currency union was often more damaging than most people realized. Both of them disrupted flows of trade and the profitability of each country's installed base of manufacturing and service capacity. Both of them slowed employment growth and shattered the dreams of would-be entrepreneurs. Both of them dealt serious blows to the prices of financial assets, and in a less immediate fashion hurt the prices of all assets.

The threat of disbandment and currency depreciation also caused damage. For nations under pressure to devalue, buyers of financial assets had to be wary of the losses they might suffer in the future, so they held back, refusing to pay current market prices for financial assets. Foreign buyers had to be especially cautious, because the full effect of devaluation would fall immediately on them, and because they knew their foreign counterparts would be thinking along the same cautious lines. The threat of devaluation compressed the prices of immobile real assets—such as, houses, farms, commercial property, and unincorporated businesses—to levels that could be supported by local buyers, because when the time came to sell, the only buyers might be locals.

The Maastricht meeting began like the others before it had: National spokespersons laid out the pressure points and nonnegotiable positions of their respective governments. The treaty appeared likely to get watered down or shelved completely. Then, at the very last minute, well after all the newspapers had all printed their morning editions, the prime ministers set aside their bargaining points, dropped their demands, signed the treaty, and then went home to their much-neglected beds.

Their *volte-face* was striking and caught the press by surprise. There had been no prior indication that the treaty was going to pass the gauntlet of conflicting demands and caveats. Yet, at the last minute, the prime ministers signed it, putting aside all their objections and blurring all the lines in the sand they had drawn earlier.

Reaction to the signing was muted and skeptical. In the days and weeks following the signing, many of our colleagues and business associates in Europe discounted the importance of the treaty. They scoffed at the idea that the voters of the individual countries would approve it. Then, as an afterthought, they asserted that the currencies of Europe might someday be united, but certainly not as early as 1999. To them, the fast-track alternative to currency unification was obviously preposterous.

The years immediately following the Maastricht Treaty gave credence to the views of cynics and skeptics. As Table 1.1 shows, from 1993 to 1996, at the most two of the 14 European Union (EU) countries met all the Maastricht conditions for membership in the European Monetary Union (EMU). But the cynics and skeptics were wrong. European currency unification triumphed over the impediments that had always prevented it. To be sure, Sweden and England withdrew from the exchange rate agreement, and therefore, did not qualify to join. There was the Danish vote against the treaty, and a very close, but favorable, vote in France. Only Greece did not meet the economic and exchange rate criteria. Nevertheless, after 1996, the consensus in favor of unification strengthened and solidified so that the only remaining questions were what the new currency would be called, which countries would qualify to join the EMU in the first round, and what the exchange rates would be in May 1998 when they were to be frozen for all time.

Table 1.1
Countries Meeting the Maastricht Treaty Conditions

Year	# Countries	Countries Qualifying
1993	0	None
1994	2	Germany & Luxembourg
1995	2	Germany & Luxembourg
1996	1	Luxembourg
1997	14	All EU nations qualified except Greece
1998	14	All EU nations qualified except Greece

The triumph, speed, and completeness of unification were breathtaking and almost inconceivable. How could something so monumental catch so many by surprise? One explanation is that the gains from currency unification in Europe had grossly outgrown the defendable benefits of local control over currencies, and as a result, the balance of power shifted in favor of unification. Evidence of these huge net gains had been clear to many observers for years, but enough grassroots support had to coalesce for national leaders to be jogged to act.

Our views on the net benefits of currency unification were dominated increasingly by the potential wealth effects that could be realized by increasing the value of Europe's new and existing asset base. Reduced risk meant lower interest rates and higher asset values. Business people and financial experts in Europe must have recognized how much more their existing assets would be worth after currency unification. For some of the EU nations, the government debt alone was already greater than 100% of their annual gross domestic products (GDP). Rough estimates of these nations' financial asset values were commonly known, and it did not take a financial expert to realize that the gains from currency unification could amount to at least 20% of annual GDP. These enormous gains alone could overwhelm the losses nations would suffer from giving up their separate local currencies.

What kept the currency unification process rolling at top speed was the rise in securities prices. As investors began to accept that devaluations were a thing of the past, the prices of financial assets rose. There were setbacks in 1992 when the Danes voted not to approve the Maastricht Treaty and when the United Kingdom, Ireland, Spain, Portugal, and Italy were forced to devalue. Nevertheless, by 1995 the rally in bond and stock markets was underway, and the trickle of capital gains turned into a torrent. The aggregate amount of stock market value created between year-end 1994 and year-end 1998 was $2.7 trillion, excluding the United Kingdom,

Exhibit 1.1
Annual Compound Growth Rates of Stock Market Capitalization, 1994–1998

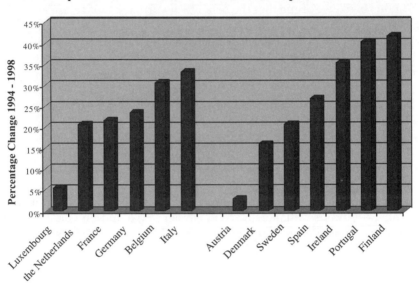

and $3.9 trillion when the United Kingdom was included. It quickly became apparent that the gains were going to be much greater than 20% of annual output; and for some nations, these total gains exceeded 200% of their GDP. Of the satellite countries, Finland, Portugal, Ireland, and Spain benefited most. Their securities markets experienced powerful rallies that carried the prices of domestic securities to levels that had never before been achieved. Members of the core six countries that benefited the most were Italy and Belgium. These were the two countries with the largest debt-to-GDP ratios. Italy was the only one of the core six that devalued its currency in 1992.[1] Exhibit 1.1 provides the annual compound growth rates of stock market capitalization for the countries grouped as the core six and the ones that joined later.

From May 1998 onward, the euro was a done deal. The countries that qualified for first-round membership in the EMU froze their exchange rates relative to one another, and their central banks signaled that they would vigorously resist any speculative raids against their currencies as the clock ticked toward the official launch date of January 1, 1999.

The path-breaking market unification gave rise to the dramatic boom in asset prices in the context of low inflation. The starting point for this book is the identification of economic gains that resulted from European monetary unification. Even the euro's most vocal advocates did not imagine how great its benefits would be, and their main (flow-based) justifications for creating a unified currency have turned out to be of secondary importance when evaluated against the increases in member countries' asset values.

In this book, we argue that the benefits of currency unification are low-hanging fruit that used to be overlooked but now are large, ripe, in plain sight, and easy to pick. Countries that are willing to work toward this mutually advantageous end can harvest this rich fruit. We compute how much value can be created if major regions such as Asia and Latin America unified their currencies. We also show several variants of the gains from currency unification for Asia and Latin America (for example, partial unification, dollarization, and full unification).

You might ask, A single currency for Asia? Have you lost your senses? To many observers, this idea is utopian and clearly out of the question. There are just too many nations with too many intractable technical and political impediments to currency unification. The mere idea of currency unification for Asia—with or without one or two of the region's major countries—sounds outlandish, but it is instructive and potentially profitable to consider currency unification for such a large and diverse region in order to see what the driving forces are and what obstacles would impede the progress of this institutional innovation.

We show how currency unification could start with just two nations and quickly attract neighboring countries. The virtue of a unified currency comes when supranational management brings increased policy credibility, because the pressures within any one country would not be strong enough to break the union's commitment to price stability and prudent supervision. As soon as a small group of Asian countries—for example, Thailand, Indonesia, and the Philippines—begins discussing currency unification seriously, the prices of assets in each of the three countries would begin to rise. The day the unification became a certainty these asset prices would rise even more. The full development of this argument may convince the reader that currency unification in Asia, though politically infeasible, would generate a massive windfall gain if it somehow became a reality.

A single currency for Latin America does not seem to be such a far-fetched idea. Three Latin countries have declared the U.S. dollar their official currency,[2] and several others have "dollarized" partially. For some types of transactions, the Americas are already a single-currency zone. This book does not argue that the remaining Latin American countries should "dollarize"; that is a decision every country has to make for itself. Instead, we compute the increase in asset values that would accompany dollarization for the purpose of making these nations aware of the huge opportunity cost of maintaining independent currencies. Our calculations have several variants, which are based on the level of unification that the region would reach. At this writing, Latin American countries have vastly heterogeneous degrees of financial market development and thus have big differences in their levels of securitization, but all of them have much lower degrees of securitization than the developed countries.

The wealth-generating effects of currency unification are not just one-time windfalls that are never repeated. After our analysis of the primary effects of currency unification, we describe dynamic processes of wealth creation that last beyond the initial quantum leap. The decline in a nation's currency risk unleashes an array of beneficial growth-generating forces, such as increased rate of output, intra-regional trade, specialization, and logistic efficiencies. These long-term benefits are the focus of some of our scenario calculations.

Rising output levels create higher productive asset valuations. This book includes spreadsheet models that simulate this feedback and develop trajectories for countries' GDP and the market value of their productive assets. The main spreadsheet model scrutinizes the linkages between growth of financial wealth and growth of the real economy. Beginning with a random disturbance that raises output and the market prices of financial assets, the model shows how the rise of financial wealth can raise the growth rate of variables that affect day-to-day well-being.

In this book, investors will find methodologies for predicting securities prices. The predictions apply to securities issued in regions with high unification potential—Asia and Latin America, in particular—and they emerge logically from the valuation parameters and calculations in our numerical illustrations and spreadsheets. The forecasts are for a hypothetical company's generic bonds and common stock, but our prediction methodology can easily be adapted and refined to specific bonds and stocks in each country. Readers are encouraged to use this book's framework as part of the information base for their long-term trading strategies. We feel that this framework is important for conceptualizing an important set of factors influencing investment decisions. Of course, sound trading strategies should include many aspects, undergo constant revision in light of the short-term and long-term outlook, and be congruent with the trader's individual situation and tolerance for risk.

To highlight the differentials in economic wealth among regions, the way they have changed over time, and their expected future trajectory, we provide a set of time series maps that resize nations by their financial asset values rather than their land mass. For example, we show how the relative sizes of the equities markets of North America, Europe, and Japan shifted dramatically from 1980 to 1990 to 2000. The visual differences brought out by the maps are indeed striking, and so are the magnitudes of dollars that the maps represent.

NOTES

1. "World Stock Markets," *Standard and Poor's Emerging Stock Market Factbook, 2001* (New York: McGraw-Hill, 2001), pp. 32–33. This is also the source of the data in Exhibit 1.1.

2. The three countries are Ecuador, El Salvador, and Panama.

Chapter 2

Financial Wealth Phenomenon

INTRODUCTION

A massive accumulation of financial assets has materialized like a super-tanker gliding quietly out of the fog. It has already grown large enough to rearrange preexisting orders of precedence and power relationships and to blot out much of the familiar economic horizon. Showing no signs of erosion, this accumulation is expected to continue growing at a rapid rate for many decades to come.

Reaction to this massive accumulation of financial wealth has been mixed, and rightly so, because it has created an iconoclastic link between wealth and power. Unlike the past when wealth was in the hands of individuals or groups who consciously exercised power, today's financial wealth belongs to a new group that is neither organized in any formal way nor focused on wielding power. The owners of this financial wealth scarcely seem to be aware of their clout. Only on rare occasions does the group speak with one voice; and when it does have a high degree of consensus, the group is clumsy in exercising its power, because it has no articulate way of expressing commands or signaling wishes.

The group of owners communicates its instructions, often in the form of whispered or mumbled buy and sell orders. These directives can cause dramatic short-term movements in financial asset prices, especially when they are abruptly conveyed because of changes in perceived risk and/or potential return. Through their uncoordinated actions, the group achieves its objective of prodding managers to deliver higher returns, but it is at the expense of creating greater volatility in financial markets.

An ironic twist is that this group of new owners did not seek power; rather, they acquired it inadvertently as a result of the geographic concentration of world financial wealth and the decentralization and democrati-

zation of control over these funds. The geographic concentration and democratization of wealth has caused a growing portion of global investable
financial capital to be channeled through a shrinking number of institutional investors (for example, mutual funds, hedge funds, and pension
funds). At the same time, decisions about the placement of these funds are
being made increasingly by ordinary middle-class investors who are
mostly American, European, and Asian. The shift in the balance of power
has been quick and unwitting; and over the next two decades, the accumulation of financial wealth and power is expected to accelerate and in-
tensify.

Middle-class investors have been empowered, and their empowerment
has begun to emasculate portfolio managers, lending officers, and investment specialists. In the past, lending officers and directors of large banks
had more influence, but now they have been pushed to the sidelines. Portfolio managers, who once had the spotlight, have also been upstaged.
There is a clear, almost irresistible, reversion to the mean of investment returns. Sophisticated portfolio specialists, who try to differentiate themselves by earning a few basis points more than their competitors, cannot
all succeed. Within a short time, successful investment strategies are imi-
tated and then no longer yield extraordinary returns. Exceptionally tal-
ented portfolio managers attract so much new money to manage that their
performance tends to fall back toward the market average. Once the man-
darins of capitalism, investment strategists and portfolio managers increasingly are becoming playthings subject to the whims of middle-class
investors. These investors—who are nervous neophytes susceptible to
panic and who display "herd" behavior and other frailties—now are the
driving force behind the financial flows that bring prosperity to countries
or entire regions. They are also the investors who can bring nations
quickly to their knees if they fall out of favor for real or perceived reasons.

This shift in the locus of financial power has many business implications. One of the most obvious is that countries need to work hard to make
themselves appealing to investors, especially unsophisticated foreign
portfolio investors. Cumulatively, the middle-class savers—who are located halfway around the world and devote about five minutes a month
to their choices of mutual funds—often have more to say about a country's
prosperity than the patriarchs of local business dynasties. This statement
is not an exaggeration now and is on track to become so true in the coming decades that one day we will all look back and think it was always so.

In many countries, policy makers have not yet come to terms with the
new order of precedence, and they try to manage their economies toward
prosperity by following the old rules; for example, they continue to assert
that the local financial services industry needs protection. According
to this outdated conventional wisdom, international financial services
providers do not fund all the necessary and beneficial local projects. In-

stead, the coldly analytical international capital markets siphon money from countries regardless of need and invest it in countries that are thousands of miles away. It is far better, according to this view, for domestic financial services firms to recycle local savings into the local community, and for that reason, they deserve protection.

This argument for protection had a certain internal logic and appeal that rarely withstood the test of time. Nevertheless, many people believed that it produced local jobs and real growth. They parroted the rationale for protection, which was that the international financial services firms had unfair advantages, and used some clever maneuvers to deliver higher returns. Financial speculation, according to this view, was more profitable than investing in bricks and mortar, and that was why international financial services firms could deliver higher returns.

Proponents of this international immiseration theory were convinced that it was all just paper-shuffling trickery, tax evasion, and money laundering that was producing superior track records in foreign multinational companies. Local financial services firms were creating meaningful employment for deserving local citizens who needed the jobs. The local firms, in this characterization, were not defrauding widows and orphans, dodging taxes, or bribing government officials, and because they focused on what might be called "real business activity" instead of financial legerdemain, they were sure to lose market share and go out of business as soon as the protection was taken away. This view held the center of public opinion for many years.

Meanwhile, populations aged. Middle-class people everywhere began thinking about and planning for their retirement, and as soon as they did, many realized that there would not be adequate provisions for comfortable twilight years. Under closer scrutiny, protected local financial services providers were exposed for their inefficiencies and low returns, especially in contrast to international financial services firms that offered well-designed savings vehicles with high and stable returns. Not only did these financial instruments have low credit risk, but they also offered international protection against inflation, devaluation, taxation, and the risks that accompany nondiversified wealth. Local savings products could not compete; and once it became clear, public opinion shifted, albeit slowly. Eventually, enough pressure was placed on political leaders for them to shift their opinions. The new direction in thinking was based on the obvious ground that local savers should have the right to invest abroad, and from this came more sweeping and revolutionary realizations.

NATIONAL CURRENCIES — ARE THEY NEEDED?

A major and really shocking realization was that most countries no longer derived net benefits from having local currencies. Public opinion flirted with this point as it became increasingly clear but could not quite embrace it. So much of history, tradition, and notions about the prerequisites for sovereignty have been based on the issuance of a national currency. For many people, the national currency was as much a part of their identity as the flag or the national anthem. As small children, they had learned how to handle the national currency. The coins had nicknames, and local sayings referred to them. People still repeated the sayings, even if the coins were no longer in circulation, or if the rising price index relegated them to quaint aphorisms that old people prattled. Every language has its analogs to penny candy, nickel cigar, two-bit ideas, dime novel, and two-dollar pistol. So the national currency was embedded more deeply in people's minds than the arguments in favor of protecting local financial institutions.

Not every nation has a chauvinistic love of the domestic currency. In many countries, especially ones experiencing hyperinflation, people do not hold the local currency. Of course, they might willingly keep a small amount of it on hand for local everyday purchases, but the cost of holding a large amount of these funds (in terms of deteriorating purchasing power) is too great. Residents in every walk of life learn quickly to convert their ever-withering currency into gold, dollars, euros, or anything of more reliable value. At the most visceral level, by minimizing their domestic currency holdings, they vote against their national currencies and in favor of currencies that retain value.

Often, governments have passed laws that were intended to force citizens to hold local currency and to channel their savings into securities denominated in the domestic currency. Capital controls of all kinds, such as taxes, exchange control boards, and outright restrictions, have been passed to restrict the possession of foreign currencies. The United States, for example, blocked Americans from owning gold bullion from 1934 to 1971; and from 1963 to 1974, the government tried to discourage them from investing too much capital abroad by implementing measures, such as the Interest Equalization Tax.[1] Similarly, the German Bardepot scheme from 1972 to 1974 controlled capital inflows in order to gain better control over the German domestic money supply. From 1991 to 1998, Chile restricted capital inflows by means of its *encaje* program in an attempt to reduce the nation's vulnerability to capital flight. Measures taken under the *encaje* program were intended to limit the funds that could flow from Chile in times of trouble, change the composition of such capital flows, and reduce the central bank's need to react to such controls.[2] Other countries had even more elaborate schemes to keep their citizens from diversifying their holdings. In some cases, criminal penalties, including the death sentence, were applied to violators of these capital controls.

In December 2001, Argentina froze bank deposits and created a dual exchange rate system. In January 2002, it extended the freeze on bank deposits and restricted conversion of local currency into dollars at the official exchange rate. Argentina permitted an escape valve by allowing local currency dealers to exchange pesos for dollars at the market-determined rate, but the public was still outraged.

Why do governments fight so hard for citizens to hold 100% of their day-to-day transactions balances and 100% of their savings in local currency? The cost of enforcement is high, and the effort that people devote to circumventing currency controls could be more productively applied. The conventional reason has been "seignorage," which was developed during the Middle Ages and has been practiced in varying forms since that time. The lord of the manor, who had the right to coin money, would issue coins and declare that they be circulated in his domain at a value exceeding the value of their gold or silver content. The feudal lord could capture a profit by taking, for example, 100 ounces of gold, mixing it with 50 ounces of base metal, and then issuing 150 one-ounce coins, mandating that each coin serve as legal tender with the value of one ounce of gold. The lord's subjects tolerated this practice and sometimes welcomed it, because they needed a currency that served as legal tender and because this practice of debasing the coinage brought revenue to the lord's exchequer in a way that was less burdensome to the citizenry than other forms of taxation. Because of its brutal clumsiness, no one advocated barter, and having more currency in circulation was regarded as a needed boost for the local economy to prosper. So if the lord's policy were successful, the people would gain. According to the practitioners of seignorage, issuing debased coinage is not taxation when it is done well. In the modern era, a successful practitioner of this policy has been the U.S. Federal Reserve.

The lord's gains were easier to calculate than the people's gains (or losses), and as a result, there was a constant temptation to overdo the coinage-debasing trick. As primitive as the debasing schemes were, lords who issued too much coin were always smart enough (and careful enough) to make sure the excessive issuance damaged the people before it damaged them. Reaping such ill-gotten gains was not difficult, despite the damage, because lords spent their funds first, thereby placing the burden on their subjects who accepted the currency in subsequent rounds of spending. Usually, "accepting" the currency was more a matter of law than choice, which is why the lords required that the currency be used as legal tender for all private and public debts.[3] Is it any wonder that in nations where such legal tender laws have existed, goods mysteriously disappear from the shelves at precisely the time when buyers have so much money to spend?

Citizens who become victims of both currency debasement and laws mandating the currency's use tend to vote in the only way they can—namely, exchanging their ever-depreciating currencies (for instance, newly minted coins) for products that will hold their value, such as precious metals. In such nations, the velocity of money tends to rise rapidly, adding to the growing problem of inflation that was brought on by the overissuance of currency.

This brief homily of the feudal lord who succumbed to the currency debasement temptation serves as a summary of the entire sad and turbulent history of currency mismanagement. Time has shown that modern statesmen and princes of every stripe have fallen victim to the same temptations that ruined the feudal lords.

Nevertheless, the damage caused by debasement was tolerated only if four prerequisites existed. First, gold (or some precious metal) existed as the refuge against inflation. Second, only a small segment of the population owned the relatively few financial assets available to purchase. As a result, if these financial assets lost value, the net economic effect on the economy was relatively small, because the losses fell most heavily on groups which were living well above subsistence. Third, retirement was not an entitlement. Relatively few people spent their twilight years in retirement as we know it today, and very few of those who lived long enough could afford retirement.

The final and most powerful reason for tolerating currency mismanagement was that in young, growing populations, debtors were more productive than creditors, and the financial markets were not sophisticated enough to incorporate expected inflation into contracts. People who were approaching the end of their working years saved and lent their savings to people who were beginning their productive years. The borrowers used the financing to pay for training, houses, and equipment that raised their productivity. Even though unexpectedly high inflation transferred wealth from savers to borrowers, it was hoped that spending on new productivity-enhancing equipment would increase output enough so that society could provide for the elderly whose savings lost some of its purchasing power.

ADVANTAGES OF CURRENCY UNIFICATION

As populations age and as more people accumulate financial assets, the costs of currency mismanagement become more visible and less tolerated, and it becomes apparent that the damage outweighs the benefits. An example illustrates why. Consider the mythical country of Ruritania where, in the 1970s, the average inflation rate was 12% per year and local government bonds yielded 16% per year.[4] The median age of the population was 25, and voters relied on the state pension scheme to take care of them from age 60 onward. This pension scheme had no financial assets. It paid retirees out of collections from the working population. Total financial assets in Ruritania were 30% of GDP, and the majority of these financial assets were short-term bonds or bank deposits. The high inflation did not damage the holders of most of these financial assets, because they had short-term maturities and the markets incorporated expected inflation into the nominal yield.

Now consider Ruritania in 2001. The population is older, and three decades of deficit spending have increased the amount of government bonds in existence. Government bonds outstanding are 60% of GDP, corporate bonds are 20% of GDP, and common stock is 50% of GDP. Government bonds have a longer average maturity than they did in 1970. Half of them are still short-term bonds, but the other half is composed of ten-year, fixed-rate bonds. The yield on these fixed-interest bonds is 16% (the same as in 1970), and the yield on ten-year, fixed-rate corporate bonds is 18%. The country's economic growth rate is 3% per year, and the price/earnings (P/E) multiple of the common stock is 7. Financial assets are worth 135% of GDP. Half the government bonds, all the corporate bonds, and all the common stocks have nominal values that are vulnerable to inflation.

Now suppose that Ruritania controls inflation by unifying its currency with those of contiguous or nearby countries. This policy slows inflation, because Ruritania transfers control of its currency to a supranational central bank, which can resist pressures from any one country to inflate and only inflates when the majority of the countries in the currency union would benefit.

Suppose this new monetary regime drops expected inflation (and the percentage change in the exchange rate) to 5% immediately, and financial market participants believe that this drop is permanent, because Ruritania has abdicated its control over monetary policy and control now resides with a supranational entity whose policies will have a strong bias against inflation. How will prices of Ruritanian securities react? The value of long-term government bonds, corporate bonds, and stocks will all rise. If the real, risk-free rate of interest and country risk premium remain the same, newly issued government bonds will now yield 9%[5] and corporate bonds will yield 11%.[6] Using standard financial formulas, one can calculate how much bond and stock prices will rise. The rise in long-term government bond prices will be equal to 46% of GDP, and corporate bonds will rise by about 34% of GDP. Because long-term bonds comprise 40% of GDP, their appreciation will increase wealth by approximately 34% of GDP. The rise in common stock prices will be equal to 50%[7] of GDP, and the total gain to owners of Ruritanian securities will be 84%[8] of GDP. In short, as long as currency unification reduces the nation's inflation rate and this reduction is reflected in lower nominal interest rates, huge immediate gains accrue to domestic holders of financial assets. Such gains are enormous by any standard, clearly larger than even the most optimistically estimated gains from unification.

When the European currencies were unifying to create the euro, numerous private and public studies tried to quantify the advantages of unification.

These studies pointed to the operating cost efficiencies for international cash management systems that would result from EC companies handling one currency rather than 11 currencies. Just by eliminating the bid–ask spreads and bank fees on currencies, it was expected that unification could reduce foreign exchange and hedging costs by $30 billion per year (approximately 0.4% of GDP).[9] Some estimates of the cumulative cost saving ranged from 1% to 2% of the company's revenues. But in summing the costs and benefits, most of the attention was directed toward gains in flow variables, such as increases in trade flows, capital flows, and real GDP as well as reductions in cost. We believe that too little attention was (and is) paid to gains in stock variables, such as economic wealth, which in most cases are both quicker to rise and far larger than the flow gains.

European currency unification is the example that motivates this book. Much of the inspiration behind this currency union, which was fully accomplished in 2002, can be traced back to the post–World War II desire to end European conflicts. During the 75 years between the late eighteenth century and World War II, Germany and France had fought three wars. It was hoped that a successful currency union would make future wars too expensive. Clearly, an economic union diminishes the possibility of war, but it does not completely extinguish all of the social, political, and economic sources of conflict. One only has to look at the tragic losses that resulted from the U.S. Civil War, ethnic-based struggles in Eastern Europe and the former Soviet Union, and the splitting of Czechoslovakia into Slovenia and the Czech Republic to see that this road many not be optimal.

Because the gains from currency unification are not evenly distributed among either the participating countries or groups within participating countries, its adoption is typically controversial, even within countries that reap the largest gains. For this reason, the realization of the EMU owes much to visionary statesmen such as Jean Monnet, Robert Schuman, Konrad Adenauer, and Alcide De Gasperi.

In this book, we will develop a methodology for calculating net benefits that can be applied to any group of countries or to any region at any point in time. The methodology used to calculate the net gains will be as applicable to the European unification as it is to currency unifications in Asia or Latin America. As well, it can be used to evaluate past currency unification efforts, such as the 1865 Latin Monetary Union,[10] the 1873 Scandinavian Monetary Union,[11] Benelux,[12] the 1967 East Africa Community,[13] and the United States, when the creation of the Federal Reserve in 1914 completed a currency unification process that had begun in the early 1860s.

Each of these unifications spurred trade by eliminating a key economic uncertainty: exchange risk. Prosperity was stimulated, in part, because low-cost producers from farther away could compete. Previously, their products were less competitive, because the cost of hedging made them uncompetitive. Thus, unifying the currencies had the same effect as lowering the cost of transportation: it increased the size of the market and fostered more complete specialization. Our belief is that currency unification can be a direct and immediate source of economic well-being for participating nations, but such gains come with the cost of reduced national autonomy. We believe that much of the perceived loss from unification is attached to a false sense of allegiance to national currencies, and in the strong light of evaluation, the economic costs of retaining such currencies are greater than the benefits most countries (especially developing nations) derive. The road to a unified currency is usually a long journey with transitory intermediate milestones such as free trade areas, customs unions, common markets, and ending in a currency union. The process of moving toward a unification forces separate national markets to converge, as they did in Europe between 1950 and 1999. The full removal of intra-union tariffs, capital controls, and the establishment of a common currency is itself just an intermediate step toward fiscal and regulatory harmonization.

NATIONAL BALANCE SHEETS

Because the focus of international financial statistics is mainly on flow variables, such as production, income, saving, and investment, the massive and far-reaching redistributions that are occurring in the ownership of global financial wealth are not captured. There is a meaningful difference between income and wealth that is already important for the international financial markets and will become of increasing concern to the baby-boom generation as it reaches retirement age.

Assets have to be owned by someone—and that someone has to have a nationality. Claims on a nation's assets are *liabilities* when they are owned by outside (that is, nonresident) creditors, and they are called *net worth* when they are owned by insiders (that is, resident owners). Unfortunately, few countries report national balance sheets. National financial statistics are remarkably incomplete and inconsistent in reporting nations' financial and real assets, liabilities, and net worth. To show the distinction, it is easy to find the figure for U.S. GDP, but it is quite difficult to find figures for the value of all real and financial assets in the United States. Until these figures are available for all countries, it will be difficult (or impossible) for statisticians to determine accurately which nations have rising equity bases.

It is important to have information that quantifies how each country has invested its own savings, the relationship between assets and liabilities, and who owns the liabilities. These facts are needed to evaluate a country's economic position because of changes in important economic variables, such as exchange rates, interest rates, and risk. National balance

sheet information is important for clarifying many economic mispercep-
tions. For instance, there is no stigma with being a net debtor if the borrowed funds are invested wisely in productive assets. Similarly, a net
creditor position is not a mark of strength if it results in anemic domestic
demand and the diversion into foreign investments of capital needed for
domestic growth.

Centuries of orthodoxy dictate that only assets can create wealth and
that liabilities take away flexibility, because countries and companies cannot always borrow as much as they want. The conventional view is that liabilities are not wealth; they only assign assets to their legal owners after
the assets have been created. These defining premises of orthodoxy are
brought forward in the debate about the enormous U.S. net debt to foreigners. For some, this debt is a clear sign of weakness and profligacy; for
others, the large net debt is proof that the guiding principles of the republic, laid down by the Founding Fathers, are alive and vibrant. Capital
comes to the United States as immigrants do, seeking opportunity and relief from oppression. If recent macroeconomic performance is a relevant
indicator, the large U.S. liabilities to foreigners do not seem to have hurt
growth. The productivity of the borrowed capital probably raised the
country's growth rate, as did the productivity of the immigrants who
came to contribute their energy and skills. This optimistic assessment of
U.S. liabilities to foreigners will be put to the test, because the U.S. net
debtor balance is projected to grow.

Liabilities to foreigners do matter, but a nation's indebtedness to foreigners undermines its sovereignty no more than it does for any debtor
company. Creditors want to be repaid, and for this reason, liabilities are a
source of the pressure to perform that policy makers, corporate managers,
and portfolio managers feel so keenly. If a national boundary separates the
bondholder or the stockholder from the assets, a new layer of repayment
risks must be considered. For instance, if the bonds or stocks are denominated in a currency that is different from the holder's home currency, the
foreign investor's position is more vulnerable.

Even though foreign portfolio investors face many risks that are greater
than those faced by domestic investors, there is one area in which this vulnerability is considerably smaller: Foreign portfolio investors are less
threatened by the pressures and persuasions that local oligarchs can bring
to bear on local citizens. There is less need for foreign portfolio investors
to be alert to the subtle signals and displays of class authority that would
cow local citizens, because local citizens (and direct investors) have a
much larger stake in the country as a percent of their total assets. Instead,
foreign portfolio investors can go blithely about their business and continue to press for higher returns. Liabilities speak quietly when they are
small, but as they get larger, and as a country's balance sheet shows more
debt as a percentage of assets, the liabilities speak with more clarity. The

foreign portfolio investors put out their own signals, whisper their own commands, and force the local oligarchs to take notice.

INVESTMENT DEMOCRATIZATION

It is for this reason that liabilities do matter and the democratization of investment decisions is of particular concern. How do middle-class investors form their opinions? Is this group of individuals more or less likely to be influenced by waves of optimism or pessimism than investment professionals? William F. Buckley once said, "I'd rather entrust the government of the United States to the first 400 people in the Boston telephone directory than to the faculty of Harvard University." Little did he know how close he would come to predicting the rules of the cross-border investment dance. Few would have forecast that middle-class investors would become the judge, jury, and enforcer of rules, which they had set themselves.

Financial power used to be centered in Wall Street, Threadneedle Street, and Shinjuku-cho. A few hundred top managers controlled much of the flow of credit. J.P. Morgan in his heyday could give a large loan to an applicant just because he thought the man should have the funds. Morgan's personal judgment was all the justification that was needed.

Many of those same top financial managers attempted to exert political influence. Their efforts in the political arena were easy to see and easy to categorize. Their methods varied, but their objectives were usually predictable. The familiar left-versus-right dichotomy was a workable way of classifying the positions that managers of big banks would take. The political influence of big banks was easy to neutralize, because top financial people were easy to caricature and demonize. Political cartoonists could portray them as bloated puppet masters who took delight in evicting widows and orphans and in lighting cigars with $50 bills.

Today's dispersed financial control is hard to see, in part, because as much as one-third is in offshore centers, which do not disclose investment details. To most observers, today's financial regime looks very much like the old framework of centralized control. The resemblance is superficial, but nonetheless deceiving. More funds than ever flow through the hands of financial managers. The big difference is that now the managers have less discretionary authority over the money. Managers have to keep track of it, and they are responsible for ensuring that the funds are swept into accounts that earn the highest possible return every minute. Funds flow in a barbell pattern from hundreds of millions of savers to millions of users through relatively narrow financial arteries. They cross national, ethnic, social, and religious boundaries. In the process, financial centers earn fees for acting as custodians and investment agents, but their independent control is waning.

Throughout the twentieth century, political figures have complained about the economic consequences caused by "hot money" and the "gnomes of Zurich." For years, capricious, trigger-happy portfolio managers have been blamed for pulling funds out of one country and pouring them into another. The difference today is the magnitude of the pool of funds that moves rapidly in search of high returns. In the time period 1994–1998, for example, the aggregate amount under management in hedge funds rose from $378 billion to $622 billion, an average annual compound increase of 13.3%.[14] At the same time, the productive capacity of the world grew by a cumulative amount less than 12.6%.[15] These facts have raised the clout of middle-class investors mightily, and their clout is on track to gain a position of absolute dominance over the other institutions of the social contract. Political, legal, cultural, and religious authorities are losing power quickly to a group that is numerous, located in rich neighborhoods of a few countries, and in competition with itself. The members of this group are trying for superior investment performance by purchasing investments that they expect will earn above average returns and unloading investments that fall out of favor. An abundance of public information is available to make investment decisions.

ACTIVE VERSUS PASSIVE FUNDS

The total pool of financial wealth can be divided into actively managed and inactively managed funds. The distinguishing features of active management are short cycles of accountability and transparency that involve daily marking-to-market, quick and easy procedures for moving capital out of one fund and into another (or from one manager to another), and fast decisions to jettison portfolio managers who underperform and to replace them with new ones. Almost any type of asset can be held in an actively managed vehicle: stocks, bonds, real estate, precious metals, or tangibles; and there are numerous actively managed investment vehicles from which to choose. So, middle-class investors see no reason to accept below-average performance for any of their assets at any time in their lives.

The pool of actively managed financial assets has grown in size relative to the pool of inactively managed financial assets. As recently as 1988, the total world value of listed common stocks was only $9.7 trillion, and less than $2 trillion of these were held in actively managed portfolios.[16] By year-end 2000, the total world value of listed common stocks had risen to around $36 trillion, and as much as $12 trillion may have been held in actively managed portfolios.[17] The total value of all financial assets has grown rapidly, as fast as 20% per year between 1995 and 2000, but the pool of actively managed assets has grown spectacularly: at least 30% per year for the same time period. The actively managed pool has emerged so recently that it is highly unlikely that most informed people have had time to incorporate its true importance into their frame of reference.

The pool of funds that is being actively managed is already larger than other important economic and financial magnitudes on earth and is growing much faster. It dwarfs the financial resources of governments, outstrips the gross dollar value of trade in goods and services, and is approaching the dollar value of annual world output. For the past eight years, the annual growth rate of this pool of funds has averaged three to five times the growth rate of world trade, and six to ten times the growth rate of world output. From 1990 to 2001, the annual growth rate of assets of actively managed mutual funds was 18.6%. For the same period, the annual growth rate of trade in goods and services fluctuated in the range of 1% to 12.5% and averaged 6%, and the annual growth rate of output for the period was 2.8%.[18]

The monthly growth of this pool of actively managed funds is larger than the value of all financial assets in many countries. For example, one month's accumulation is larger than the value of all financial assets in Thailand and Australia combined. Included are not only all securities listed on the Thai and the Australian stock exchanges but also all bank deposits in those two countries, including deposits held abroad by Thai and Australian citizens.

In its *Annual World Wealth Report* (1998 and 2001),[19] Merrill Lynch/Cap Gemini Ernst & Young revealed that the wealth of "high net worth (private) individuals" in the global asset management industry had reached $25.5 trillion—up from $7.2 trillion in 1988 and $19.1 trillion in 1997. With anticipated annual growth of 12%, it was expected to top $44.9 trillion by the year 2004. The sum is already larger than the total value of all financial assets in Japan at current prices—an immense amount, on the order of $20 trillion. Most Japanese financial assets are held in non-dynamic form—for example, in postal savings accounts, life insurance policies, or cross holdings of common stock—which are held for decades regardless of performance. Japanese pension fund assets are now being managed more actively, and middle-class investors in Japan are now buying mutual funds, including mutual funds that invest outside Japan, but perhaps as little as $1 trillion of Japanese financial assets are currently held in dynamic form.

Active portfolio management is gaining market share, and accountability of financial managers is becoming more widespread. Pressure to perform now applies to a pool of funds that is approaching $20 trillion. The remaining financial wealth, which now is worth approximately $80 trillion, is held in ways that do not transmit pressure to perform as directly and powerfully and that do not demand as much accountability.

Projecting these growth rates into the future is an informative exercise. With reasonable assumptions, by 2015, the size of the pool of funds invested in actively managed mutual funds and pension funds will reach eight times the value of world output, 25 times the value of world trade, and over 200 times the annual tax revenues of the federal government of the United States.

What makes this trend even more remarkable is that it has only just begun. Currently, only about 15% of the portfolios that are classified as "globally diversified" are invested internationally. This percent is substantially below proportionate levels of international capitalization but is, ironically, above what many investors feel is a comfortable level. With time, the level of international diversification will increase and therein lies the concern.

COUNTRY SIZES RESTATED

The extreme size disparity among the pools of financial wealth held by national groups is an important feature of the financial landscape. For example, the annual increase in pension fund holdings of Chileans would be sufficient to buy (at current prices) 100% of the face value of all financial claims of Ecuador and Bolivia combined. Familiar economic statistics on flow variables such as GDP and personal income do not reveal this fact. They show a disparity of income and output per capita. The inequality may seem large, but it is dwarfed by the disparity in financial wealth per capita. The population and GDP figures for the three countries are as follows: Chile's population is 14.2 million, and its GDP is $69.8 billion; Ecuador and Bolivia have a combined population of 18.9 million and a combined GDP of $22.3 billion. Therefore, Chile's per capita GDP is $4,915, whereas Ecuador and Bolivia average $1,180. These figures show that Chileans enjoy a higher standard of living than Ecuadorians and Bolivians. A layman might confuse income with wealth and think that none of the three countries is wealthy—certainly not wealthy enough to buy a substantial share of the other's capital market assets.

In reality, Chileans add so much to their retirement savings accounts each year that they could, in theory, buy all the outstanding financial assets (at current prices) of each of several smaller Latin American countries. Figures for annual income or output obscure the sudden accumulation of financial wealth in Chile. Income and output figures also distract attention from the key weaknesses of the economies of Ecuador and Bolivia: underdeveloped finance sectors and low degrees of securitization.

Financial wealth data show how important it has become for countries to have modern, competitive finance sectors, and how much difference it makes when a country's financial assets begin to be held in active vehicles. Financial wealth data, combined with exchange rate trends, also show how quickly a country can move ahead or fall behind in the wealth rankings. Comparisons between countries that are based on output per capita change slowly. A poor country would need decades for its output per capita to catch up to a richer one's higher standard of living. Take, for example, a poor country with one-tenth the per capita GDP as a rich country, but with real GDP growing at triple the level of the rich country (for example, 9% versus 3%). Even at this highly accelerated rate of real growth and assuming all else remained the same (for example, population growth rates), it would take the poor country over 40 years to close the income gap.

This is not the case for wealth. In the recent past, there have been several startling jumps in wealth per capita and also some dismaying declines. Wealth is much more volatile, and its magnitudes are much larger. Country-specific securitization figures for 1988 and 1997 are summarized in Appendix 1. They reveal that big gains in wealth were made by Chile, the United States, Greece, the United Kingdom, Spain, Finland, Taiwan, Singapore, and Poland. Staggering declines were the fate of Japan and South Korea. Figures for 1999 show that countries such as Thailand, Indonesia, Venezuela, and Russia suffered shuddering reductions in their levels of securitization; and in 2001, the countries that suffered precipitous drops were Argentina and Turkey, whereas Russia recovered sharply. The nations that scored gains had increases in securitization, stock market rallies, and strong currencies. The declining countries endured local stock market declines, devaluations, or both.

Importantly, two of the declining countries had high saving rates. Countries with high saving rates used to be considered successful, because saving was believed to result in capital formation and per capita income growth. Now, a high saving rate is no longer enough to ensure star performance. Today's stars are the countries that are the most successful at raising the market value of their income-producing assets. The modernity of the finance sector is a determinant of the level of wealth per capita.

THE DOLLAR AS LODESTONE AND THE EURO AS THE NEW MAGNET

Middle-class investors around the world have shown a preference for using and holding U.S. dollars. The foreign exchange value of the dollar has remained strong despite chronic U.S. current account deficits, which have averaged in excess of $30 billion per quarter over the past 20 years and $74 billion per quarter since the Asian crisis of 1997 (see Exhibit 2.1). Between the beginning of the Asian crisis in July 1997 and March 2001, the dollar rose by 22% (that is, 5.6% per year) on a trade-weighted basis (see Exhibit 2.2). This result may be contrary to what many people might have guessed, but upon closer inspection, it stands to reason. It was unmistakable that U.S. consumers put considerable downward pressure on the U.S. dollar (that is, upward pressure on the value of Asian currencies) through

Exhibit 2.1
U.S. Current Account Deficits: 1978–1998 (In billions of U.S.$)

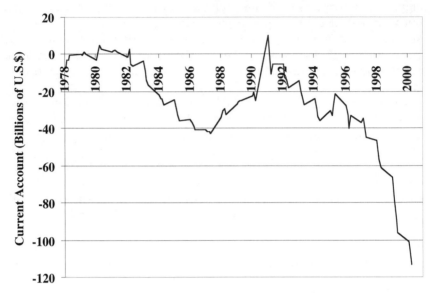

their purchases of Asian imports, but this supply of dollars was more than offset by Asian investors who demanded dollars in order to purchase financial assets denominated in U.S. dollars. Increasingly, as international capital markets have become larger, it has been the flow of investment capital and not the flow of goods and services that has determined short-term movements of international exchange rates. Dollars seemingly lost through open import doors do not depreciate a currency if they flow willingly back in through the open capital windows.

It is important to note that if the U.S. dollar rises in relation to other currencies, the relative magnitude of the U.S. dollar pool of actively managed financial assets will become larger. The strong dollar has allowed U.S. companies and companies that list their shares on U.S. stock markets to acquire business assets outside the United States at bargain rates. U.S. firms have used less of their debt capacity, or issued fewer new shares, to acquire assets abroad. These assets have contributed to the increase in financial wealth that is attributed to the United States. Of course, this wealth does not belong entirely to U.S. citizens, but they benefit from the spillover effects.

Because of its sophisticated capital markets, the United States attracts many foreign firms that sell their shares on U.S. stock markets. As a result, additional capital flows toward the United States from individuals who have not immigrated but choose to have U.S.-based assets. The United

Exhibit 2.2
Trade-Weighted Value of the U.S. Dollar: July 1997–March 2001

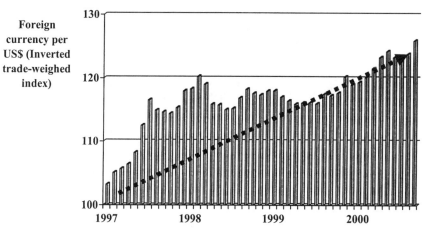

States benefits by being able to export additional financial services, and it also benefits in terms of *measured wealth*. When a non-U.S. company whose shares are listed on a U.S. stock exchange, such as Telefonica of Spain, buys another non-U.S. company—for example, the cellular telephone provider for the city of Sao Paulo, Brazil—U.S. stock market capitalization increases and trading volume on the New York Stock Exchange increases. U.S. investors who own shares of Telefonica of Spain gain as do U.S. workers in the financial services sector who execute these trades.

FORECASTS OF COUNTRY SIZES

Relative figures for the financial wealth of countries are already startling. Exhibit 2.3 shows the distorted features of a world map with the sizes of countries measured by financial wealth instead of by land area. Resizing the world by wealth would make North America immense and would inflate considerably the size of Western Europe. Africa, a continent of considerable geographic size, would become smaller than Portugal. Japan, due to its advanced stage of development, would become an enormous island in the Pacific, larger than all of mainland Asia; and South America would become the size of a tiny teardrop below an enormous North America face.

Between 1988 and 1997, these disproportions became even more skewed; and if recent growth rates continue, Exhibit 2.3 shows how even more outlandish they were by the end of 2001 (also see Appendix 2). Under these circumstances, financial wealth will accumulate in the ac-

Exhibit 2.3
World Market Capitalization: 1988, 1997, and Projected 2001

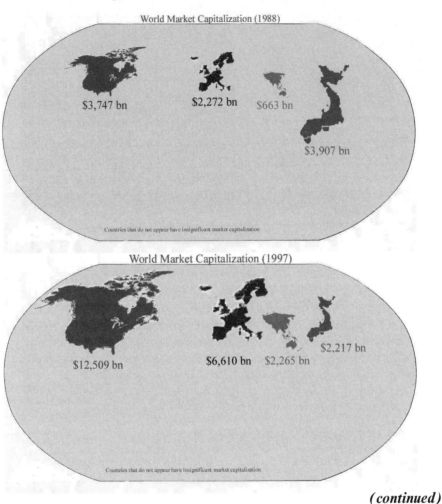

(continued)

counts of the people who already hold most of it. These people will be mainly citizens of countries that have permitted and encouraged savings to be put into actively managed vehicles.

FORECASTING REGIONS' FINANCIAL WEALTH

Forecasting aggregate world financial wealth is made easier by our having a reasonably good idea of the number of savers and their average monthly portfolio accumulation. At the same time, the job of forecasting is

Exhibit 2.3
World Market Capitalization: 1988, 1997, and Projected 2001
(continued)

World Market Capitalization (2001 forecast)

$14,731 bn $7,323 bn $2,695 bn $1,197 bn

Countries that do not appear have insignificant market capitalization

complicated by the relative difficulty of predicting the average annual rates of return that savers will earn. Nevertheless, by putting sensible confidence intervals around the historic average, we can at least get a hint of the magnitudes involved. Most difficult for our analysis is to forecast the annual growth rates of a country's and a region's financial assets. In Chapter 8, we show a method for forecasting the growth rate of a country's financial wealth. This is a basic model that provides estimates intended to show orders of magnitude. We cannot hope it will give accurate results except in relative terms and in the context of future events. Nevertheless, it is worthwhile to go through the exercise, because the method makes use of a key variable that we discuss extensively in this book, namely, the country risk and the factors that lower it. Any forecast of a region's financial wealth must depend heavily on how country risk fluctuates in future time periods. If country risk for the major countries of a region declines, the financial wealth of the entire region will rise, the stock and bond markets of the region will boom, and a cycle of prosperity will commence.

Recent events include examples of cycles of prosperity and cycles of shrinking financial wealth. Asia, after the 1997 crisis, saw its financial assets become undervalued relative to the previous decade's trends; and Latin American financial assets, after the "tequila" devaluation of December 1994, suffered a long period of erratic, depressed prices. These periods of regional decline contrasted with the emerging markets' boom from 1989 to 1993.

The pattern has been for world financial wealth to rise erratically, with growth rates in excess of 11% per year over the past 20 years and periods of higher growth in that time frame, especially from 1994 to the first quarter of 2000. At the same time, individual countries have experienced violent booms and crashes of financial wealth, of much greater percentage magnitude, and in shorter time frames. Despite the high volatility, some forecasts can be made of individual countries' financial wealth, and from there one can develop regional forecasts. We attempt to do this after developing the methods in the chapters ahead.

CONCLUSION: WHISPERED ORDERS

A new financial power group has emerged, which should not be categorized in terms of nationality or in a framework of traditional geopolitical agendas. Its interests are neither country-specific nor nationalistic; on the contrary, this power group's interests are hot-wired to world-level concerns. The threats to it are abstract and quite visceral. With few exceptions, the group's members live in comfort and enjoy physical security. Thus, they can focus on threats that are more remote, because the immediate travails and headaches of daily life are no longer of such immediate concern.

The question that now hangs in the air is, In what directions and toward what destinations will the new overlords take us, regardless of whether they become aware of their power and learn how to wield it? It will become increasingly important for politicians, central bankers, businesses, and financial analysts to identify the variables that most heavily influence the decisions of middle-class investors. These variables may not be the same as the ones used by highly trained economists, financial analysts, or government treasury officials to describe a nation's economic health. For instance, a country with a current account deficit that is over X% of GDP may not be in financial difficulties; but, if investors use this X% threshold for their decisions, it could result in massive capital outflows and endogenously cause an economic downturn. To reduce economic volatility, politicians and central bankers will have to identify and manage the factors that influence the decisions of middle-class investors or control the announcement effects that surround them. To be successful, businesses and financial analysts will have to anticipate these factors and act quickly before they change. Over time, the factors that most influence the decisions of middle-class investors should converge toward those used by economists and government officials, but like all supertankers, shifts in direction can be long in coming and, in the meantime, considerable short-term hardships and instability could occur.

A sobering question now hangs over financial markets: How many countries still gain from having their own currency? The facile answer, the nationalistic answer, and the orthodox answer are all losing their preemptive legitimacy. The question is up for reexamination. The macroeconomic aggregates are no longer in the proportions they used to be. The standard computations no longer come out so obviously in favor of the old answers.

NOTES

1. The Interest Equalization Tax was a 15% U.S. federal tax on the interest received from foreign borrowers. It was intended to penalize U.S. investors purchasing foreign debt and, therefore, to make foreign debt issues less attractive to U.S. dollar holders.

2. Christopher J. Neely, *An Introduction to Capital Controls, Review—Federal Reserve Bank of St. Louis* The data on how much was invested in hedge funds each year is from Nashville, Tenn.: Van Hedge Funds Advisors International, 2001. Available at http://www.hedgefund.com/universe.htm.

3. In some nations, such as the United States today, legal tender meant that the currency had to be accepted for public and private debts. It did not mean that currency had to be accepted for transactions involving goods and services.

4. 12% expected inflation + 4% real interest rate = 16%.

5. 5% expected inflation + 4% real rate of interest = 9%

6. 5% expected inflation + 4% real rate + 2% credit risk premium = 11%.

7. When expected inflation was 12% per year, the P/E ratio was 7.1 (for example, P/E = $1/(k_e - g) = 1/(.20 - .06) = 1/.14 = 7.1$), where the 20% average cost of equity, k_e, is composed of a 12% expected inflation, a 4% real, risk-free rate of return, and a 4% risk premium for the average common stock. If expected inflation drops to 5%, the cost of equity falls to 13% (that is, 5% expected inflation, 4% real, risk-free rate of return, and 4% risk premium), and the P/E ratio rises to 14.3 (that is, $1/(.13 - .06) = 14.3$). If prior to the decline in expected inflation the P/E ratio was 7.1 and afterward the P/E ratio was 14.3, then the market price of the average stock must have doubled, thereby increasing the market capitalization from 50% of GDP to 100% of GDP. As a result, the increase in capitalization is by 50% of GDP.

8. 50% + 34.4% = 84.4%.

9. IFO Institute estimated that transaction costs saving would be about 1% of GDP for bank, commission, personnel costs, and non-personnel costs.

10. This union included Italy, France, Belgium, Switzerland, and later Greece and Spain.

11. This union included Sweden, Norway, and Denmark.

12. Benelux was a currency union between Luxembourg and Belgium.

13. This union included Kenya, Tanzania, and Uganda.

14. Data on dollars under management in hedge funds is available from Van Hedge Funds Advisors International, Inc. of Nashville, Tennessee through their Website: http://www.hedgefund.com/universe.htm.

15. The annual growth rate of world productive capacity was 3% per year or less during that time frame. Note that $(1.03)^4 - 1 = 12.6\%$.

16. Source for the $9.7 trillion figure is *Standard and Poor's Emerging Markets Data Base, 1995 Factbook* (New York: Standard and Poor's, 1996), 14–15. For the amount in actively managed portfolios, consider that U.S. equity mutual funds in that year had only $194.8 billion under management. The source for that figure is *The Mutual Fund Factbook,* Investment Company Institute website: http://www.ici.org.

17. For the $36 trillion figure, the source is World Bank, *World Bank 2001 World Development Indicators* (Washington, D.C.: International Bank for Reconstruction and Development, 2002), 278–281. For the $12 trillion figure, consider that U.S. equity mutual funds had $3,962.3 billion under management, 20 times more than in 1988. The source for the $3,962.3 billion figure is *The Mutual Fund Factbook.*

18. Data are for U.S. mutual funds and are from *The Mutual Fund Factbook.* Data for annual growth of world trade in goods and services and for annual growth of world output are from World Trade Organization, *International Trade Statistics 2001,* http://www.wto.org/english/res_e/statis_e/its2001_e/stats2001_e.pdf, 2–3.

19. *World Wealth Report 2001,* Merrill Lynch/Cap Gemini Ernst & Young, Available at: http://www.ir.ml.com/news/ML051401.pdf

Chapter 3

Economic and Monetary Integration

INTRODUCTION

Tariffs, quotas, and exchange controls have been a part of international financial relations for centuries. Nations often resort to them in order to accomplish macroeconomic goals, such as improving their current account deficits, reducing the level of unemployment, and leveling the playing field of international trade. Regrettably, protectionist legislation has survived despite countless studies showing that it rarely improves the balance of payments, reduces unemployment rates, or levels the playing field. In short, protectionist legislation hurts the many to help the few.

Prosperity is highly correlated with low trade barriers, open borders to immigrants, and unrestricted capital movements—all of which are goals of economic integration. Nonetheless, finding the right mix of integration is tricky, because everything has a cost, and because economic integration raises controversial, philosophical concerns about the sacrifices that countries should make in the name of integration. It also raises very practical questions related to the net benefits (or net losses) of integration and how they can be measured prior to the union.

A relatively recent controversy between Germany and France is illustrative of a deep philosophical division within the EU that has been brought to the surface. In spring 2001, German Chancellor Gerhard Schröder proposed a vision for the EU that would turn Europe into a federation of states, much like the United States. But, creating a "United States of Europe" is not the goal of everyone. Shortly after Schröder's provocative proposal, French President Jacques-René Chirac proposed a counter vision for the EU that maintained Europe as an association of independent sovereign nations. As of 2002, this controversy has not been resolved and is not expected to be resolved for years to come.

For nations wishing to distance themselves from the policy of protectionism and to integrate their economics with other countries, there are seven levels of economic integration from which to choose. A monetary union is just one of them. Countries interested in forging closer ties can begin the process of integration with *preferential trading agreements*, which reduce the level of protectionism on *selected* goods and services. The European Coal and Steel Community, which was the *wunderkind* of early European integration efforts and the forerunner of the European Community, was an example of a successful preferential trading agreement.

Free trade areas are a higher level of economic integration, because they abolish restrictions on *all* products traded among member nations. At the same time, they permit members to maintain their own independent trade barriers relative to nonmember countries. The Canada–U.S. Free Trade Agreement (FTA), North American Free Trade Agreement (NAFTA), European Free Trade Association (EFTA), and Latin American Free Trade Area (LAFTA) are (or were) examples of such unions.

The third highest stage of economic integration is a *customs union*, which has all the features of a free trade area but goes one step further by requiring member nations to agree on a uniform level of protection relative to nonmember countries. Establishing a standardized level of protectionism is a relatively large step for any country to take, because in so doing, the country relinquishes a portion of its national autonomy to supranational rules and institutions.

A *common market* is the fourth most advanced integration arrangement. It has all the features of a customs union (that is, it permits the free flow of goods within the union and establishes a common external level of protection), and it also opens the borders of member nations to the free, intra-union flow of labor and capital. Citizens of nations belonging to a common market should enjoy the same rights and benefits as resident nationals. Moreover, intra-union capital market transactions and money market transactions should be treated in a nondiscriminatory manner. The European Common Market (ECM), which is one of the best twentieth-century examples of a common market, was first set in motion at the Treaty of Rome on March 25, 1957, and developed into a full common market by the 1990s. The 1961 Central American Common Market (CACM), though far less successful than the ECM, is another example of a relatively recent effort to integrate a handful of Latin American economies.

The three most advanced levels of economic integration are a *monetary union,* an *economic union,* and a *political union.* A monetary union has all the features of a common market but adds a supranational authority responsible for conducting monetary policy. An economic union has supranational authorities who are responsible for conducting fiscal policy. A political union has supranational authorities conducting foreign and military policies.

Exhibit 3.1
Seven Levels of Economic Integration

Economic unions and political unions can be formed without having supranational monetary authorities. Similarly, monetary unions can be established without creating supranational economic or political authorities. In fact, there appears to be no theoretical or empirical reason why any level of integration requires the formation of a monetary union or why a monetary union requires any level of economic or political union. For example, the U.S. Constitution was signed in 1787, thereby creating in the United States a political and economic union, but it was not until 1914 that the United States had a central bank that was responsible for monetary policy. Similarly, during the nineteenth century, Germany had an economic union and political union before it had a common currency. By contrast, since January 1, 1999, the European Monetary Union (EMU) has existed without the European Union (EU) becoming a political union.

Exhibit 3.1 shows the seven levels of economic integration, with a monetary union positioned as the fifth step up the staircase of the economic integration process. If one viewed this stratified triangle as a guide for achieving integration, then a monetary union should be created only after a common market is formed. The usual way of describing integration is as a succession of steps with new levels of convergence building on the ones already accomplished, and we have followed this convention in our exposition up to this point. It is a mistake, though, to believe that every group

Exhibit 3.2
A Monetary Union Enhances All Forms of Economic Integration

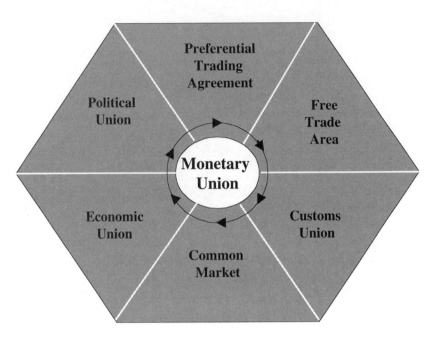

of countries wishing to integrate will have to pass through that exact sequence of steps. A monetary union can be formed at any stage of economic development, and it can be formed with other nations that may be at different stages of development. It is not necessary for the nations unifying their currencies to have previously integrated their economies in other ways. Nations that are truly committed to integrating their economies should consider a monetary union, even at the earliest stages of their convergence.

Exhibit 3.2 shows an alternative relationship between monetary unions and other forms of integration. Rather than a pyramid or staircase (as Exhibit 3.1 depicts the positioning), the seven dimensions of integration have a hexagonal form with a monetary union forming a (potential) common core.

Few would argue with the conclusion that the United States has derived significant advantages from having a monetary, economic, and political union, but at the same time, it should be equally well understood that these benefits came with considerable costs. The Civil War, for instance, was in large part an economic clash between the industrial North, which wanted unrestricted agricultural imports but controlled industrial imports, and the agricultural South, which wanted just the opposite. Prior to the Civil War, the North and South were, economically speaking, two different countries in terms of labor mobility, per capita income, capital–labor ratios, and culture.

It is not difficult to understand why successful, lasting monetary, economic, and political unions have been the exception rather than the rule. Even when economic integration has created significant *net* advantages, vested interest groups, who stood to lose, have fought vigorously to subvert change and to maintain the status quo. Nevertheless, continuing rounds of integration will be as much a part of our future as they have been of our past, because nations are lured by the obvious and potentially enormous benefits that can result from larger markets and lower trade restrictions.

Nearly two centuries ago, David Ricardo gave the world the concept of comparative advantage. He demonstrated how the world as a whole would benefit if nations could focus their production on areas where they have *relative* international production advantages. Apart from that theoretical argument in favor of comparative advantage, free and open markets make economic sense, because they reduce costs in other ways: They permit economies of large-scale production, sharpen competition, improve management (for instance, due to the threat of acquisition), enhance product quality, pressure companies to use state-of-the-art technology, and increase efficiency. Economic integration provides more for everyone, and unlike competition among companies, where one company's gain is often another company's loss, trade and specialization are not zero-sum games. The success of one nation does not have to come at the expense of another.

MORE ABOUT MONETARY UNIONS

Monetary unions offer member nations numerous benefits, among which are:

1. the elimination of foreign exchange uncertainty, which leads to greater imports, exports, and foreign direct investments,
2. the abolition of competitive devaluations,
3. greater specialization in trade and finance,
4. economies of scale,
5. increased competition, and
6. rationalization (that is, mergers, acquisitions, and labor count reductions in an effort to remain competitive),
7. reduced transactions costs (that is, no need for bank accounts in each country, no bid–ask spread or foreign exchange commissions to pay),
8. reduced borrowing costs,

9. deeper and broader equity, debt, money, and derivative markets,

10. enhanced monetary policy credibility, and

11. more predictable purchasing power of income and investment returns within the monetary union, and therefore more mobile labor and capital.

To date, only Benelux, a currency union with multiple objectives, has been successful long enough for the weight of opinion to have classified it as an outright success. Other currency unions have failed, often for good reasons. For instance, the Latin Monetary Union and the Scandinavian Monetary Union were forced to disband at the beginning of World War I because of the lack of both a single central bank and the political leadership capable of resisting restrictive trade controls (for instance, tariffs) during periods of rising domestic unemployment.

The success of any common market (or other trade liberalization schemes based on economic integration) is based on six major economic factors, which are the

1. number of participating nations,

2. distance between member nations,

3. level of pre-union protectionism,

4. extent to which member nations' exports are competitive with each other (that is, rather than being complementary),

5. level of pre-union trade among the member nations, and

6. level of post-union protectionism relative to nonmember nations.

The ideal combination is for a monetary union to be formed among a large number of nations that are in close geographic proximity and conduct a majority of foreign trade with each other in internationally competitive industries. Such a union would provide companies with wider markets that could be exploited due to the relatively inexpensive transportation costs. The higher the pre-trade barriers, the greater would be the gains from a union; and the lower the post-union barriers (that is, relative to nonmember countries), the less there would be to lose. To illustrate two countries that would not benefit from a monetary union, consider Ecuador and Malaysia. These two are far apart geographically, and they do not trade very much with each other. The only condition they meet is that both countries' export industries are internationally competitive.

CONDITIONS FOR A SUCCESSFUL MONETARY UNION

Financial variables—such as prices, wages, interest rates, commodity prices, exchange rates, and real GDP—act like economic shock absorbers to cushion a nation's economy from real and financial shocks. For example, prices adjust when there is a sudden disruption in the supply of some commodity. Because there are so many shocks, without fluctuations in prices, the real economy would lurch along like a car traveling on a rutted road. The shock absorbers handle some of the disturbances, and the more they handle, the less bumpy is the passengers' ride. Every economic shock causes a certain amount of dislodgment, and the more disturbance absorbed by any one of the economic shock absorbers, the less that has to be absorbed by other variables. That is why governments are so preoccupied with grain reserves, petroleum reserves, foreign exchange reserves, and "safety nets" for citizens who suffer when an economic shock hits.

If it is true that exchange rates are economic shock absorbers, then why would any nation willingly give up this source of stability and flexibility? The answer is that governments seek to create the smoothest economic ride for their citizens. If the nation's well-being is tied heavily to the international sector, in general, and to a particular foreign country, in particular (for example, it might have a large trading partner, such as the United States), then minimizing the exchange rate instability could create a smoother ride. The more important the international sector, the greater are the benefits from eliminating exchange rate fluctuations; but, net benefits will result only if a nation's other economic shock absorbers are flexible enough to take up the added pressure that will be put on them.

When a nation sacrifices its monetary autonomy and merges its currency with a supranational currency, its chances for success are increased if certain factors are present. For instance, there should be a high level of labor and capital mobility among the member nations in the monetary union, and there should also be considerable price flexibility. The more mobile resources are and the more flexible prices are, the less need there is for exchange rates to equilibrate differences in relative inflation rates and productivity levels. As well, the introduction of a common currency increases labor market, capital market, and product market transparency, which should raise labor mobility and create pressure for convergence of pensions, unemployment benefits, yields, prices, and taxes.

Monetary unions in nations that have similar broadly diversified domestic industrial bases also have greater chances for success. Having similarly structured economies means that external shocks will affect the member nations in parallel ways and require comparable macroeconomic policy responses. The closer the structure of their economies, the less chance there will be for policy disputes about macroeconomic polices. Having a diversified industrial base is also important, because it increases each nation's economic stability by reducing the effect of any external shock. For example, if a country's GDP is tied mainly to oil, then any change in the price of oil is likely to have a major (often destabilizing) effect on the domestic economy.

Finally, monetary unions have greater chances for success if there is a supranational fiscal authority with significant power to tax and spend according to the needs and priorities of the union as a whole and an ability to temporarily offset economic hardship by taxing Peter to pay Paul. In that way, the supranational fiscal authority responds to regional disparities and thus does not need to obey the dictates of individual member countries. For instance, in the United States, if New England is booming and the Southeast states are languishing, the national government can moderate the unevenness by collecting taxes from the booming states and redistributing them, in the form of unemployment compensation, to the slower-growing states. Because the U.S. government collects between 20% and 39% of each marginal dollar, it has substantial clout.

COSTS AND BENEFITS OF A MONETARY UNION

Flexible exchange rates are ideal for some economic environments but not for all. To understand why this is true, consider whether it makes sense for a nation, regardless of size, to have its own currency. If it were always advantageous, then by similar reasoning, states, provinces, and cantons (many of which are the size of countries) should also have their own currencies. But if each state, province, and canton should have its own currency, then why shouldn't each region, city, suburb, and individual have one too? Clearly, if each individual had his/her own currency, the transaction costs of making even the simplest purchases would be so high that they would far outweigh any advantages. By inductive reasoning, as the size of an economic entity expands from an individual to a region to a nation and beyond, there must be a point at which the benefits of a common currency outweigh the disadvantages (for example, transactions costs). This section discusses in further detail the factors that determine the costs and benefits of an optimal currency union and how these factors are likely to change over time.

Performing a cost–benefit analysis of economic integration is a bit like doing an econometric study on the advantages and disadvantages of getting married. The problem is that many of these costs and benefits are not quantifiable and are largely unknown until the relationship develops. Moreover, estimates are subject to wide variation, because our understanding of the process is still too primitive for precise answers. Nevertheless, such analyses are often important, because they help us understand where costs and benefits are likely to reside (or, at least, where a priori reasoning indicates they should reside).

Exhibit 3.3 puts this notion into graphical perspective. Economic integration has costs and benefits that vary directly with the level of integration. The upward-sloping "Integration Benefits" curve in Exhibit 3.3 reflects the *total benefits* that a nation derives from integration. These ben-

Exhibit 3.3
Gains, Losses and Net Gains from Integration

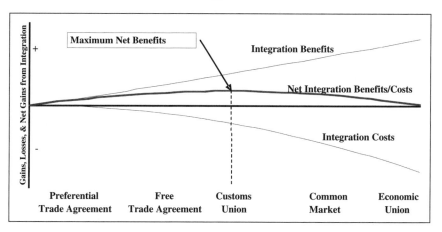

efits are in the form of lower tariffs (trade creation), wider consumer product choice, better quality, economies of scale, efficiency gains, greater labor
and capital mobility, and increased competition.

The downward-sloping "Integration Costs" curve reflects the *total* costs a
nation suffers from having reduced national autonomy in determining its
macroeconomic policies and from the trade diversion effects that result
when a common external wall of protection is erected. The loss of a nation's
ability to independently determine monetary and fiscal policy could be
great if it resulted in a higher average level of cyclical unemployment. The
country would lose some or all of its ability to pursue independent macroeconomic goals, such as lower unemployment, higher growth, or lower inflation, and it would compromise the nation's ability to defend itself from
external shocks, such as changes in international interest rates and exchange
rates. For countries starting with high debt and high deficit positions, their
policy responses would be severely impaired in times of recession.

The optimal level of integration is the one that maximizes the *net* benefit to the nation. If there are no net benefits, then an autarkic position (no
integration) should be chosen. In Exhibit 3.3, the "Net Integration Bene-
fits/Costs" line is at a maximum at the customs-union level. A monetary
union is not listed as one of the integration alternatives in Exhibit 3.3, because monetary unions are treated as a complement to any of the other integration alternatives.

What would (or should) happen to the level of integration if a currency
union were formed? The answer depends on whether the net benefits
from the currency union are positive or negative and fixed or variable. As
Exhibit 3.4 shows, if the benefits are positive, fixed, and front-loaded (that

Exhibit 3.4
Wealth Gains Plus Typically Measured Gains from Integration

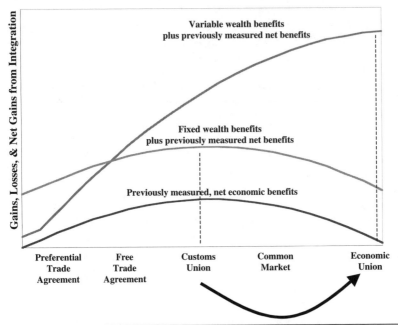

Variable benefits from a monetary union shift the optimal level of integration from a customs union to an economic union.

is, merely creating a one-off increase in economic benefits), then the optimal level of economic integration should stay the same. By contrast, if the net benefits of the monetary union are positive and variable (that is, rise with the level of integration), then the inclusion of these benefits should promote integration beyond the customs-union level.

For example, currency unions reduce transaction costs (for example, by eliminating bid–ask spreads) and reduce or eliminate cross-currency risk, thereby cutting nominal interest rates. Lower nominal interest rates raise the prices of fixed income securities and other assets (for example, real estate). The drop in nominal interest rates results in a huge increase in wealth. If this increase in wealth were the only benefit from a monetary union and if these benefits were all front-loaded, then the level of integration should remain the same. By contrast, if the benefits were variable, perhaps reflecting lower transaction costs and increased real (GDP) growth, then these benefits would increase with the level of integration, thereby promoting more advanced levels of integration. In Exhibit 3.4,

Exhibit 3.5
Possibility of Net Losses at Every Level of Economic Integration

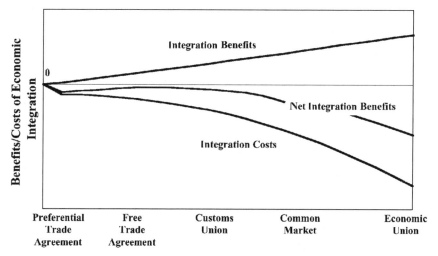

these variable gains have the effect of increasing the optimal level of integration from a custom union to an economic union.

Even if the gains from a monetary union were positive and variable, this does not mean that the level of integration should always rise. Exhibit 3.5 provides an example in which the net benefits are negative at all levels of integration. Even though the creation of a monetary union would provide net benefits, they would not be sufficient to offset the losses from integration. As a result, the optimal position for this nation would be to refuse all offers to integrate with any other nation.

It is also possible for the creation of a monetary union to result in net losses, in which case its creation would make no sense. Such an outcome could occur, for example, if the loss of independent monetary decision-making power simultaneously raised both the nation's average level of cyclical unemployment and the variability of GDP enough to offset the gains from the monetary union. Any nation that adopts fixed exchange rates and imposes no trade or exchange controls sacrifices its ability to conduct independent exchange rate policy and monetary policy as tools of macro-management. This trade-off is often called the "Impossibility Trilogy."

CONCLUDING QUESTION: DID EUROPEAN ECONOMIC AND MONETARY INTEGRATION CREATE NET BENEFITS?

The EMU has now been fully implemented, but euro-skeptics remain. It is, therefore, appropriate to ask whether European integration benefits exceeded the costs. The timely version of this question is whether monetary convergence solidifies and consolidates earlier gains or whether it casts in concrete a suboptimal arrangement?

This is a loaded question, because something "optimal" can look ugly standing alone but beautiful relative to the next best alternative. The original 11 nations forming the EMU did not have the ideal set of conditions for a monetary union. Intra-union resource mobility was strikingly low, there was no strong supranational (taxing and spending) authority to temporarily redistribute revenues, intra-union prices were rather inflexible (at least they were inflexible downward), and trade among EU nations varied between 10% and 20%, which is significant in absolute terms but not close to the volume of trade among the U.S. states.

Differences in language, culture, and levels of unionization explained a large portion of the labor immobility, but even *within* many European countries, labor mobility has been found to be low relative to nations such as the United States. Having highly mobile labor markets and developing them is one of the major keys to success for a monetary union. With high labor mobility, any asymmetric shocks to one economy (for instance, an increase in the price of oil that helps the Netherlands but hurts Germany) could be abated in part by the migration of labor from high unemployment areas to areas with greater employment opportunities. These attributes make Europe seem less than ideally suited for integration.

No assessment of European union can be complete without taking into account an effect that is often overlooked. A major criterion for judging the suitability of any currency union should be the effect that such a union has on the value of participating nations' financial and real wealth. In Europe's case, this effect was decisive. The next chapter explores more fully the development of European integration and its effect on financial wealth.

Chapter 4

European Monetary Unification

INTRODUCTION TO THE EUROPEAN MONETARY UNION

The European Monetary Union (EMU) became a reality on January 1, 1999, when 11 countries irrevocably fixed their currencies to each other, surrendered monetary policy to the European Central Bank, and created a common currency called the euro. On January 1, 2002, these same countries plus one more (Greece) began using, for the first time, physical euro coins and bills, and in February 2002 the period of dual currency circulation ended and the physical currencies of the 12 European Union (EU) nations were relegated to museums.

During the 1993–1999 period, the EU nations pursued contractionary monetary and fiscal policies in an effort to bring their economies into convergence and to meet the conditions they had mutually imposed on themselves for their monetary union. To be sure, these policies brought some hardship. Unemployment was higher than it might otherwise have been, and there was a loss of potential GDP; but lower interest rates and reduced exchange rate risk have created billions of dollars of wealth in just a short span of time—and the EMU has just begun. When enough time has passed for historians to put the events, causes, and effects into perspective, the EMU is likely to be recorded as one of the most significant economic milestones of the twentieth and twenty-first centuries. Clearly, it is a crowning and fitting tribute to visionary statesmen, such as Jean Monnet, Robert Schuman, Konrad Adenauer, and Alcide De Gasperi, who fought diligently and tirelessly for a dream that few thought was attainable.

Since the very earliest stages of European economic integration over a half century ago, the creation of a common currency was the dream that few believed could become real. As late as the mid-1990s, there were serious doubts as to whether the scheduled start of the EMU and the creation of the euro would happen on time. Postponements were expected, but in the end, the 1999 starting date (almost miraculously) held. The EMU survived in spite of having widely varying political systems, legal institutions, cultures, economic performance, public debt levels, and ten different languages. When success finally came, it proved that reason and persistence could triumph over parochial nationalism and skepticism, and it showed that, with tenacity and determination, governments could create a whole that was greater than the sum of its parts.

A common European currency now holds sway over the world's largest trading block—an area that includes approximately 300 million consumers. By comparison, the EMU is almost 10% larger than the U.S. market. For that to have happened, a truly precedent-setting event had to occur. For the first time in history, countries ranking among the world's *most developed* voluntarily abolished their own domestic currencies and transferred monetary power to a supranational authority.

The EMU and full monetary convergence were the final destination at the end of a long journey. The European countries began modestly to integrate their economies shortly after World War II with a relatively uncomplicated arrangement called a "preferential trading agreement." Then, over the following 50 years, they built on their successes and mutual interests to advance integration to higher and more sophisticated levels of economic unification. In the next section, these alternative integration agreements are explained along with some of the trade-offs the European countries had to make when they adopted them.

ROAD TO A EUROPEAN MONETARY UNION

The creation of a common currency in Europe took approximately 50 years. The path taken was neither straight nor smooth. Nevertheless, from modest beginnings, the member countries persevered and overcame many obstacles.

Cooperation during the Immediate Years after World War II

During the early post–World War II years, world attention was focused mainly on political issues. The United States wanted to build an independent Europe that could stand on its own against Communism (that is, the Soviet Union) and that could weave Germany into a central (but controlled) role. But, political strength required a healthy economy, and, thus, it was impossible to disentangle U.S. political goals from economic necessity of reconstruction.

The Marshall Plan (Economic Recovery Program)—whose purpose was to prevent starvation and to begin the process of repairing war-torn Europe—was proposed on June 5, 1947, passed by the U.S. Congress on April 2, 1948, and signed by President Harry Truman on April 3, 1948. Europe responded immediately to the U.S. offer of help by convening the Conference of European Economic Co-operation in Paris in July 1947. Following this conference, the Organization for European Economic Cooperation (OEEC) was established; and over the subsequent four years, it helped to administer the $13.3 billion of Marshall Plan aid appropriated by the U.S. Congress.

In addition to administering the Marshall Plan funds, the OEEC was also responsible for liberalizing European trade and freeing restrictions on current account payments. Clearing account balances were so fragile after World War II that European nations controlled their imports through a combination of exchange controls, import licenses, and bilateral clearing agreements. To remedy the payment gridlock caused by the bilateral clearing agreements, the OEEC established the European Payments Union (EPU) in 1950. The EPU provided multilateral clearing of accounts and the extension of limited amounts of credit (mainly in the form of clearing balances). Its goal was to eventually restore full current account currency convertibility in Europe. So successful was this effort that, in 1958, having accomplished its goal, the EPU was abolished and replaced by the European Monetary Agreement, which provided for convertibility of member nations' currencies. But even though convertibility for current account transactions had been achieved, full capital account convertibility would have to wait almost 35 more years.

The European Coal and Steel Community

The formal process of European unification began on April 18, 1951, when the Treaty of Paris created the European Coal and Steel Community (ECSC). The ECSC was created for the specific purpose of building a unified European market in coal, iron, and steel; but it was clear from the start that broader objectives—such as moving Europe toward a federation of states and beginning the healing process between France and Germany— were in the minds of many. Advocates believed that an economic union would dilute the power and aggression of Germany, a country that, within a span of 75 years, had battled France in the Franco-Prussian War (1870–1871) and led the world into two wars. The hope was that an economic union would make war too expensive, and conflict could be avoided in the future.

The six original nations that formed ECSC—France, West Germany, Italy, Belgium, the Netherlands, and Luxembourg—were the same countries that formed the European Economic Community (EEC) in 1957. The ECSC is commonly referred to as a "preferential trading agreement," but in at least one respect, its structure went well beyond the scope of such agreements. The ECSC's executive structure was financially independent and had the power to exert supranational decision-making authority over member nations. This supranational executive authority became the basis for the European Commission of the European Economic Community (EEC).

The ECSC was a success, not only because it coincided with a dramatic increase in the production of coal, iron ore, and steel; but also, and more importantly, because it was able to prevent volatile price movements that usually characterize commodity markets. The ECSC's accomplishments were so impressive that one might have expected Europe to move rapidly toward full economic and monetary union, but in the end, it took a half century to accomplish this goal.

Perhaps time in years is not the best metric to evaluate the speed of economic integration. Each stage of unification bestows on member nations economic advantages that have to be savored; and sufficient time has to elapse for members to make requisite economic, political, cultural, and environmental changes that lay the foundation of future progress. It could be that the real lesson to be learned from the European integration experience is that nations need a generation or more to learn to cooperate and to make the changes that are essential and fundamental for the creation of an economic *and* monetary union.

The European Economic Community

The EEC was created at the Treaty of Rome in March 1957 and began operations on January 1, 1958. Its founding members committed themselves to the creation of a unified market, which meant:

1. establishing closer relations and eliminating customs duties among member nations,
2. co-coordinating macroeconomic policies,
3. erecting a common external tariff for the community,
4. establishing a common agricultural and transport policy, and
5. creating a European social fund and European investment bank.

To minimize any trade distortion effects, the union decided that the common external tariff it erected would be no greater than the average, pre-union tariff level of all member nations. To diminish the labor and capital market distortions, the union sought to liberalize resource markets and harmonize regulations, thereby promoting intra-union factor movement. Unfortunately, success in promoting the intra-union movement of labor and capital lagged seriously behind the liberalization of trade in goods and services.

By 1958, the EEC members had established the European Monetary Agreement, which provided for the convertibility of member nations' currencies. But the 1960s were turbulent years. It was becoming increasingly clear that the U.S. dollar would not survive as the foundation for the international monetary system. Currency revaluations by Germany (1961 and 1969) and the Netherlands (1961) and a currency devaluation by France (1969) added to the instability.

In 1967, the Europe Economic Community merged with the European Coal and Steel Community and the European Atomic Energy Committee to form the European Community (EC). By July 1968 the EC had finished erecting the common external tariff wall of its customs union (18 months ahead of schedule). EC membership increased in 1973 with the admission of Denmark, Ireland, and the United Kingdom. Membership increased again in 1981 when Greece joined and in 1986 when Spain and Portugal became members.

By 1986, total membership had reached 12 countries, and interest among nearby nations (mainly Austria, Finland, Sweden, and some Eastern/Central European nations) was growing. The EC had already done the lion's share of work to reduce trade barriers, and it was proceeding, though less successfully, toward liberalizing international capital flows. Starting in 1990, EC members took serious aim at dismantling their exchange controls, and by 1994, the customs union became a common market.

Exchange Rate Mechanism and the Path to Monetary Union

Concerned about the U.S. dollar's disproportionate position in the international monetary system and skeptical about the U.S. commitment to maintain the dollar's value in the face of growing U.S. current account deficits, European representatives met at the 1969 Hague Summit in the Netherlands and took a significant step toward creating a European monetary union. They appointed Pierre Werner, prime minister and finance minister of Luxembourg, to lead a committee with the purpose of laying out the steps necessary for the formation of a common European currency.

The resulting "Werner Report" in 1970 was a progressive and visionary document. It proposed a three-phase program to be completed by 1980 with irrevocably fixed European exchange rates and a unified system of central banks. Stage 1 focused on the reduction of exchange rate fluctuations among member nations; stage 2 sought to achieve free, highly integrated intra-union capital markets; and in the final stage, countries were to permanently fix their exchange rates relative to one another. The EC approved the "Werner Report" in 1971, but unfortunately, it crashed almost immediately on the rocks of economic turmoil in the early 1970s.

Persistent U.S. current account deficits and massive currency specu-lation put so much downward pressure on the U.S. dollar that on August 15, 1971, President Richard Nixon broke the dollar's fixed link to gold. His unilateral action abolished the international monetary system that had been constructed a quarter century before at Bretton Woods, New Hampshire. The Smithsonian Agreement was quickly pieced together to replace that of Bretton Woods, but because of continuing worldwide balance of payments pressures and an oil crisis, it collapsed in 1973. As a result, the world's major currencies were cut loose from their familiar fixed moorings, and they began to float relative to one another.

Members of the EC were free from the constraints and obligations of an exchange rate system that was based on the U.S. dollar. But, even though this new freedom was a welcome blessing relative to the U.S. dollar, it had the undesired effect of increasing the volatility among European currencies. As a result, a core of European nations (specifically, Belgium, Germany, Luxembourg, and the Netherlands) in 1972 fixed their exchanges rates within a narrow band ($+/- 2.25\%$) relative to one another and permitted the band to fluctuate vis-à-vis the U.S. dollar. To reduce their vulnerability to speculative currency flows, many of these nations (for instance, France and Italy) imposed exchange restrictions that attenuated the power of short-term capital movements to affect their exchange rates. From 1972 to 1973 (that is, while the Smithsonian Agreement was in force), the exchange rate system among these European nations was called the "snake in the tunnel," because the EC's narrow exchange rate band (the snake) fluctuated within a broader band (the tunnel) relative to the U.S. dollar. After the Smithsonian Agreement was abolished in 1973, the European exchange rate arrangement was called, simply, the "snake," and ultimately, it became the foundation for the European Monetary Union in 1999.

The "snake" was able to weather many storms during the 1970s, but by 1977, only five of the nine EC nations (Belgium, Denmark, Germany, Luxembourg, and the Netherlands) participated in the exchange rate agreement. There was growing concern about the disruptive effects an unstable dollar was having on European economies and an equally serious apprehension that the German mark was increasing its dominance in the EC. A show of support was needed so that the EC would keep progressing toward monetary union, and it came at the December 1978 Brussels Summit when German Chancellor Helmut Schmidt and French President Valéry Giscard d'Estaing strongly supported the further development of a European currency union . In March 1979, eight European nations formed the European Monetary System (EMS) and the Exchange Rate Mechanism (ERM), under which central banks of EC member countries were required to intervene in the foreign exchange markets to keep their currencies within a 4.5% band (that is, $+/-2.25\%$) of their individual parity exchange rates.[1] The European Currency Unit (ECU), which was a weighted average of the combined basket of member nations' currencies, then floated against the dollar without intervention points.

The EMS was plagued by revaluations of various member nations' currencies, and by 1987, the strong need for harmonized macroeconomic policies became clear. Central banks were becoming no match for the resources of international currency speculators. Without cooperation, the highly mobile international pool of "hot money" in the capital markets could overwhelm any exchange rate limits set by the EMS.

In 1988, European Council created the Committee for the Study of Economic and Monetary Union (also known as the Delors Committee). The final report of this committee proposed a broad, skeletal framework for the implementation of a European economic and monetary union (that is, in the form of a single currency and supranational central bank). At the Madrid summit meeting in April 1989, the European Council approved the Delors Plan. Like the "Werner Report" some 19 years earlier, the Delors Plan outlined the creation of a monetary union in three successive stages.

During Stage 1 (June 1990–January 1992), members of the EC were expected to begin the process of converging and coordinating their economic policies, increasing central bank cooperation, removing the remaining intra-union trade and capital barriers, linking their currencies through the ERM, adding some important members (for example, England, Portugal, and Spain) to the ERM, resisting currency realignments, and creating procedures for budgetary policy coordination. As a result of these efforts, the Single European Market began in 1993 and the EC changed its name to the European Union (EU). By 1994, the EU had become a full common market. Within Europe for the first time in history, goods, services, and capital could move freely. Restrictions on labor movement had also been relaxed, but the actual movement of labor among EU countries was insignificant.

The first stage was disrupted by the withdrawal of the British pound and Italian lira in 1992 from the ERM. To salvage the exchange rate agreement, the exchange rate bands, for all member currencies except the Dutch guilder, were widened in July 1993 to 30% (that is, $+/-15\%$ on either side of parity). Stage 2 of the Delors Plan, which began on January 1, 1994, focused on increasing policy coordination among nations and creating independent central banks. "Independent" meant that governments could no longer rely on central banks for either overdraft facilities or for automatic refinancing of public debt. Exchange rate fluctuations were to be narrowed, and increasingly more of the union's macroeconomic policies were to be managed by supranational authorities. During the second stage, the European Monetary Institute (EMI) was to begin operations.

The EMI was established on January 1, 1994, with the mandate to monitor member nations' compliance with the Maastricht Treaty convergence criteria and to prepare for its central bank responsibilities when the EMU began. The EMI had the task of increasing cooperation among the individual EU central banks, as well as ensuring that technical obstacles, in terms of monetary polices, financial regulations, and payments systems, were gone before Stage 3 began.

During Stage 3, member nations were to permanently fix their exchange rates and place control of monetary policy solely in the hands of the European System of Central Banks (ESCB). In May 1998, 14 of the 15 EU nations qualified for admission to the EMU, but only 11 became founding members. Greece was the only EU member that did not meet the Maastricht Treaty economic conditions. EU rules required that any nation qualifying for admission must join the monetary union, but Denmark, the United Kingdom, and Sweden were able to opt out voluntarily.

The Maastricht Treaty and the Period Thereafter

One of the most important treaties for the eventual unification of European currencies was the Maastricht Treaty (Maastricht, the Netherlands), which began in 1991, was signed on February 7, 1992, and was ratified by all member nations by November 1993. For all practical purposes, this Treaty was just an extension of the Delors Plan, making only small relative changes in implementation timing and the transfer of power to a supranational central bank. The Maastricht Treaty set a timetable for beginning Stage 2 (1994) and Stage 3 (1999) of the Delors Plan. Among the many issues discussed at this meeting were trade, foreign affairs, immigration, defense policy, workplace safety, citizenship, health, consumer protection, and tourism, but clearly the most important topics were those connected to the formation of a single currency and the transfer of power to a supranational monetary authority.

The European Monetary Union's chances of success were judged to be greater if member nations' economies converged prior to the union. To this end, the Maastricht Treaty laid down the five convergence criteria that nations would have to meet to qualify for EMU entry in 1999 (see Table 4.1). Fulfillment of these conditions would be determined on May 3, 1998, but the evaluation would be based on the country's performance in 1997. Only those countries judged to have met these criteria would be allowed

Table 4.1
Maastricht Treaty Convergence Criteria[2]

Criterion 1

The Member State must have "a price performance that is sustainable and an average rate of inflation, observed over a period of one year before the examination, that does not exceed by more than $1\frac{1}{2}$ percentage points that of, at most, the three best performing Member States in terms of price stability. Inflation shall be measured by means of the consumer price index on a comparable basis, taking into account differences in national definitions."[3]

Criterion 2

The "Member State is not the subject of a Council decision under this Treaty that an excessive deficit exists."[4] The reference value for the government deficit is "3 percent of the planned or actual government deficit to gross domestic product at market prices."[5]

Criterion 3

The reference values for the ratio of government debt to gross domestic product at market prices is 60%.[6]

Criterion 4

The Member State must respect "the normal fluctuation margins provided for by the Exchange Rate Mechanism of the European Monetary System without severe tensions for at least the last two years before the examination. In particular, the Member State shall not have devalued its currency's bilateral central rate against any other Member State's currency on its own initiative for the same period."[7]

Criterion 5

"Observed over a period of one year before the examination, a Member State [must have] . . . an average nominal long-term interest rate that does not exceed by more than 2 percentage points that of, at most, the three best performing Member States in terms of price stability. Interest rates shall be measured on the basis of long term government bonds or comparable securities, taking into account differences in national definitions."[8]

---

to join as founding EMU nations. But gaining European Council approval for entry was only half the chore. The other half was convincing domestic parliaments, legislatures, and/or popular opinion in a national referendum to accept the terms.

The intent of these preconditions was to bring the member nations to the point at which the transition to a unified currency would be the next natural step. The fear was that without substantial convergence the currency union would fail, because the member nations' economies would be too dissimilar. One of the convergence indicators addressed concerns

Exhibit 4.1
Debt-to-GDP Levels for EU Nations: 1997

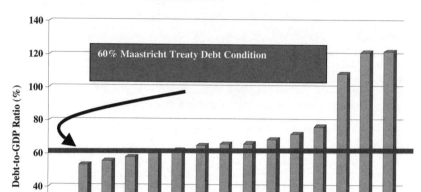

about the union's inflation rate. Low inflation countries, such as Germany and the Netherlands, feared a common currency would fail if the EMU's inflation rate stabilized at the high end of the members' average. They lobbied strongly for convergence at the low end of the inflation range. Similarly, there were fears that, if a common currency was created among nations with excessive debt levels, the economic stress from these debt positions could put undue pressure on the European Central Bank (ECB) and force an easing of monetary policy, thereby increasing the inflation rate.

The deficit and debt conditions were "soft" in the sense that countries that did not meet them could still be members of the EMU so long as it was judged that they were going in the right direction. As Exhibit 4.1 shows, Belgium, Greece, and Italy were well above the 60% limit in 1997. Denmark, Austria, Germany, Ireland, Portugal, Spain, Sweden, and the Netherlands were closer to meeting the goals but still above the limit.

The job of meeting the Maastricht Treaty conditions would have been a lot easier if the policies needed to attain them could have been enacted without the sacrifice of other macroeconomic goals, such as unemployment and GDP growth. How simple it all would have been if (as shown in Exhibit 4.2) member nations could have enacted macroeconomic policies that would act jointly, like a giant piston, to push their economies closer to the Maastricht Treaty goals.

Exhibit 4.2
Convergence Criteria: The Hope

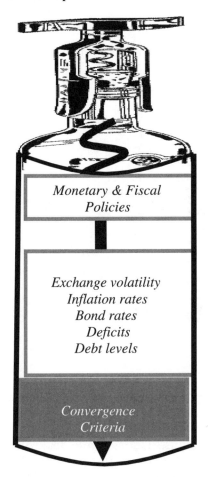

The real world involves trade-offs, and the EU confronted a large one. Because the Maastricht convergence criteria were aimed at reducing simultaneously exchange rate volatility, inflation, interest rates, deficits, and debt levels, the appropriate macroeconomic policies required contractionary monetary and fiscal policy. As Exhibit 4.3 shows, these policies slowed Europe's economic growth and raised the level of unemployment. During the 1990s, the EU (especially in comparison to the United States) suffered from an economic malaise termed "euro sclerosis" (that is, sluggish GDP growth and low job creation).[9]

High and rising unemployment rates (see Exhibit 4.4) complicated the task of reaching the Maastricht Treaty's debt and deficit goals. To be sure,

Exhibit 4.3
Convergence Criteria: The Reality

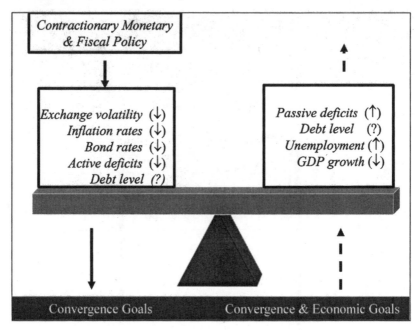

Source: European Monetary Institute. http://www.ecb.int/ and U.S. Department of Labor, Bureau of Labor Statistics. FRED http://www.stls.frb.org/fred/

discretionary reductions of government spending and increases in taxes helped to reduce these nations' *active deficits* (that is, full-employment deficit), but the *actual deficits* (that is, the deficit used in the convergence criteria) increased, because nations had to deal with higher transfer payments and lower tax receipts as their unemployment rates rose.[10]

After the Maastricht Treaty conditions were established, European nations entered a rather disconcerting period of noncompliance, but then economic conditions over the years between 1991 and 1999 were turbulent ones. The union was shocked in 1992 when Ireland, Italy, and the United Kingdom dropped out of the ERM. The turmoil was so disruptive that the EU was forced in 1993 to widen the band of permissible exchange rate fluctuations between member countries' currencies. The previous limits of +/− 2.25% were expanded to +/− 15% (that is, a 30% band of fluctuation). This pressure along with continued strains caused several member nations, notably Portugal and Spain, to devalue their currencies several times over the subsequent years.

The Maastricht Treaty was immediately controversial. Even though it was eventually ratified by all European Union members by 1993, ratification was not without difficulty. In 1992, a popular referendum in Denmark

Exhibit 4.4
EU and U.S. Unemployment Rates: 1990 to 1999

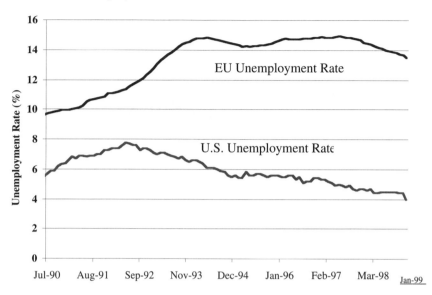

rejected the country's participation in the treaty. This rejection raised doubts about the likelihood that this common currency would ever become a reality, and it started a wave of currency speculation that destabilized many European currencies. In a second referendum, Denmark ratified the Maastricht Treaty, but ratification for Denmark (and for the United Kingdom) was subject to an "opt-out" provision that allowed it to remain outside the EMU (but to remain a member of the EU), even if it qualified in 1999 for admission.[11]

Turmoil surrounding ratification of the Maastricht Treaty generated considerable unease in the currency markets and led to increased speculative activity. In addition, the reunification of East and West Germany brought significant pressures on the Bundesbank (Germany's central bank) to keep the inflation rate in check. Reunification called for massive federal expenditures, which were financed by borrowing. As a result, when Germany's fiscal spending skyrocketed, monetary policy became restrictive. The combination of expansionary fiscal policy and contractionary monetary policy worked together to raise real interest rates. In an effort to prevent their currencies from depreciating relative to the mark, the European central banks were forced to intervene in the foreign exchange markets, which caused their money supplies to fall. As a result, Germany faced resentment for the contractionary effect its economic policies were having on other European economies, which

Table 4.2
Country Performance Relative to Maastricht Treaty Criteria

	Inflation	Deficit as % of GDP*	Debt as % of GDP	ERM Participation	Long-term Interest Rate **
	Jan. 1998	1997	1997	March 1998	
Reference Value	2.7%	3%	60%		7.3
Country					
Austria	1.1	2.5	66.1	Yes	5.6
Belgium	1.4	2.1	122.2	Yes	5.7
Denmark	1.9	-0.7	65.1	Yes	6.2
Finland	1.3	0.9	55.8	Yes	5.9
France	1.2	3.0	58.0	Yes	5.5
Germany	1.4	2.7	61.3	Yes	5.6
Greece	5.2	4.0	108.7	Yes	9.8
Ireland	1.2	-0.9	66.3	Yes	6.2
Italy	1.8	2.7	121.6	Yes	6.7
Luxembourg	1.4	-1.7	6.7	Yes	5.6
Netherlands	1.8	1.4	72.1	Yes	5.5
Portugal	1.8	2.5	62.0	Yes	6.2
Spain	1.8	2.6	68.8	Yes	6.3
Sweden	1.9	0.8	76.6	No	6.5
UK	1.8	1.9	53.4	No	7.0
Average	**1.6**	**2.4**	**72.1**		**6.1**

Notes:
* Negative values for the government deficits indicate surpluses.
** Bonds with average 10-year maturity. Rates averaged over the previous 12 months. Bolded figures indicate non-compliance with Maastricht criteria.

Source: European Commission

already had unemployment rates above desired levels and real GDP growth rates below preferred levels. This growing resentment added to fears of currency realignment within the EU and stimulated even more currency speculation.

Because the EU had systematically begun to dismantle its exchange controls in 1990, member currencies were much more vulnerable to speculative attacks. As mentioned, massive currency movements starting in September 1992 caused the lira and the pound to withdraw from the ERM and caused Spain to devalue its currency. By July 1993, the EMS widened the allowable band of exchange rate movement to 30%, thereby temporarily retreating from its goal of a unified currency system. When pressure on exchange rates in March 1995 caused the depreciation of both the Portuguese escudo and Spanish peseta, no one expected that these two countries would be able to meet the Maastricht Treaty's two-year rule (that is, exchange rate compliance over the 1996 to 1998 period).

In fact, there was widespread skepticism about whether any but a couple of EU countries could meet the Maastricht Treaty conditions, and as the years passed, this skepticism became even more widespread. In an attempt to meet the exchange rate stability requirements of the Maastricht Treaty, Finland and Italy rejoined the ERM in 1996. Table 4.3 shows that, at most, only four nations met the Maastricht Treaty conditions between 1991 and 1996. In 1992, only one country met the criteria; and in 1993, none qualified for membership in the EMU. It was remarkable that so few nations had satisfied the requirements, but what was more remarkable was that most of the nations that attained the Maastricht Treaty goals did so by resorting to accounting gimmicks and fiscal smoke and mirrors that magically made the nations' economies look financially healthier than they were. For instance, France swapped pension liabilities for up-front cash; Italy imposed a one-year euro tax; and Germany selectively excluded hospital expenses and fiddled with pension and welfare reform.

When the European Monetary Union was created on January 1, 1999, the European System of Central Banks[12] also began operations. The European Monetary Institute officially became the European Central Bank (ECB), the national central banks became branch banks of the ESCB, and the ESCB was charged with charting the course of EU monetary policies. Quite astonishingly, at the same time, the Economic and Finance Committee (ECOFIN) was given responsibility for the EU's exchange rate policies. The wisdom of this division of power is still being debated. Because exchange rate policy is so closely entwined with monetary policy, many doubt the practical viability of such a division of power.

The ESCB was structured along the lines of the U.S. Federal Reserve. Two decision-making bodies—the Governing Council and the Executive Board—govern it. The Executive Board resides in Frankfurt, Germany,

Table 4.3
Countries Meeting the Maastricht Treaty Conditions

Year	# Countries	Countries Qualifying
1993	0	None
1994	2	Germany & Luxembourg
1995	2	Germany & Luxembourg
1996	1	Luxembourg
1997	14	All EU nations qualified except Greece
1998	14	All EU nations qualified except Greece

and is composed of six members, who hold eight-year terms and are appointed by the European Council. The Governing Council of the European Central Bank[13] is composed of a six-member executive board and the
12 central bank heads.[14] It decides by simple majority or in some cases by
qualified majority. The central banks play a role similar to the 12 Federal
Reserve Banks in the United States.

Article 107 of the Maastricht Treaty was written to ensure the ESCB's independence from political influence. Even though politics will surely play
a role in the appointment of ECB members, on paper, the ECB's charter
provides it with more independence than the U.S. Federal Reserve. The
Federal Reserve was created by the U.S. Congress in 1913, and its charter
could be changed at any time by Congress. By contrast, the charter for the
ESCB was created at the Maastricht Treaty by a unanimous vote of EU
member nations. Consequently, it would take a similar unanimous country vote (and not the act of just the European Parliament) to change the
ESCB's charter.

The Maastricht Treaty (Article 105) states that "the primary objective of
the ESCB shall be to maintain price stability" and "without prejudice to
the objective of price stability, the ESCB shall support the general economic policies in the Community." Moreover, "the ESCB shall act in ac-
cordance with the principle of an open market economy with free
competition favouring an efficient allocation of resources." The ECB has
been given the exclusive right to authorize the issue of euro banknotes
and coins, but operational implementation of this responsibility has been
delegated to the national central banks. It is not permitted to directly finance the deficits of member nations (Article 104b).

The Maastricht Treaty convergence criteria determined which countries could qualify as founding members of the EMU, but consideration
also had to be given to the criteria for nations seeking entry after the
EMU was up and running. For member nations that qualified, but chose

not to join in 1999 (for example, Denmark, Sweden and the United Kingdom), the European Commission would continue monitoring to ensure that their economic policies and conditions remained in compliance with the Maastricht criteria. As well, the admission of new nations would require easily understood (transparent) criteria. To this end, the European Council signed the Stability and Growth Pact (Amsterdam, July 1997) for the purpose of giving member nations a reason to continue pursuing cyclically balanced budgets or budget surpluses after the EMU began. Failure to meet the requirements could result in examinations, advice, recommendations, publication, and, if needed, the imposition of sanctions.

At the June, 1977 meeting in Amsterdam, Holland, the EU established the legal framework, stability pact, and a new exchange rate arrangement to coordinate the economic and exchange rate policies of the EMU countries and those that remained outside the union. The new voluntary exchange rate system (ERM-II), was similar to the original Exchange Rate Mechanism under the European Monetary System, except that external currencies were linked to the euro rather than to the currencies of individual member nations. A 30% band of fluctuation relative to the euro was permitted. ERM-II was crucial for countries desiring to enter the EMU and wishing to fulfill the exchange rate requirement of the Maastricht Treaty.

The story of European monetary unification has a happy ending. On January 1, 1999, the euro was launched in dematerialized form (that is, in checking account form) with the 11 member nations' currencies irrevocably tied to the euro, just like pennies, nickels, dimes, quarters, and half dollars are tied to the U.S. dollar. On January 1, 2001, Greece became the newest EMU member, and on January 1, 2002, physical euro coins and notes began to circulate. By February 28, 2002, the euro had become the sole currency of the EMU member nations.

THREE LESSONS LEARNED ABOUT MONETARY UNIONS

From centuries of experience with economic integration, we have learned three important lessons. First, the potential benefits of integration act initially like huge economic magnets to attract member nations, open lines of negotiating dialogue, and, if successful, actually begin the process of reducing trade barriers, integrating economies, and unifying currencies. The second lesson is that initial economic magnetism fades quickly and its polarity seems to reverse when nations confront, as they must, the costs of integration—even if these costs are relatively small and the net benefits are huge. It is for this reason that most nations rarely move beyond the initial stages of integration. Now that the European Monetary

Exhibit 4.5
Countries Likely to Enter EMU in the Coming Years

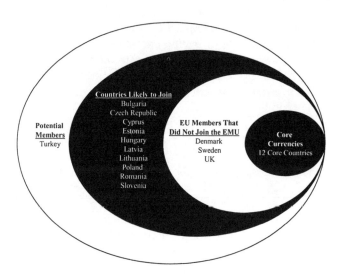

Union is a reality, the question is whether this achievement will create sufficient centripetal forces to make withdrawal extremely difficult and expensive. The world has had so few historic examples of such advanced currency unions that the answer is not obvious.

The final lesson is that monetary unions are helpful in absorbing *financial shocks* to a nation's economy, but they can do little to cushion nations from *real economic shocks.* Weather-related catastrophes, embargoes, wars, and technological changes are real-side effects that are not blunted by the existence of a unified currency. As a result, changes in supply and demand that are precipitated by real economic shocks can have sizable effects on nations' wages, employment, prices, growth in GDP, and real interest rates.

Consider the effects of rapidly rising U.S. oil prices due to a war or to orchestrated reductions in production (perhaps cartel related). When the price of oil rises, the New England states spend more of their income on oil but transfer spending power to the oil-producing states in the Southeast. As a result, New England suffers when there are higher energy prices. By contrast, the Southeastern states also pay more for oil, but their purchasing power does not escape the Southeastern region and therefore the negative economic consequences are abated. Having a common currency in both parts of the United States does little or nothing to ease the economic effects of this real economic shock.

Exhibit 4.6
The European Union and Prospective Members

Souce: http://www.eurunion.org/legislat/agd2000.htm

FUTURE EUROPEAN MONETARY UNION MEMBERS

Since its beginning in 1957, the European Union has expanded its membership four times, adding nine new members to its ranks. Over the coming decade, it is very likely that ten to 13 additional countries will join the EU and the EMU (see Exhibit 4.5). Transition for the nations desiring EMS membership is likely to be easier for those that have already linked their currencies to the euro. Even before the birth of the ERM in 1999, the Bulgarian leva, Czech koruna, Hungarian forint, and Polish zloty moved in line with the German mark. These nations have, for all intents and purposes, already emasculated their central banks by transferring monetary policy decisions to the European Central Bank in Frankfurt.

Clearly, Denmark, Sweden, and the United Kingdom are the most likely candidates for near-term membership in the EMU, because they opted not to join in 1999. There are at least 13 other nations, mainly in Eastern and Central Europe (see Exhibit 4.6), that are primed to join the EU in relatively short order. Three of them are Eastern European (the Czech Republic, Hungary, and Poland), four are Balkan (Estonia, Latvia, Lithuania, and Slovenia), and two are Mediterranean/Asian (Cyprus and Turkey). These aspirant member nations are in highly varied stages of development, and some are not ready for immediate entry (for example, Bulgaria, Latvia, Romania, and Slovakia). Because of their different stages of development and convergence, the process of admitting all of them to the EU could take 20 years or more.

The Czech Republic, Cyprus, Estonia, Poland, and Slovenia began negotiations to enter the EU in 1998; and Bulgaria, Latvia, Lithuania, Malta, Romania, Slovakia, and Turkey followed shortly thereafter, in 2000. At the 1993 Copenhagen meetings, the EU established criteria for Central and Eastern European nations seeking entry to the EU. Among these criteria were the existence of functioning markets, rules of law, respect for minority rights and human rights, and an ability to handle the responsibilities (for instance, competition, environment, health, public administration, and safety) of EU membership. At the EU's 1995 Luxembourg meetings, only five of the Central and Eastern European nations were given fast-track consideration.

There are fierce controversies surrounding EU expansion that could seriously jeopardize its progress. To join the European Monetary Union, countries seeking membership will, of course, have to meet the Maastricht Treaty requirements, and many analysts doubt seriously if these countries are at a stage of economic and social development that would make entry into the EU seamless. If they do gain entry, the demographic statistics are worrisome. The 12 most likely new members would enter the EU with an average per capita GDP that is less than one-third of the average of the current 15 EU countries. They would increase the EU's GDP by a paltry 4%, but, at the same time, increase the EU's population by 30%.

As daunting as the macroeconomic concerns are, there is a host of noneconomic issues that seem to be even more problematic. For instance, there is apprehension that aspirant nations do not have sufficient levels of investment in and commitment to the environment, financial and banking sophistication, corporate governance laws, freedom of the press, enterprise restructuring, human rights, minority rights, and commitment to the fight against corruption.

At the EU's meeting in Nice, France (2001), a deal was struck for the enlargement of the union, which would require changing some EU institutions in preparation for the expansion to 28 or more countries. The Nice meeting was heated for several reasons, inter alia, because some of the smaller EU nations (for example, Belgium and Portugal) feared losing

Exhibit 4.7
Currency Unions Have a Gravitational Attraction

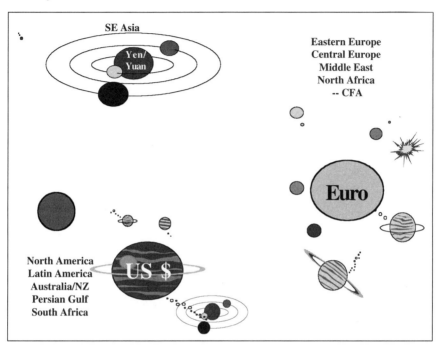

their relative voting power, and they were concerned that the EU's decision to use majority voting in 30 new policy areas, rather than the national veto system, could work to their disadvantage.[15] Germany and Austria were apprehensive that expansion would stimulate an uncontrolled surge of labor across their borders and into their workforces. Spain was frightened that expansion would result in the loss of EU aid (approximately €50 billion), because it no longer would rank among countries with the lowest per capita income.

A visible sign of how serious this controversy has become was Ireland's popular referendum in June 2001 in which Irish voters rejected the EU's expansion plans, which were drawn up at the Treaty of Nice in December 2000. Ireland's eventual endorsement in 2002 was vital to the process, because approval by all 15 EU member nations is required for the treaty to take effect. The Irish rejection cast a giant cloud over how fast expansion will take place.[16]

The real question regarding the EU's expansion is not *if* expansion will take place but *when* it will take place. Because they offer such enormous potential benefits, currency unions exert a relentless pull on other currencies, especially on neighboring currencies, in the same way that large planets (see Exhibit 4.7) exert a strong gravitational pull on smaller,

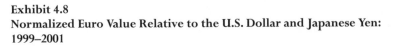

Exhibit 4.8
Normalized Euro Value Relative to the U.S. Dollar and Japanese Yen:
1999–2001

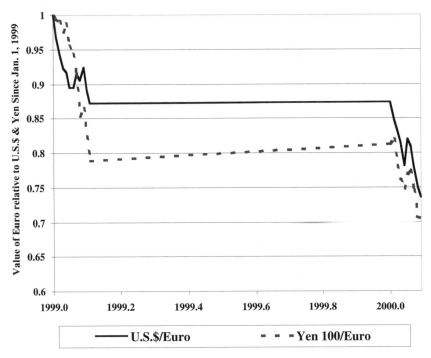

nearby planets. Together, the EU, Japan, and the United States account for approximately 70% of the world's production. Many economic observers have predicted that Japan, China, or the Association of Southeast Asian Nations will form a third currency block. In Chapter 7, we explore several new possible currency unions in Asia and Latin America to see how much value they might create.

THE EURO AND ITS FUTURE

The first referendum on the euro was in the foreign exchange markets. Many observers expected the euro to be strong, and they equated a strong euro to a vote of confidence. If that is the criterion of success, then the new currency did not perform as well as its advocates had hoped it would. Exhibit 4.8 shows that, between its birth on January 1, 1999 and 2001, the euro fell against the U.S. dollar and the Japanese yen.

Despite the euro's pallid performance vis-à-vis the dollar and the yen, it did achieve many successes. Most important, the market prices of financial assets in the euro zone rose sharply. Bonds and common stocks both went up. The rallies in financial asset prices justified the effort and the pain that the member nations imposed on themselves during the years prior to the launch date. Member nations forced the high inflation countries to comply, at least for a time, with the strict Maastricht criteria, and they forced the high-debt countries to curb their fiscal deficits and sell state-owned assets. They disciplined themselves so that they would be able to accomplish convergence at the low end of the inflation rate range. That is how the euro acquired instant credibility as a low-inflation currency.

Bond traders viewed the euro as a continent-wide extension of the mark, not as a continent-wide extension of the peseta or the escudo. Its weakness in foreign exchange markets was not a judgment about its future purchasing power or its unsoundness in its design or implementation. The implied inflation premium in euro-denominated government bonds was consistently lower than the inflation premium in dollar-denominated government bonds. The ESCB's autonomy and mandate to control inflation convinced investors that it would successfully defend the purchasing power of the new currency unit.

Instead, the euro's decline happened, because its birth coincided with a strong and broad-based bull market in the United States. U.S. financial markets exerted a force of attraction that pulled funds away from European capital markets, especially during the 1999–2000 period. Nevertheless, enough buying power remained in European capital markets to fuel strong rallies in the prices of blue chip European common stocks. Also, the euro's credibility as a store of value remained strong, as bidders kept the prices of euro-denominated bonds at the high prices they had reached after May 1998, when the euro, from the point of view of bond traders, became a fait accompli.

The euro's launch was a brilliant success in the real economy as well. European economic growth, which had been sluggish for a generation, picked up, and unemployment fell steadily for the first two years after January 1999. There are many explanations for this economic revival, and in fairness to all points of view, it is important to acknowledge that the rise in growth and employment may have been due to the euro's depreciation in the foreign exchange markets. Exports rose and tourism flourished throughout the euro zone. There were also regulatory changes that allowed hiring new employees on part-time, temporary contracts.

Another explanation for the economic revival is that after the new currency came into effect, governments could go back to their old higher levels of spending within the limits of the Stability and Growth Pact. They had restrained themselves to qualify for membership in the new club and now gave themselves the luxury of a small celebration. They would not have to finance the expenditures with tax collections or with bond issues denominated in the old, high-interest currencies. Instead, they could issue bonds denominated in euros and take advantage of the new currency's image of strength as a store of value.

So the economic revival has many possible explanations that do not attribute much importance to the new currency. Nevertheless, the euro's launch sent a signal to market participants everywhere that Europe was willing to sacrifice national priorities and parochial interests to achieve a supranational goal: a truly unified European economic space. Launching the euro on schedule silenced many skeptics and showed investors that they could safely start businesses that depended on accessing a wider western European market. In that sense the euro's launch was massively successful as a signal. The investment climate made a quantum improvement, and many people acted in response to the signal.

Thinking of the euro's launch as a signal helps to explain why the European nations put themselves through such rigors between 1993 and 1998. European policy makers made it clear from the earliest discussions of monetary union onward that they were going to establish their common currency on a sound footing. Their actions affirmed that prudent objective at every moment, even when currency instability was severe. They showed, by allowing their economies to stagnate, that they were serious about holding themselves to strict criteria. If necessary, the euro's launch would proceed with only a select handful of nations qualifying as charter members of the club. The fainthearted and the backsliders would not make the grade. These countries would have to qualify at a later date, if they could muster the resolve to qualify after failing the first time. One major reason for this consistent signaling and for the real pain and inconvenience was to show everyone, including themselves, that the euro was a sound currency, deserving the same level of credibility that the dollar and the Swiss franc command.

The Europeans bought credibility for their new currency, and the cost they paid was worth the value they obtained. To see the trade-off, let us consider the period from 1992 to 1998 and calculate the effect on the value of financial assets of the new, low-inflation currency. Suppose that prior to the unification there were two zones: a low-inflation zone with the interest rate on five-year government bonds equal to 5%, and a high-inflation zone with the interest rate on five-year government bonds equal to 14%. Also suppose that the two zones were the same size (that is, each zone accounted for 50% of the total economic activity of the euro zone). In the high-inflation zone, suppose that there were government bonds outstanding in an amount equal to 70% of annual output, and common stocks with market values equal to 30% of annual output. The price/earnings (P/E) multiple of those common stocks would be 7.7.[17] In the low-inflation zone, suppose that there were government bonds outstanding in an amount equal to 70% of annual output and common stocks with market value equal to 60% of annual output. The P/E multiple of those common stocks would be 12.5.[18] For simplicity, suppose that all the bonds were five-year, fixed-coupon, noncallable bonds, and before the currency unification, they were all trading at 100% of face value.

Now consider what would happen if the currency unification came about without the fiscal and monetary discipline that Europe imposed on itself. Financial market participants might reasonably fear that the new currency would come with high inflation and, therefore, these partici-pants would adjust the prices they would be willing to pay for all the fi-nancial assets in the zone. In effect, they would apply the 14% discount rate that characterized the high-inflation zone to the financial assets in the low-inflation zone. The market prices of the government bonds in the low-inflation zone would fall. Prior to the unification, they were worth 70% of annual output of the countries in the low-inflation zone. After the unifica-tion they would be worth only 48.4%[19] of annual output in the low-inflation zone. This would be an enormous loss, in the amount of 21.6%[20] of annual output in the low-inflation zone. And that would not be the only loss. The market prices of common stocks in the low-inflation zone would also fall. For simplicity, suppose that the companies in the low-inflation and high-inflation zones were so similar that the only difference in their stock market valuations came from the difference in long-term interest rates in the two zones. In that case the stock prices in the low-inflation zone would fall by about one-third, from 60% of annual output to 38.4% of annual output.

In this simplified case, we can see that the loss to holders of bonds and common stocks in the low-inflation countries would be the enormous amount of 43.2%[21] of annual output of the low-inflation zone. Since we have assumed that the low-inflation zone constitutes 50% of the entire euro zone, the loss would be 21.6%[22] of annual output of the entire euro zone.

This computation shows that monetary unification would have de-stroyed value if European countries had unified their currencies in a way that allowed high inflation to become the norm throughout the euro zone. Unifying the currencies created value in financial markets, mainly because it spread the discipline of low inflation to the countries that previously had tolerated high inflation. Now let us compute how much financial wealth Europe's stern policy on convergence criteria would create in our hypo-thetical example. Market participants believed that the euro would have low inflation, and so they applied the 5% rate to the five-year bonds of the countries that had previously had high inflation. They bid up the prices of those government bonds, and after the prices reached the new equilibrium, the total market value of the bonds reached 97.3% of annual output, an im-provement of 27.3% from the 70% they had been worth before the unifica-tion. The total market value of common stocks, because of the simplifying assumptions we have made, would rise from 30% to 46.9%[23] of annual out-put. In total, therefore, the value created would be equal to 44.2%[24] of an-nual output of the high-inflation countries. Since we have assumed that the high-inflation countries constitute 50% of the entire euro zone, the gain would be 22.1%[25] of annual output of the entire euro zone.

To see the trade-off and why the EU pursued fiscal and monetary conservatism, let us put our calculated gains and losses in terms of economic growth. We saw that the EU would have lost the equivalent of 21.6% of its asset prices (stocks and bonds) if its monetary and fiscal policies after the union converged to the high inflation countries' levels. This loss is equivalent to about 3% per year loss for each of the seven Maastricht transition years, and these losses would be coming on the back of already weak economies. By contrast, pursuing convergence to the low-inflation countries' levels would have the effect of increasing asset values by 22.1%, which is a gain in GDP of approximately 3% per year. In other words, the difference between inflationary policies and noninflationary policies was the equivalent of 6% difference in GDP growth for each of seven years.

These calculations show why the Europeans were so insistent that all the countries wishing to join the currency unification meet stringent eligibility criteria. If the Europeans had rushed into a currency unification without putting themselves through the rigors of satisfying the Maastricht criteria, and if they had failed to put in place the checks and balances that guard against inflation, the euro might have come into existence as a high-inflation currency. These calculations indicate that, in that scenario, the result would have been unsatisfactory.

THE FUTURE OF THE EURO CAPITAL AND MONEY MARKETS

In what direction will the European capital market move in the future? If the structure of EU capital markets moves closer to that of the United States, then considerable changes will have to be made. Exhibit 4.9 shows, in nominal amounts, the composition of the EU's capital markets compared to the United States and Exhibit 4.10 standardizes these figures in terms of 100%. The EU capital markets show a striking reliance (both in absolute terms and relative terms) on bank loans relative to stock market capitalization and public debt. In the future, as the EU securitizes assets and continues to develop its capital markets, the composition of the European capital market should move steadily toward the U.S. structure.

The continued advance of the EMU will accelerate the development of European corporate bond markets, but rapid progress will mean breaking down excessive regulation (for instance, legal and tax obstacles) and beefing up the relatively narrow institutional investor base. Dismantling these barriers will likely be a primary theme over the coming years.

European securities markets have become more integrated and liquidity-driven due to the deregulation of financial intermediaries; and the con-

Exhibit 4.9
Composition of EU and U.S. Capital Markets: 1996 Figures in Trillions of U.S.$

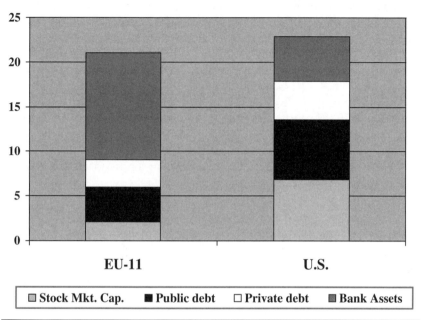

Source: International Monetary Fund and Bank for International Settlements.

vergence of macroeconomic policies since the Maastricht Treaty was ratified in 1993 has spurred capital mobility. As well, large issues of sovereign
debt have improved the efficiency of the secondary market in bonds, so the
yields that investors realize with government securities have reached levels that provide alternatives to bank deposits. Nevertheless, to remain internationally competitive, the EMU must continue to develop larger, more
liquid secondary markets in government debt. The European Central Bank
could play a part in this development by relying less on setting minimum
reserve requirements and more on conducting open market operations.

In the future, legal risks along with risks associated with credit, liquidity,
and settlement will become the most important determinants of government
security prices. Because government liabilities will no longer be backed by a
sovereign ability to print and coin money, the government debt markets will
be stratified in a manner similar to the state and municipal debt markets in
the United States. The Maastricht Treaty specifically chose a "no-bailout"
policy so that nations would not be able to rely on the European Central
Bank for support. As a result, the EU nations may have to turn to the International Monetary Fund (IMF) if they run into debt repayment problems.

Over the coming years, the euro will encourage securitization, harmonization of market practices, and greater pricing transparency. There will be substantial efforts to ease member country restrictions on the allowable investments of pension funds and insurance companies as the market practices of members are harmonized. Consolidation of the European financial services industry will continue along the lines of the United States. Currently, the EU has 16 futures and options markets, with the top three exchanges (that is, Deutsche Terminborse [DTB], Marché à Terme International de France [MATIF], and the London International Financial Futures Exchange [LIFFE]) putting extensive competitive pressure on each other. To remain competitive, more money market instruments will have to be developed that are alternatives to bank deposits, as well as screen-based, order-driven trading systems (along the lines of the Swiss system) that automate all aspects of the stock and bond markets.

DID THE EUROPEAN MONETARY UNION CREATE WEALTH? ESTIMATES BEFORE AND AFTER UNIFICATION

After currencies unify, relinquish their national identities, and forge a single supranational currency, we have argued that bond and stock prices should be higher than they were before the unification. It should also be true that the weaker the preexisting currency was and the stronger the supranational currency, the greater should be the price appreciation. The European convergence gives several examples of price appreciation, and some of these are dramatic. It is worthwhile to examine these price changes to see the timing and magnitude of the gains and to see what factors may have accounted for the gains.

The security appreciation did not follow immediately after the Maastricht Treaty was signed. Before people could begin to treat the monetary convergence as a fait accompli, there were several major and highly visible steps that Europe had to accomplish in order to convince themselves that they were really going ahead. After the borders really came down for movement of goods and capital and after the national referenda to ratify the Treaty had been held, Europeans could direct their attention to the idea that monetary convergence was going to happen. From the viewpoint of 1992, both 1999 and 2002 seemed a long way into the future, so there was no pressing urgency to buy securities to profit from the coming rise. Besides, up until 1997, so few countries met the Maastricht guidelines, and the business climate was so anemic that few analysts thought a full currency union would become a reality (see Table 4.3). Nevertheless, there were some rays of sunshine. For instance, a stock market boom began in 1996 in several edge countries, such as Finland and Spain.

There are several possible explanations for the stock market booms that happened in Europe during the 1996–2000 time frame, with particular strength in edge countries. We examined data for Helsinki, Madrid, and Milan and found that all three experienced rises of 150% or more from January 1996 to January 1999.[26] These dramatic rises have many possible explanations besides the one we adduce, and we provide these reasons so that the reader can see how many favorable forces converged to produce these stock market rallies.

1. All governments in Europe were taking steps to control inflation and were publicizing those steps.

2. Telecommunications companies, especially Nokia in Finland and Telefonica in Spain, were doing very well and were attracting many new shareholders who paid premium prices for the shares. Since these companies have relatively high weightings in the indexes we studied, their success accounts for part of the rise.

3. Pension funds were gaining importance and their managers were able to press for shareholder value. The dominant view still focused on stakeholder value, but the balance was shifting.

4. Brussels was gaining influence, and the European standard for protecting minority shareholder rights was higher than in some edge countries.

Our explanation for the stock market rallies is that there was a decline in both country risk and the risk of exchange rate depreciation. After January 1, 1999, and effectively after May 1998, these countries could not devalue or inflate unilaterally, no matter what emergency might have arisen. To see the effect that the drop in country risk would have on the price of a typical common stock, consider the following example, which uses a standard formula for the price of a common stock.

$$P = E/(k_e - g)$$

where P is the stock price, E is earnings per share, k_e is the cost of equity, and g is the growth rate of earnings.

Dividing both sides by earnings per share E, we can derive:

$$P/E = 1/(k_e - g)$$

Using typical pre-unification values for k_e and g of 14% and 5%, we calculate:

$$P/E = 1/(0.14 - 0.05) = 1/(0.09) = 11.1.[27]$$

In other words, before the run-up to currency unification, the average P/E ratio should have been as low as 11 in some European countries. After unification, the cost of equity would fall, in this example to 11%, and the

Table 4.4
**Stock Market Capitalization as a Percent of GDP Before and After
Currency Unification**

Country	1990	1999	Change
Germany	22.2%	67.8%	+45.6%
Italy	13.5%	62.2%	+48.7%
Spain	21.7%	72.4%	+50.7%
Finland	16.6%	269.5%	+252.9%
Not in the Union			
UK	85.9%	203.4%	117.5%

Source: World Bank, *World Development Indicators 2001*, IBRD, 2002, pp. 278–281.

expected growth rate of earnings would rise, in this example to 6%, and the new P/E ratio would rise to 20:

$$P/E = 1/(0.11 - 0.06) = 1/(0.05) = 20.$$

This combination of inputs would cause an approximate doubling of stock prices, which is a less dramatic move than what occurred from 1996 to 1999. The question is what investors were thinking that made them pay so much. They could have been taking note of all the favorable developments during that time period and buying, because they lowered their country risk assessments and because they raised their forecasts of earnings growth. In the example, we lowered the cost of equity by 3% and raised the earnings growth forecast by 1%. Investors evidently made larger adjustments than we assumed they did to their assessments, but it is difficult to tell what relative importance they assigned to the many favorable trends that were going on at that time.

To complete the discussion regarding the stock market rallies in Europe during the 1996–1999 period, we note the magnitude of wealth that the stock market rallies delivered to asset holders. As of January 1990, before monetary unification began, European stock markets were relatively small and inactive. Their market capitalizations and other indicators of size were small compared to the larger markets in New York and London. By 1999, the stock market capitalization had risen to substantially larger shares of GDP, as shown in Table 4.4. This enormous windfall was (and is), in our view, indicative of the major benefit that currency unification can bring.

In addition to the stock market rallies, there were rallies in the government bond markets of the countries joining the euro. We have selected two bond markets—Italy and Spain—to illustrate these rallies. Italy was one of the original six countries to join the EU, but its currency was chronically weaker than those of the other original six members. Spain was an edge country, joining the EU at the late date of 1986, and during the early 1990s,

Exhibit 4.10
EU and U.S. Capital Markets: 1996 Standardized Figures Relative to 100%

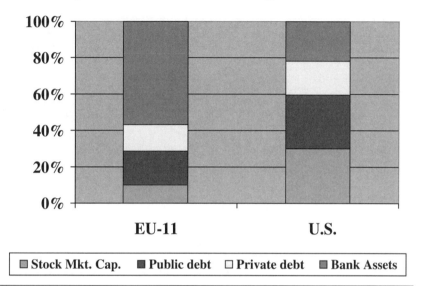

Source: International Monetary Fund and Bank for International Settlements

pundits questioned whether Spain would be able to meet the Maastricht criteria and join the euro in the first round.

Both government bond markets enjoyed strong rallies from 1995 to the end of 1998. A graph of the monthly yields for these government bonds shows that these rallies were in sharp contrast to the meandering fluctuations for the period 1992–1994 and for the year 1999. Instead of randomly fluctuating from positive to negative territory and back again, ten-year government bonds earned positive yields nearly every month from mid-1995 to the end of 1998. For Italy, in a span of 44 months (from April 1995 to December 1998), there were only six occasions when the monthly yield was negative. Also, when the yield for a month was negative, it was never very negative, but when it was positive, it was sometimes strongly positive. The annual compound yields for 1995, 1996, 1997, and 1998 were 21.5%, 31.0%, 18.9%, and 15.9%, respectively (see Exhibit 4.11).

For Spain, during the time period from April 1995 to December 1998, the pattern was very similar. There were also only six occasions when the monthly yield was negative, but, again, it was never sharply negative, and the annual compound yields were very high, as they were in Italy. For 1995, 1996, 1997, and 1998, the annual compound yields were 24.2%, 27.8%, 14.8%, and 15.7%, respectively (see Exhibit 4.12).[28]

There are several possible explanations that parallel closely the rallies in the stock market. To give a balanced treatment of these explanations, we

Exhibit 4.11
Italian Government Bond Rally: 1995–1998 Cumulative Value in Lira

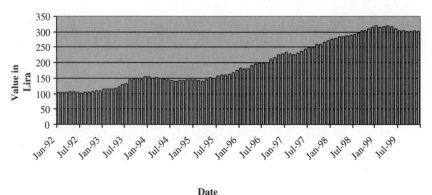

Date

begin with two that are conventional and do not relate directly to the monetary convergence. First, inflation was declining in these countries and in other industrial countries during that period. Second, the fiscal deficits of both Italy and Spain were being reduced. These are two plausible reasons for the rallies, but there was, in our opinion, too much strength to the rallies for these reasons to be the full explanation.

Our explanation for the rallies is that the euro was going to be a more stable currency than the lira or the peseta. For that reason, bond investors bid up the prices of Italian and Spanish government bonds as the approaching monetary convergence gained credibility. The Italian and Spanish governments were going to give up their authority to devalue or inflate their currencies unilaterally. Bondholders were going to gain protection. Italy and Spain would have only two choices after the convergence: pay or default. The politically easier ways of lowering the debt burden—inflating or devaluing—were becoming less feasible and, finally, impossible. For that reason the bonds rallied.

CONCLUSION

After overcoming many real impediments, Europe finally achieved the dream of unifying its currencies. The process was a struggle, because the European countries were not ideally suited to form a monetary union. Europe is too large and its economies are too dissimilar to constitute a textbook example of an optimal currency area, and people do not move from one part of Europe to another very willingly. Wisely, the architects of European economic integration began the journey with a preferential trading agreement for coal and steel. This was a good starting point, because in the 1950s, Europe's national coal, iron, and steel industries needed mar-

Exhibit 4.12
Spanish Government Bond Rally: 1995–1998 Cumulative Value in Pesetas

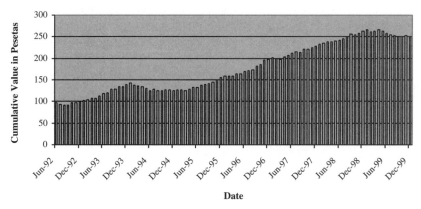

Date

kets, access to financing, and stable prices for their products more than they needed protection. Success in this continent-wide initiative turned the popular imagination away from the conflict and devastation of World War II. The monetary concomitant—the European Payments Union—went hand in hand with economic integration and became one of the first visible signs that full economic and monetary integration could be achieved.

NOTES

1. The Italian lira fluctuated within a 6% band until January 1990, when it reduced its currency fluctuation to the normal 4.5% band. The British pound, Spanish peseta, and Portuguese escudo fluctuated within a 12% band (that is, +/–6%) relative to the parity rate when they first joined the EMS. In the post-1979 period, bilateral exchange rates among the EU nations were adjusted and periodically realigned. In total, there were 11 realignments between 1979 and 1987.

2. "Protocol on the Convergence Criteria Referred to in Article 109j of the Treaty Establishing the European Community the High Contracting Parties," *Treaty on European Union.* Available: http://europa.eu.int/en/record/mt/protocol.html.

3. Ibid., Article 1.

4. Ibid., Article 2.

5. "Protocol on the Excessive Deficit Procedure the High Contracting Parties," *Treaty on European Union.* Article 1. Available: http://europa.eu.int/en/record/mt/protocol.html.

6. Ibid.

7. "Protocol on the Convergence Criteria," Article 3.

8. Ibid., Article 4.

9. Over the 20 years prior to the ERM, the United States created 38 million new jobs, of which 31 million were in the private sector. During the same period, the EU created five million new jobs, of which one million were private. The fiscal and monetary discipline that the countries imposed on themselves to comply with the Maastricht Treaty explains part of this enormous difference in job creation performance but not all of it. The other causes of Europe's under-performance in job creation were its high tax rates, over-regulation, labor market rigidities, minimum wage, as well as relatively high non-wage costs and unemployment benefits. See Martin Feldstein, "The Political Economy of the European Economic and Monetary Union: Political Sources of an Economic Liability," *Journal of Economic Perspectives* 11, no. 4 (Fall 1997): 40.

10. The actual deficit is composed of the active deficit plus the passive deficit. The active deficit is measured at full employment and does not include the effects of a nation's automatic stabilizers. The passive deficit rises with the level of unemployment rate due to higher transfer payments and lower tax receipts. The active deficits of EU nations fell, but their actual deficits rose because of the more than offsetting rise in the passive deficit.

11. When the Maastricht Treaty was passed, Finland, Greece, Italy, Sweden, and the United Kingdom were not participating in the EMU.

12. The ECB plus the 12 national central banks make up the ESCB.

13. It is similar to the Federal Open Market Committee, which is composed of the seven Board of Governors members and five members of the 12 Federal Reserve Banks.

14. Each central bank head is chosen by the national government of the respective member nation.

15. Individual nations will maintain their veto rights in the areas of taxation, social security, asylum, immigration policy, subsidies to poorer regions, and trade in financial services.

16. Ireland was the only EU country with a Constitution that required a referendum. Other nations required just parliamentary approval. For the vote in 2001, only about one-third of the Irish voters showed up at the polls and a slim majority defeated the EU's expansion plans.

17. The P/E ratio is derived from the formula: $P/E = 1/(k_e - g)$. For this example, suppose g, the growth of earnings per share, is 5% in both zones, and the risk premium is 4% in both zones. Then, k_e, the cost of equity capital, would be 18% in the high inflation zone and 9% in the low inflation zone. Using the P/E formula, we find that $P/E = 1/(0.18 - 0.05) = 1/.13 = 7.7$.

18. Because the cost of equity capital, k_e, would be 13% in the low inflation zone, we find that $P/E = 1/(0.13 - 0.05) = 1/.08 = 12.5$.

19. The 48.4% figure comes from valuing a five-year, 5% coupon bond to yield 14% and then multiplying this value by 70%.

20. $70\% - 48.4\% = 21.6\%$.

21. $21.6\% + 21.6\% = 43.2\%$.

22. $43.2\% * 50\% = 21.6\%$.

23. 30% * (12.5/8) = 46.9.

24. 16.9% + 27.3% = 44.2%.

25. 44.2% * 50% = 22.1%.

26. In particular, Madrid rose 188%, Helsinki rose 218%, and Milan rose 152% during that time frame. Source: Bloomberg News Service Dedicated Terminal: Datastream Data Service provided through Bloomberg, and calculations by the authors.

27. At the beginning of 1996, the composite yield on ten-year European government bonds was 7.44%. Source: European Central Bank website: http://www.economagic.com/em-cgi/data.exe/ecb/t3- 02- 05+2. If the risk premium for the average common stock was 6.56%, then the cost of equity would have been 14%. Note that 7.44% + 6.56% = 14%. If the expected growth rate of earnings was 5%, then the P/E ratio would be 1/(0.14– 0.05) = 11.1. Data from Bloomberg News Service Dedicated Terminal indicate that P/E ratios for Spain and Italy in mid-1995 were slightly higher than this already (that is, a P/E of 13 and 19, respectively).

28. Data from Merrill Lynch Global Index System reported on Bloomberg. Data are for monthly returns on an index of ten-year government bonds for both countries. Annual returns are from the same source. For the graphs, we computed a cumulative total amount for an initial investment of 100 units of local currency and graphed the monthly values of that total.

Chapter 5

The Development of a Common Currency in the United States and Germany

INTRODUCTION

The dollar is the common currency of all 50 U.S. states. Whether you are in Kennebunkport, Maine, or 5,100 miles away in Honolulu, Hawaii, a dollar is worth a dollar. It comes as a surprise to many that this was not always so and that the adoption of a common currency occurred long after the U.S. Constitution was signed. In fact, something resembling the dollar, as we know it, was not created until 1863-1864 (over 75 years after the Constitution) and a lasting U.S. central bank did not begin operating until 1914. Compare this to nations such as Sweden, England, and France where central banks were established in 1668,[1] 1694, and 1800, respectively.

How did the United States survive so long without a common currency and without a central bank? What compelled the nation to unify its currency? Were the states of the union ideally suited for a common currency? Were the same issues discussed during the establishment of a common U.S. currency as were discussed with the founding of the euro, the common Euroland currency? Did states have to qualify, as the European nations did, to become members of the U.S. common currency? Providing a historical perspective and putting these questions into a broader context are the goals of this chapter. Fortunately, most of the practical and theoretical issues behind the creation of a common U.S. currency parallel the issues in our previous chapter on European monetary unification.

THE DEVELOPMENT OF A COMMON
CURRENCY IN THE UNITED STATES

The Early History of U.S. Money

From 1492, when Columbus first came to America, until the Revolutionary War in 1775, much trade was done by means of barter. "Money" existed in the American colonies in the form of a potpourri of commodities (usually having some practical use) such as animals (for example, deer, raccoons, and dried fish), animal skins,[2] wampum, musket balls, produce (for example, grains of various kinds and tobacco), beads, and pins.

Coins also circulated at that time, but there was always a persistent shortage of them, thereby forcing the colonies to rely on easily transferable, small-denomination commodity and paper currency. The coin shortage was the result of the colonies' persistent trade deficit with England, English prohibitions against coinage in the colonies,[3] and British Navigation Acts (1650–1765; repealed 1849) that restricted the export of British silver coins from Britain. To fill the void, Spanish, French, and Portuguese coins (mainly silver) played a relatively large role in the colonial money supply.[4]

In colonial times, there were no real (incorporated) banks as we define them today. There were some private individuals and businesses that issued paper notes, but they were usually for special purposes and were often backed by land. As well, state governments issued bills of credit, which were secured by anticipated tax collections or backed by specie. Inflation rates varied from colony to colony, depending heavily on the rate of paper currency issuance by the state government. For instance, in the late 1740s and in 1750, New England experienced such high inflation rates that in 1751 the British passed a currency act requiring these colonies to have specie backing for any bills of credit they issued.

The path to a common U.S. currency was not linear, and in the end, it would be an exaggeration to say that the adoption of a common currency was the result of a thorough congressional cost–benefit analysis of optimal currency areas, because it was not. The decision was mostly the result of Civil War financing needs and the sheer unmanageability of having thousands of different currencies issued by state banks. A system of federal banks together with a common currency was a means to address the government's endless search for ways to finance its budget deficits and simultaneously to put an end to the anarchic issuance of paper money by state banks.

Throughout U.S. history, most of the federal government's financial crises occurred during times of armed conflict. As a result, wars were major stimuli behind the creation of a national currency, but the need to finance government spending was not reason enough to create a mo-nopoly currency by federal mandate. Federal banks could have existed (and did exist) side by side with state banks, and therefore, federal notes could have existed side by side with state bank–issued notes and did. In fact, there were two separate 20-year periods in the eighteenth and nine-teenth centuries (that is, from 1791 to 1811 and from 1816 to 1836) during which U.S. federal notes competed head to head with state bank–issued currencies.

At the outset of the U.S. Revolutionary War in 1775, the Continental Congress issued paper money, called "continentals," to help finance the enormous cost of the war. The continentals were not backed by gold or sil-ver; rather, their value was dependent on expected post-bellum tax rev-enues and, therefore, were redeemable only if the colonies won their independence. To promote their acceptability, the Continental Congress imposed penalties on anyone refusing to accept continentals, but even with these sanctions, the continentals were unsuccessful—and for good reason: They were over-issued and the government tried to legislate their value. By 1779, the total of all issued continental notes was slightly over $240 million.

If the world has learned any lesson over a millennium of monetary his-tory, it is that the value of money cannot be legislated. Money is the cre-ation of human necessity and not of government edict. The excess supply of continentals[5] caused their market value to drop below their official value, and with this decline came depreciation. By 1781, continentals had fallen to 0.2% of their original value.[6] Even though they were virtually worthless to holders, continentals served a very valuable service, because they helped to finance a war that the colonies won. The alternative to cur-rency issuance would have been for the Continental Congress to tax colo-nial citizens, which would have been the height of irony since the colonies were already rebelling over excessive British taxes. By printing notes to finance spending and creating rampant inflation, the Continental Congress produced the same effect as taxes, but by politically more ac-ceptable means.

At that time, most Americans were self-sufficient farmers, transporta-tion was primitive, manufacturing and trade were limited, and the mar-ketplace was immature. As a result, there was considerable controversy over the role and need for a central bank. On one side were Alexander Hamilton and his followers who advocated centralized banking, as well as the development of industry, expansion of commerce, and concentra-tion of government power. On the other side were Thomas Jefferson and his followers, who advocated atomistic farming, decentralized banking, and a relatively weak federal government.

Most of the fighting during the Revolutionary War had ended by 1781, so colonial financing needs became less pressing. Nevertheless, financing was still an important consideration for the long-term economic health of the new nation. To address the financial needs of the young country and a cash-strapped federal government, the Bank of North America was chartered in 1781. The bank was a public company that was owned by both the government and private individuals. It lent to private and public customers, accepted deposits, and issued its own notes. The success of this bank prompted the creation of state banks such as the Bank of New York (1784), the Bank of Massachusetts (1784), and the Bank of Maryland (1790). Even though the Bank of North America is regarded as having been generally well run, it lost its charter in 1785.[7]

The Revolutionary War ended in 1783, and the U.S. Constitution was signed in 1787. During the interim period, the colonies returned to printing bills of credit in highly varying amounts, and credit over-expansion led to a recurrence of many prewar monetary problems. As a result, when the Constitution was drafted, it addressed some of the obvious monetary shortcomings of the prewar and postwar periods, although not all of them.

The U.S. Constitution had the effect of creating a common market among the 13 original colonies. Citizens were "entitled to all privileges and immunities of citizens in the several states,"[8] which included the rights of free trade,[9] travel, and migration among the states. In addition, states were required to give full faith and credit "to the public acts, records, and judicial proceedings of every other state."[10]

The Constitution was as important for what it did not create as it was for what it created. For instance, it made no provision for a central bank, treasury, or federal banking system, and because it did not explicitly prohibit individual states from chartering banks and regulating the issuance of paper money, it was assumed that permission was implicitly granted.[11] Numerous banks within each state competed openly against each other, and the value of their banknotes varied directly with the reputation of the bank and inversely with the distance the bill traveled from the issuing financial institution.[12]

Article 1, section 8, clause 5 of the Constitution gave Congress the "power to ... coin money, regulate the value thereof, and of foreign coin, and fix the standard of weights and measures." In 1792, Congress established a national mint in Philadelphia and defined the dollar in terms of fixed weights of gold and silver, thereby putting the United States on a bimetallic monetary standard. In these early years, the power *to coin* money was not interpreted as the power *to print* it. Consequently, the U.S. federal government did not issue paper money in any form until 1864. From 1792 until 1864, the U.S. federal government focused mainly on standardizing the weights and measures for the metal content of coins and on determining whether the United States should have a silver, gold, or bimetallic monetary system.

Attempting to maintain a bimetallic monetary standard was a folly because of the constant discrepancy between the official price and market price of gold and silver. The problem was that the official price of gold relative to silver was set by the government, but the market price of gold relative to silver varied from day to day with the forces of supply and demand. Debtors and consumers wanted the cheapest way to repay debts or purchase products, so whenever the gold–silver market price was out of line with the gold–silver official price, the public would spend the coins whose official value was above the value of the gold or silver they contained, and individuals would hoard or melt down the coins whose gold or silver content had a market value greater then their official value.[13] Even though the United States was officially on a bimetallic standard from 1791 to 1879, because relative prices were almost always misaligned, the nation was on a de facto silver standard from 1791 to 1834 and on a de facto gold standard from 1834 to 1861.

It would be a gross overstatement to imply that the laissez faire U.S. monetary system was bad for the nation. Not surprisingly, the established eastern regions (in general, the creditor regions) disliked the lack of order, because they saw in this helter-skelter world of noncentralized state banking a threat to low inflation and bank stability. By contrast, the emerging western regions of the United States (predominantly the debtor regions) welcomed the flexibility and rather loose availability of funds provided by competitive, entrepreneurial state banks. A bank's success in many central and western towns or regions depended almost entirely on the prosperity of the local community. Banknotes were often backed by land, and if the local economy was successful, land prices rose, loan defaults were relatively low, and the banks thrived. By contrast, regional economic malaise caused community land prices to fall, loan defaults to rise, and banks to fail. If communities failed, its residents moved on, and this type of marginal experimentation continued.

The Federalists won a major victory in 1791 when Congress, at the urging of Alexander Hamilton,[14] created the (First) Bank of the United States (see Exhibit 5.1).[15] This bank was established to manage the nation's war debt, help finance newly created deficits, and move the country toward a common currency. Its $10 million capitalization was funded predominantly (about 80%) by foreigners, and it competed head to head with state banks by issuing its own paper notes, making loans, purchasing securities, and taking in deposits.

The bank's growth was spectacular, because it became the fiscal (that is, depository and paying) agent of the U.S. government. With eight branches that stretched from Boston to New Orleans, it was geographically dispersed, thereby allowing the bank to efficiently transfer funds from region to region. Unlike the small state banks, whose notes usually circulated at varying discounts throughout the United States, notes of the (First) Bank

Exhibit 5.1
(First) Bank of the United States (1791–1811): Philadelphia, PA

Source: The IHA, Independence Hall Association, Carpenters' Hall, 320.
Used by permission of the Independence National Historical Park.

of the United States circulated at par throughout the nation. The bank was
so successful that by 1811 its notes comprised approximately 20% of the
U.S. money supply.

Historians have been generally positive in their evaluation of the management and performance of the (First) Bank of the United States.[16] It was
well run and provided both liquidity and financial stability for the U.S.
economy. One of its most important, but controversial, functions was to
exert central bank powers over the unevenly regulated state banks. The
bank had power without any real authority, and one way it wielded its influence was to accept state banknotes only if they were backed by specie.
Another tactic was to set up deposit accounts in the state banks by using
them as correspondent banks. To test the soundness of its correspondent
banks, the (First) Bank of the United States would frequently withdraw its
deposits and demand payment in specie. The threat of mass redemption
forced these state banks to restrain their credit activities, and it put enormous pressure on them to act in financially prudent ways.[17] Many of these
state banks resented this intrusion into their otherwise profitable (albeit
often fraudulent and unethical) businesses.

James Madison, who succeeded Thomas Jefferson as president from
1809 to 1817, was philosophically opposed to the (First) Bank of the
United States, but he was also a realist who recognized the bank as a valuable source of public financing. Financing was important to the Madison

Exhibit 5.2
Second Bank of the United States (1816–1836): Philadelphia, PA

Source: Independence National Historical Park, 313 Walnut Street, Philadelphia, PA.
Used by permission of the Independence National Historical Park.

Administration, because it was soon embroiled in economic and territorial disputes with France and Spain, as well as the costly War of 1812 with England. When the bank's charter expired in 1811, President Madison supported the issuance of a new charter, but even his support and the support of many others were not enough to extend the charter.

The renewal of the (First) Bank of the United States lost in the House and Senate by just one vote. Defeat was the result of successful campaigns by an interesting blend of overlapping vested interest groups. One group of opponents was fearful of the bank's dominant foreign ownership.[18] Another group objected to the bank on philosophical grounds, claiming that the U.S. Constitution gave Congress no explicit power to charter federal banks.[19] State bank owners formed the most vocal and venomous group of opponents, because the national bank acted simultaneously as a competitor (for deposits, loans, and banknotes) and as a strict (central bank-like) disciplinarian.

The abolition of the (First) Bank of the United States was a victory for xenophobes, creditors, and state banks. Its demise was coincident with dramatic increases in financing needs owing to the War of 1812. Consequently, the number of state banks exploded, and this wave of expansion continued until 1816 when Congress established the Second Bank of the United States (see Exhibit 5.2).

Modeled after its recently departed relative, this new federal bank, which began operations with three and one-half times as much capital as the (First) Bank of the United States, also issued its own paper notes, made loans, purchased securities, issued both deposits and banknotes, and grew rapidly in size by becoming the fiscal agent (that is, depository and paying agent) of the U.S. government. Because of its large relative size, the Second Bank of the United States had considerable clout in the financial affairs of the United States, and it took on the responsibility of financially disciplining state banks. The exercise of these quasi-central bank functions was supported strongly by conservative bankers, creditors, and, in general, National Republicans, but it was bitterly opposed by state bank owners, debtors, and most Democrats.

Despite its relatively good performance, the charter of the Second Bank of the United States expired in 1836 and was not renewed. Many of the same groups that opposed the (First) Bank of the United States also opposed the Second Bank of the United States. There were those who opposed it on constitutional grounds, others wanted easier credit availability, and, of course, state banks disliked the competition and central bank enforcement activities of the Second Bank. As well, Nicholas Biddle, the head of the Second Bank of the United States, made a series of political blunders that helped President Andrew Jackson,[20] an opponent of the bank, win a narrow congressional vote that revoked the charter.[21]

History has placed quite a large burden of blame on Biddle's political ineptitude, but such interpretations distract from a key fact: the matter did not come up for a vote again. It died there, indicating either that most of the country did not want a national bank at that time or that the creation of such a bank was not high on the list of priorities. America's experience with the (First) and Second Banks of the United States soured public opinion toward central banks and national banks. As a result, it was not until 1863, over a quarter of a century later, that the United States chartered another national bank, and it was not until 1914 that a U.S. central bank was created.

After the Second Bank of the United States was abolished, state banking became a very lucrative business, and the number of chartered state banks blossomed. To operate a state bank required obtaining state charters, and these charters usually required special acts of state legislatures. All too often, political favoritism, extortion, bribery, and corruption played major roles in determining who received a charter. To correct these abuses, states such as Michigan (in 1837) and New York (in 1838), and thereafter most others, passed "free banking" laws, which automatically approved state charters as long as applicants fulfilled certain mandatory requirements. Because special permission from the state legislature was no longer needed, the floodgates to new charters were opened, causing an immediate explosion in both the number of state banks and in the rate of bank failures.[22]

State banks and state banknotes reached their highest level of importance in the U.S. monetary system between 1836 (the end of the Second Bank of the United States) and the Civil War. This period was characterized by unevenness in state banking regulations and punctuated by outrageous examples of banking abuse. Not all states had lax restrictions, though. Many large towns and some states (for example, Louisiana, Massachusetts, and New York) were quite purposeful and strict in their supervision, but where regulations were weak, speculative loans and excessive leverage on inadequate capital fueled destabilizing expansions and contractions in regional economic activity. Because there was no longer a national bank to act as the fiscal agent of the government and because of the irregular quality of state banknotes, in 1840 Congress established the Independent Treasury,[23] which was really nothing more than a temporary depository for government deposits before they were spent.

During this period, there were literally thousands of state banks issuing tens of thousands of differently sized and shaped paper notes. These notes traded at varying discounts from par based on their perceived specie backing and the reputation of the issuing bank. Signs of the times were banknote reporter publications[24] that provided relatively up-to-date information on the value and existence of both legitimate and counterfeit currencies.[25] In large towns, a cottage industry arose of companies that specialized in exchanging the notes of one bank for another.[26] At this time, there was no central bank to regulate the banking system or to manage the national inflation rate. In fact, there was no official national inflation rate to manage. But, individuals tolerated the inconvenience and chaos in preference to a national currency that would be out of local control. Their concern was mainly with having a substantial influence over liquidity in their particular part of the country.

When the Civil War began in 1861, it brought immediate, substantial financing needs to both the northern and southern states. As a result of the war, the metallic backing to the U.S. dollar was abandoned, and it was not restored until 1879. Between 1861 and 1865, the government of the Confederate States issued its own inconvertible currency. Because there was no guaranteed backing to the currency, its postwar value was dependent on a Southern victory.[27] The Confederate currency was over-issued, thereby creating a period of severe hyperinflation in the southern states. By the end of the war, Confederate notes were worthless. Not only were they over-issued and unbacked by any precious metal or taxing power, but in 1865, they also were declared illegal in the United States.[28]

The northern states had the same urgent financing needs during the Civil War. Due to a recession that started in 1857, customs revenues flowing to the U.S. government suffered serious shortfalls and plunged the budget into deficit. The war presented, of course, an even more urgent need to finance government spending. At first, revenues were drawn from taxes and bond issues, but the growing deficit soon made the issuance of paper currency a necessity. In 1861, Congress authorized the issuance of demand notes, which were putatively redeemable in specie and usable for tax payments, but due to the exigencies of the war, these notes soon lost their specie backing. [29]

This lost specie backing did not deter Congress from issuing new notes in the form of U.S. notes. From 1862 to 1863, $450 million of non-redeemable (that is, not backed by any precious metal) U.S. notes were issued. Because their backs were printed in green ink, they became known as "greenbacks." To force their acceptability, Congress declared them legal tender (that is, acceptable as payment for private and public debts).[30]

Congress passed the National Banking Acts (1863–1864) to address many shortcomings of the undisciplined and uncoordinated U.S. financial system. To bring stricter financial order to the banks, Congress more carefully defined and regulated bank capital requirements, loans, supervision, examination, reporting, reserve requirements, asset quality, and collateral for banknotes. It also created the Comptroller of the Currency office to administer the national banking laws and to charter national banks (using free-banking principles).

To help finance federal expenditures, the acts created national banks that could serve as a marketplace for the newly issued government bonds. To induce banks to take national charters (and to induce state banks to switch to national charters), the acts allowed national banks to deposit federal bonds with the Comptroller of the Currency in return for both government deposits and national banknotes worth 90% of the bonds' value. Congress did not go so far as to declare these bank notes legal tender for private debts, but it did approve their use for *almost any* government debt.[31]

The National Banking Acts were important, because they deliberately attempted to eliminate state banknotes from circulation and to force state banks into national charters. Crucial to this effort was an 1865 amendment to the National Banking Act that put a 10% tax on the notes issued by state banks. This tax took away the profit from state currency issuance and gradually eliminated these notes from circulation. In 1878, the Comptroller of the Currency estimated that the common currency saved the United States $20 million to $60 million annually (that is, as much as 1% of the total value of goods produced).[32] In today's dollars, this translates into billions of dollars of savings.

The National Banking Acts of 1863–1864 were successful in establishing a common U.S. currency, but they were unsuccessful in abolishing the state banking system. Immediately after banknote creation became unprofitable, state banks began to switch to national charters, but the banks soon realized that they could earn even greater profits by lending newly created deposit liabilities than by lending banknotes. As a result, they shifted back to state bank charters, and, consequently, as late as 1910 fewer than 30% of the 24,514 U.S. banks had national charters.[33]

The National Banking Acts improved many of the deficiencies of the anarchic state banking system but created some new ones in the process. The core problems were an inflexible money supply and a faulty system of bank reserves. Between 1865 and 1913, the U.S. money supply consisted almost exclusively of gold coins,[34] silver (and other minor) coins,[35] gold certificates,[36] and silver certificates,[37] all of whose physical quantities (and therefore values) fluctuated with the production rates of precious metals and with balance of payments conditions rather than with the expansion and contraction of the economy. National banknotes[38] and U.S. notes were also a part of the money supply, but national banknotes were no longer printed.[39] U.S. notes, the remaining major money supply component, comprised less than 15% of the total money supply and were backed by government bonds that were on deposit with the Comptroller of the Currency. The expansion and contraction of these national banknotes were tied to changes in the national debt rather than to seasonal and cyclical changes in economic activity.

The reserve scheme of the National Banking Acts was also a problem, because it turned bank reserves into "dead money" and encouraged reserve pyramiding. Reserves became dead money, because they could not be used—for anything. They simply sat in bank vaults. These reserves were not even pooled with the reserves of other banks and used to provide temporary relief for banks in need.

Pyramiding became a problem, because small- and medium-size banks could deposit some of their reserves in larger banks. When money became tight, small banks called in their reserves from medium- and large-size banks, and the medium-size banks called in their deposits from large banks, but there was no place for these large banks to go for additional liquidity. The result was a wave of banking failures and financial instability.

In 1893, an unusually severe recession occurred in the United States that was set off by a banking crisis. The nation was harshly shaken, and only after industrialist J.P. Morgan provided financial assistance did the situation improve. This panic revealed the serious flaws in the U.S. banking system and confirmed in the minds of many individuals that serious reform was needed.

At the turn of the century, the United States officially went on the gold standard.[40] For many, this golden anchor gave reassurance that the country would not return to high levels of inflation, but any hope that it would prevent economic downturns was extinguished by the "Panic of 1907." Ill-fated, bank-financed stock speculation caused bank runs that temporarily suspended payments in nearly a dozen New York City banks and caused others to fail.

The financial turmoil was enough to spur Congress to request a thorough review of the U.S. monetary system. This review was conducted by the newly created National Monetary Commission, and it was from the Commission's recommendations that the U.S. Federal Reserve System was formed in 1913. Not since the Second Bank of the United States did the United States have a national bank with central bank responsibilities, so the Federal Reserve Act filled a gap that had lasted more than three-quarters of a century. The National Monetary Commission's report addressed four major shortcomings of the National Banking Act, namely, the lack of sufficient elasticity in the U.S. money supply, a relatively inefficient system for funds transfer (mainly the domestic and international check-clearing systems), an ineffective (nonexistent) pooling of bank reserves, and a lack of a sophisticated short-term security market that could be used by banks to assure needed levels of liquidity.

The Federal Reserve provided guidance for overall U.S. monetary policy, and by creating Federal Reserve notes and giving discount loans to banks, it offered flexibility in money supply growth. At the same time, this flexibility was supposed to be an automatic response to the economic environment and not a result of the discretionary powers of the Fed. Both Federal Reserve notes and discount loans were backed by gold, eligible paper (for example, commercial paper), and/or government bonds in the hope that the money supply would automatically expand and contract with the business cycle. The reasoning seemed logical. Increased economic activity meant greater borrowing, greater borrowing led to the issuance of more commercial paper, and more commercial paper created, automatically, a larger money supply.[41]

The Fed was also expected to improve monetary flexibility by the way it managed bank reserves. By pooling member bank reserves, the Fed could act as the "lender of last resort" for both individual banks in need of temporary help and also for the banking system in times of liquidity crisis.

From 1914 to 1933, the power in the Federal Reserve System was clearly in the hands of the regional Federal Reserve banks, but the Great Depression forced Congress to change this power structure and to vest the Fed's major decision-making powers in the hands of the seven-member Board of Governors. It is fair to say that if Congress had known in 1913 what the Federal Reserve System would eventually become, the enabling legislation that created the Federal Reserve System would never have been passed. Over the years, numerous revisions have been made in the Federal Reserve's mandate, most of which have increased its independence and centralized its power structure in the Board of Governors. As a result, the United States has moved persistently toward a common paper currency (the Federal Reserve note) and strong central bank control over the U.S. monetary base.[42]

Benefits of a Single Currency

There are few today who seriously debate whether the United States has benefited from having a common currency.[43] With a nominal GDP, today, well over $10 trillion, the combination of a common currency and a huge marketplace allows the United States to benefit from specialization, economies of scale, competition, and rationalization, as well as reduced risks in domestic and international financial transactions. The United States benefits even more than other nations that have a common currency by virtue of the fact that international transactions (that is, the average of imports and exports) are only about 14% of its GDP, leaving about 86% to transactions among domestic residents. If the benefits that the United States derives from its common currency are equal, as a percent of GDP, to the estimated benefits the European Union derives from the euro, the annual U.S. savings are approximately $100 billion, which amounts to about $750 per person in the civilian labor force.[44]

Is the United States an Optimal Currency Area?

During the 1990s, one of the most hotly debated international issues was whether the European Union was an optimal currency area. Most of these analyses used the framework developed by Robert Mundell[45] as the theoretical basis for their analyses, and they used the United States as the standard for a well-functioning currency area. Is the United States an optimal currency area? This section addresses this issue and puts it into perspective.

Four criteria can be used to determine if membership in a currency area is optimal and, therefore, if the currency union will be a success.[46] In general, a currency union's chances for success are larger if:

1. the participants are exposed to similar external shocks,
2. the shocks are symmetric in terms of their impact on participant nations,
3. the reactions to the shocks by member nations are comparable, and
4. the adjustment of any member to an idiosyncratic shock is quick and efficient.

Empirical work on criteria 1 and 2 indicates that the eight major regions of the United States are indeed subject to common external shocks and that their reaction to the shocks is generally the same.[47] More specifically, statistical tests have been conducted to determine if regional sensitivity to changes in economic variables, such as world oil prices, real U.S. GDP, and U.S. monetary policy, are similar. With only minor regional exceptions, the results indicate that these three common disturbances explain between 53% and 85% of the fluctuation in regional output. Moreover, there are many similarities in the relative importance and duration of these shocks.[48]

Criteria 2 and 3 can be evaluated by how closely changes in the real gross product of each U.S. region and/or state mirror changes in the general U.S. business cycle. Exhibit 5.3 shows that there are high correlation levels between the real gross state product of these eight major regions

Exhibit 5.3
Correlation between Regional Changes in Gross State Product and Changes in GDP

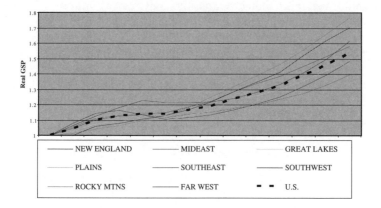

Region	Average Correlation Coefficient (1986 — 1999) *(Regional gross state product relative to GNP)*
Southwest	99.8%
Great Lakes	99.6%
Plains	99.6%
Southeast	99.6%
Rocky Mountains	99.4%
Mideast	99.4%
Far West	98.2%

Source: Bureau of Economic Analysis. Bureau of Labor Statistics, URL:
/news.release/laus.t03.htm. http://stats.bls.gov/news.release/laus.t03.htm.

and changes in the real gross domestic product of the United States. In each case, the correlation coefficients are over 96%.[49]

On a state-by-state basis, the results are similar. The correlation between changes in the real gross state product of 48 of the 50 U.S. states is over 0.93. Only Hawaii and Alabama have correlation coefficients that are substantially out of line with movements in the U.S. business cycle.

Empirical work on criterion 4 indicates that U.S. regions react relatively quickly and efficiently to idiosyncratic economic shocks. In one study, adjustment in half of the regions (Great Lakes, Plains, Southeast, and West Coast) took less than one year, and adjustment in the remaining regions (New England, Mideast, Southeast, and Rocky Mountains) occurred within three years.[50]

Exhibit 5.4
State Unemployment Rate—Average National Unemployment Rate (July 2001)

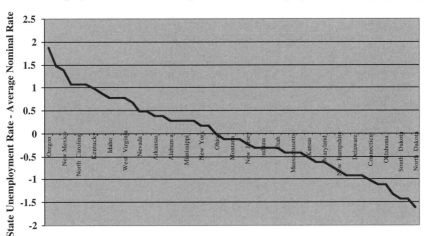

Another key to determining whether the United States is an optimal currency area is the level of economic integration in its product, labor, and capital markets. If a region's product, labor, and capital markets are integrated, then differences among their prices, unemployment rates, and interest rates should be small. Large differences could exist only if products and resources (that is, labor and capital) were immobile and therefore unable to profit from the large price discrepancies.

Exhibit 5.4 shows that, for July 2001, the differences between the unemployment rates of U.S. states, relative to the average, were small. There was a less than 2% difference between the average national unemployment rate and the unemployment rate of each state.

Resource and product mobility in the United States are promoted by the relative absence of language and cultural barriers. As well, the nation has a fairly low level of unionization compared to other countries, especially in Europe. According to the U.S. Bureau of Labor Statistics and the U.S. Bureau of the Census, union membership in the United States grew rapidly from about 12% of non-farm payrolls in the 1930s to its peak level of 35% in 1945–1946 and 1954. Since then, union membership relative to the workforce has declined, and today only about 14% of the U.S. workforce is organized in unions.[51]

Resource mobility has also been aided by the increased sophistication and reduced costs of U.S. transportation and communication systems. As a result, the U.S. states have been closely tied together throughout the twentieth century, causing prices to be more transparent, arbitrage to respond to even small price differentials, and resources to be cheaper and easier to move. Because labor has become increasingly more mobile, it has helped the nation adjust during periods when dissimilar economic shocks hit various economic regions. Studies have shown that, in the United States, the movement of labor from low employment to high employment regions is one of the nation's major adjustment mechanisms.[52]

In addition to labor and capital movement, there are other factors that help cushion U.S. regions from idiosyncratic economic shocks. For instance, the high level of fiscal federalism in the United States helps regions to adjust automatically to such disturbances. The U.S. system of federal taxes and transfer payments has the effect of diverting funds from relatively fast-growing regions to regions growing relatively slowly. The estimated level of fiscal federalism in the United States is between $0.20 and $0.45 per dollar change in GDP.[53] In other words, for every $1 decline in a region's income level, the federal government automatically cuts taxes and raises transfers by an amount between $0.20 and $0.45.[54]

Adding to the list of characteristics that makes the United States an optimal currency area are constitutional guarantees and limitations, as well as antitrust laws that prohibit the restraint of interstate trade. The U.S. Constitution empowers the federal government with the regulation of commerce relative to foreign nations and among the several states.[55] It explicitly prohibits:

1. the imposition of taxes or duties on articles exported from any state,[56]
2. the regulation of commerce or revenue to the ports of one state over those of another,[57]
3. vessels bound to, or from, one state, from entering, clearing, or paying duties in another state,[58] and
4. "states from entering into any treaty, alliance, or confederation; ... coin money; emit bills of credit; make any thing but gold and silver coin a tender in pay-ment of debts."[59]

Numerous federal antitrust laws have been passed to promote the free flow of goods and services among states. For instance, the Sherman Act of 1890 prohibits contracts and conspiracies that restrain trade among the states or with foreign nations. The Federal Trade Commission Act of 1914 seeks to prevent unfair competition. The Clayton Act, also passed in 1914, embellishes and further defines the Sherman Act in those cases in which business practices substantially lessen competition. Specifically, the Clayton Act restricts the practices of price discrimination, exclusive dealing, mergers, acquisitions, interlocking directorates, and the holding of one company's stock by another company. The Hart–Scott–Rodino Antitrust Improvements Act of 1976 amends the Clayton Act by requiring companies to notify the Federal Trade Commission before large mergers and acquisitions are completed.

Was the United States an Optimal Currency Area in 1787 or 1864?

The United States is one of the best, albeit not perfect, examples of an optimal currency area in the twentieth century, but was this the case in 1787 when the 13 original colonies hammered out the Constitution, or in 1863–1864, when Congress passed the National Banking Acts? After all, it was then and not now that a common currency was first contemplated and then implemented.

If the United States today is an optimal currency area, then it is the result of over 200 years of evolution, and to a large extent, the current U.S. monetary structure and economy are what they are *because* of the common currency.[60] In other words, due to the currency union, structural changes have occurred that have harmonized state economies and thereby improved the functioning of the currency union.

A time span of over 200 years makes a lot of difference. Was the United States ripe in 1787 for a unified currency? The level of economic integration among the participant states and currency regions was significant, labor was very mobile, and unionization was relatively low. At the same time, most citizens were self-sufficient farmers; manufacturing and trade were much less important; fiscal federalism was nonexistent; and capital markets were both underdeveloped and nonintegrated.

Evidence of the underdeveloped U.S. capital markets can be seen as late as 1913, when the Federal Reserve System was created. Congress established the 12 regional central banks with the belief that they could provide a measure of regional monetary sensitivity. As the twentieth century unfolded and capital markets became more efficient,[62] the folly of this reasoning became evident. Varying dollar discount rates from region to region became unworkable, because they allowed arbitrageurs to profit from the interest differentials and to quickly bid them away.

By 1860, there were 34 states in the Union, and the United States appeared to be even more ready for a common currency. Not only was the marketplace large and growing increasingly more integrated, but also the chaotic system of state bank notes created a huge opportunity to derive economies of scale from the adoption of a single currency. Other positive characteristics for a common currency were the significant levels of economic integration among the U.S. states and the advanced stage of labor and capital market development, relative to the early part of the century.

Dollarization in the Future

The expansion of the dollar area has been due to a combination of political, economic, emotional, and cultural factors, but there is little doubt

Exhibit 5.5
U.S. Dollar Currency Area Has a Strong Gravitational Attraction

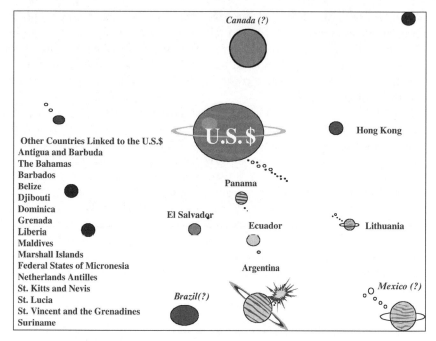

that the benefits of the dollar as a common currency have exerted a relentless pull. Just as large planets (see Exhibit 5.5) exert a strong gravitational pull on relatively smaller nearby planets, large currency areas exert a gravitational-like economic pull on smaller "nearby" currencies.

During the past few years, Ecuador and El Salvador have become part of the U.S. dollar area, and they have joined an already impressive list. Argentina,[62] Hong Kong,[63] Lithuania,[64] and Panama[65] have all adopted currency boards that link their currencies inexorably to the U.S. dollar. In 2001, the IMF also listed other relatively minor currencies that were pegged in some way to the U.S. dollar.[66] The dollarization of the world has been so unidirectional and persistent that there is more than a hint of historical inevitability to it. To be sure, many people feel that it is only a matter of time before Canada, Mexico, and Brazil abolish their currencies and adopt the U.S. dollar.

Similarities and Differences between the Creation of the Euro and the Dollar as a Common Currency

In many ways, the creation of a common U.S. currency and central bank was both strikingly dissimilar and strikingly similar to the creation of the

Exhibit 5.6
12 Federal Reserve Districts

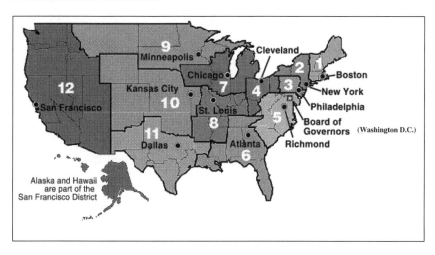

euro in 1999. On the dissimilar side, the U.S. National Banking Acts were passed with almost no mention of varying state/local deficit, debt, interest rate, and exchange rate levels.[67] There was no six-year transition period for state banks that was similar to the 1993–1999 Maastricht Treaty and no stringent conditions for joining. Transition was swift and, for some state banks, very painful.

An important difference between the Federal Reserve's mandate in 1913 and the mandate of the European Central Bank in 1999 was that the Fed was created to provide monetary flexibility, whereas the clear mandate of the European Central Bank was to ensure price stability. Congress had hoped that price stability in the United States would be assured by linking changes in the U.S. money supply to changes in the supply of gold and economic activity. These changes were supposed to occur automatically and without any discretion on the part of the Fed.

At the same time, when the European System of Central Banks was created in 1999, some member nations feared that the stringent monetary policies of Germany would dominate central bank thinking, and as a result, tight credit and an overemphasis on controlling inflation would carry much higher priorities than the goals of low unemployment and high economic growth. When the Federal Reserve began operating in 1914, one of the major fears of the central and western U.S. states was that the central bank would be run by a group of aloof and unresponsive East Coast bankers. It was for this reason that the Federal Reserve Act created 12 regional Federal Reserve banks with approximately equal financial power and a very weak Board of Governors (see Exhibit 5.6).

THE DEVELOPMENT OF A COMMON
CURRENCY IN GERMANY

The economic, monetary, and political unification of German principalities during the nineteenth century provides an excellent counterpart to similar integration efforts of the United States, because it shows that the sequence does not have to follow a prescribed pattern. German principalities formed customs unions over a quarter century before they established a common coinage system; and the common coinage system predated political unification by almost a decade and a half. Thereafter, it took an additional five years for an official central bank to be founded.

U.S. integration was in many ways like the German experience. Economic unification preceded monetary unification, and the creation of a central bank came at the end of the process. There were also dissimilarities, because the 13 U.S. states simultaneously created a political union, common market, and national coinage system when they signed the Constitution in 1787. In short, the United States accomplished three tiers of the integration process at a very early stage and with the stroke of a pen. Germany required nearly 70 years to replicate those steps.

During the nineteenth century, an atmosphere of political stability proved to be an important ingredient for the development of stronger economic ties among the German states, and for this reason, the Congress of Vienna was crucial. After the defeat of Napoleon Bonaparte in 1814, the major European powers[68] met to establish borders and to confirm the neutral status of many European nations. The negotiations resulting from the Congress of Vienna created a balance of power in Europe that brought an extended period of political tranquility. This tranquility increased labor mobility and proved to be a boon to both trade and commerce. The period after the Congress of Vienna marked the beginning of German integration.

At the turn of the nineteenth century, Germany was not the country we know today; rather, it was a collection of about 40 independent principalities and towns, each one having the sovereign right to issue money from its state-owned mint and to impose its own taxes (including customs duties).[69] These German states realized quite rapidly the advantages of eliminating inter-principality customs duties and freeing trade flows. A scattered assortment of customs union arrangements was negotiated among various states in the early 1800s,[70] and over time, the development of natural trade patterns turned the German states into three large trading blocks: a northern, a central, and a southern block.

The first significant step toward broadscale integration occurred in 1834 when the three trade blocks established a customs union called the Deutscher Zollverein (literal translation: German customs/tariff union). The Zollverein instantaneously eliminated tariffs among all participating German states[71] and it sought, as well, to standardize their coinage systems.[72] This desire for monetary consistency and efficiency was a natural consequence of the increasing volume of trade flows. Merchants demanded standardized currencies, just as they demanded standardized weights and measures.

During the 1830s, the German principalities passed two treaties that were crucial to the development of a monetary union, because together they required participants to voluntarily surrender their monetary sovereignty. The 1837 Munich Coin Treaty standardized the silver content of the gulden, which was the coin that circulated among the states south of the Main River, and gave the currency legal tender status. The 1838 Dresden Coin Convention standardized the silver content of the thaler, which was the currency of Prussia and the standard of value for most of the northern principalities. The result was that Germany then had two currencies whose values were fixed by their silver content, and so each was convertible into the other at a fixed rate determined by their content of silver.[73] Members greatly simplified their coinage system by withdrawing from circulation any currency not meeting the new standards[74] and by agreeing to denominate transactions in either the thaler or the gulden.

At the time, Prussia[75] was by far the dominant economic player among the Germanic regions, having a clear majority of the landmass, population, and industrial base. Its dominance was so great that Prussia's silver-backed currency, the thaler, became the de facto currency of the German confederation, and the Prussian bank became the union's de facto central bank.[76]

The combination of Germany's customs union and the fixed exchange rate within the gulden and thaler zones promoted both trade and factor movement across state borders. In 1857, commercial momentum was boosted when the members of the Zollverein and Austria signed the Vienna Coin Treaty (Münzverein).[77] This treaty with Austria was intended to broadly expand the Zollverein's monetary union. Unfortunately, it never accomplished this goal, because Austria continued to print nonconvertible paper currency and eventually dropped out of the agreement in 1867 after it suffered a devastating defeat in the Austro–Prussian War.

Nevertheless, the Vienna Coin Treaty was successful in other areas and, in the end, significantly furthered Germany's monetary integration efforts. Perhaps most important among its contributions were those that put Germany on a pure silver standard and purposely discouraged the development of bimetallism. The treaty accomplished this by barring principalities from minting gold coins[78] and prohibiting the exchange of gold coins for silver, thereby preventing the states from debasing the value of the thaler and the gulden. As well, it restricted principality issuance of small-denomination coins; those coins that remained in circulation were required to be fully convertible. The Treaty also granted the thaler legal tender[79] status, thereby promoting its increased use; and finally, it had the foresight to address ground rules for the issuance of paper money, which had grown substantially in use over the 1800s, especially in industrialized regions.[80]

Two armed conflicts, both of which were provoked by Prussia's Chancellor Otto von Bismarck,[81] were directly responsible for the formation of Germany's political union. The first war (the Austro–Prussian War) was fought with Austria in 1866. In a short, seven-week period, Prussia was able to crush Austria and reap significant territorial gains. Shortly after the war, Prussia organized the North German Federation, which entered the Zollverein as a block.[82] The second war was fought against Napoleon III in 1870. When France declared war on Prussia, it spurred a rise in German nationalism among the independent principalities and forged, as Bismarck had hoped, a united German response to the French threat. Prussia easily defeated France, and the victory led to the formation of the German Reich in 1870.

The political unification of Germany in 1870 had important economic implications, among which were the need to give increased priority to international trade relations and to the standardization of the country's paper currency. Between 1871 and 1873, Germany tried to expand commercial relations with its most important trading partners[83] by adopting the gold standard.[84] During the same period, Germany changed the name of the thaler to the mark and put into effect important monetary reforms. To bring the same standardization to its paper currency as was brought to coins, Germany imposed strict rules on the issuance of currency by private banks, which quickly forced them to curtail such activities.[85] In 1876, Germany transformed the Prussian Bank into the Reichsbank (the German Central Bank),[86] which became responsible for the issuance of the newly issued Reichsmark.[87]

This summary of Germany's economic, commercial, and monetary unification reveals many parallels to the U.S. experience. There were important differences in the sequencing of the steps, but it is notable that the U.S. and German experiences covered approximately the same period and ended with national monetary systems that were almost exactly the same. For the United States, the period was 1787–1864; for Germany the period was the early 1800s to 1876. Each country started the unification process by dropping tariffs in a climate of political stability, thereby deriving gains from trade. Then, they took the next step by standardizing and regulating currency issuance—first coins, and later paper currency—at the level of states or regions. Toward the end of the period, they eliminated local issuers of currency, both principalities and state-chartered banks, by penalizing them to the point at which the profitability of issuing currency was nullified. They centralized the authority to issue currency, and each country backed its currency with precious metal. Table 5.1 summarizes the chronology of these changes in the two countries.

Table 5.1
Dates of Key Events in U.S. and German Monetary Evolution

	U.S	Germany
Political Stability	1787 or 1812	1814
Customs Union	1787	1834
Standardized Coins	1787	1838
Common Market	1787	1870
Political Union	1787	1870
Standardized Paper Money	1864	1873
Central Bank	1914	1876

CONCLUSION

The experiences of Germany and the United States contrast with the experiences of England. England had a national currency convertible into precious metal and a central bank almost 200 years earlier than Germany and the United States. There are many possible explanations for this fact. We advance the following explanation, which is consistent with the argument we make in this book. In the case of Germany and the United States, there were commonalities in the sequences of events as both countries obtained the benefits of nationally uniform currencies and fixed exchange rates.

In the earliest days following political integration, the top priority for the German principalities and the United States was not an internationally accepted currency. Instead, they needed a standardized unit of value and medium of exchange for transactions among the principalities and states and with contiguous trading partners. Political integration and political stability created opportunities to trade with nearby neighbors, and those opportunities were attractive enough to influence the salient attributes of each country's monetary arrangements.

For both Germany and the United States, internal trade in goods was more important than long-distance overseas trade until the mid-to-late 1800s. In the United States, developing the frontier created demand for credit that would have been hard to satisfy if there had been a restrictive currency regime. The transition from coins to paper money created many opportunities for American ingenuity. There were credit expansions and collapses that would have been difficult to achieve under a more restrictive, East Coast–dominated currency regime. The national priority did not shift to having a national paper currency convertible into precious metal until foreign, long-distance trade became more important than local trade and easy access to credit. Local voters with a preference for inflation and debasement could win over the groups that wanted to preserve the value of financial assets and foster long-distance trade. After the frontier had been settled and after the opportunities for internal trade and credit expansion had been exploited, the priority shifted. It became more important to stabilize the value of financial assets and to facilitate transactions that spanned larger distances or longer periods of time.

England's situation from Elizabethan times onward was quite different. Internal trade was not as important as long-distance overseas trade in terms of potential profitability. Long-distance trade could be very profitable, but it was also very risky. Returns were volatile because of the intrinsic risks of distance, pirates, weather, and navigation. The rich merchants would not tolerate monetary instability and used their influence with the monarch and the parliament to impose a stable currency, convertible into gold, that would serve as a standard of value throughout the entire colonial empire. In modern terminology, England was an open economy, exposed to the vagaries of international commerce.

Germany and the United States were less open, so they could delay adopting national paper currencies convertible into precious metal. Germany and the United States also had political systems that came closer to weighting all votes equally. England had "rotten boroughs" that elected representatives to parliament but were in effect controlled by hereditary landowners. That gave more weight to the preference for monetary stability. In the United States, there were many voters who owed money and, thus, had a preference for depreciating the purchasing power of money. They voted for Andrew Jackson, who was from the frontier, because he would favor growth over "sound" money, and thus reduce the burden of what they owed. England also had voters who owed money, but their power did not sway parliament. The merchants were able to muster enough influence to put a strong paper currency into place, and keep it there.

In Germany and the United States, the balance of power shifted to favor a stable currency later, after several transformations of the economic landscape. Railroads had linked markets that previously were effectively isolated, the frontier had been settled, and intra-country long-distance trade had become more important. Debtors still outnumbered creditors, but the other factors in favor of strong national currencies gained strength, and the political system then put the new monetary regime into effect. Attention turned toward international monetary relations and the development of foreign trade relations. Thereafter, it turned toward raising and preserving the value of financial claims.

The road to a common currency for the United States was long and eventful. Although the idea of a single national currency, to be managed by a central bank, arose frequently and triumphed to some degree twice before the Civil War, the weight of public opinion at that point in U.S. history favored local autonomy. American voters tolerated the chaos that went along with the new nation's style of weak regulation, because the alternative would have been restrictive monetary policy and chronically tight credit.

The pendulum swung in favor of a national currency convertible into precious metal at about the same time in the United States and in Germany. The monetary histories of the two countries are quite different in detail but display striking parallels in chronology. Many of the same pressures were at work in both countries, and the outcomes made sense in relation to the magnitudes and profitability of the business activities that were important at the time.

Two clear patterns emerge that are germane to the argument in this book. First, the size of the optimal currency zone grew with improvements in trade and commerce. In the beginning, it was only as large as a state (or *Land*), then, in the case of Germany, it was as large as half the country, and by 1873, it grew to include the entire country. Second, the role of state-chartered banknotes in the United States and regional coinage in Germany was to facilitate transactions involving goods and services. Expansion of a currency zone is the sine qua non of financial systems with deep capital markets. In the early days, the development of broad capital markets was not as important to the United States and Germany as developing strong internal trade relationships, but as time passed, the goal of advancing the state and level of sophistication of their capital markets became increasingly more important.

NOTES

1. The Riksbank is the world's oldest central bank. See Sveriges Riksbank, *Sveriges Riksbank—The Swedish Central Bank*. Available http://www.riksbank.com/upload/4990/riksbankeneng.pdf. Accessed April 19, 2001.

2. The beaver and corn were at one time defined as legal tender in Massachusetts. See Joseph B. Felt, *A Historical Account of Massachusetts Currency* (Boston: Perkins and Marvin, 1839, 16.

3. Despite England's prohibition, the Massachusetts Bay Colony established an illegal mint in Boston in 1652 where it manufactured silver coins, including the famous "pine tree shilling." The mint operated until about 1682, when it was closed by order of parliament. Even though the Boston mint had a 30-year life, all pine tree shillings were dated 1652. This was done so that, if England discovered the illegal mint, the colonials could claim that no coins had been produced since 1652. See Federal Reserve Bank of Philadelphia, *Money in Colonial Times*. Available: http://www.phil.frb.org/education/colonial.html.

4. Because the colonies did a considerable amount of trade with Spain, France, and Portugal, coins from these nations were most available. See B.T. McCallum, "Money and Prices in Colonial America: A New Test of Competing Theories," *Journal of Political Economy* 100 (1992): 143–161.

5. Continentals grew by approximately 50% per year during the first five years of the Revolution. See Michael Bordo and Lars Jonung, *Lessons for EMU from the History of Monetary Unions* (London: iea Publications, 2000), 11–19.

6. From this experience came the pejorative English expression "not worth a continental," which is used to describe anything that has virtually no value.

7. The repeal of this charter could have been due to the conservative lending practices of the bank, which did not particularly win the heart of a federal government in need of financing.

8. U.S. Constitution, art. 4, sec. 2, cl. 1.

9. "No Tax or Duty shall be laid on Articles exported from any State." U.S. Constitution, art. 1, sec. 9, cl. 5.

10. U.S. Constitution, art. 4, sec. 1.

11. "The powers not delegated to the United States by the Constitution, nor prohibited by it to the states, are reserved to the states respectively, or to the people." Bill of Rights, amend. 10.

12. This inverse relationship was due to the transportation costs needed to return the notes.

13. "Bad" money (that is, overvalued coins whose legal tender value was greater than the market value of the metal contained in the coin) drives "good" money out of circulation is often referred to as Gresham's Law. Sir Thomas Gresham was the master of the mint in England under Queen Elizabeth I in the sixteenth century.

14. Alexander Hamilton was the first Secretary of the U.S. Treasury.

15. At the time, this bank was called the Bank of the United States. Its charter was not renewed in 1811, and in 1816, the Second Bank of the United States was formed. As a result, the word "First" has been put in parentheses to better distinguish it from the Second Bank of the United States.

16. William F. Hickson, *Triumph of the Bankers: Money and Banking in the Eighteenth and Nineteenth Centuries* (London: Praeger, 1993), 114. Also see, Edward L. Symons Jr. and James J. White, *Banking Law,* 2nd ed. (West Wadsworth: St. Paul, 1984), 12.

17. The bank could accomplish the same feat by accepting and accumulating notes of over-leveraged banks and then presenting them, all at once, to the issuing banks for redemption in specie.

18. Because about 70% of the (First) Bank of the United States' stock was owned by foreigners, there was concern about who controlled the bank and for what interest.

19. This issue was settled by the Supreme Court by *McCulloch v. Maryland, 17 U.S. (4 Wheat) 315 (1819).*

20. Jackson, the seventh President of the United States, served from 1829 to 1837. He was so furious over the actions of Nicholas Biddle and his cohorts that he withdrew all public funds from the Second Bank of the United States.

21. The Second Bank of the United States survived temporarily by obtaining a bank charter from the state of Pennsylvania, but it never regained the status it held as a national bank and eventually became insolvent.

22. Between 1836 and 1861, the number of state banks expanded by 125%. See Board of Governors of the Federal Reserve System, *Banking Studies* (Washington, D.C., Board of Governors of the Federal Reserve System, 1941), 417–418.

23. The Independent Treasury was repealed in 1841, but reintroduced and modified in 1846 and 1847. It remained active until 1921, when its functions were taken over by the Federal Reserve.

24. Some examples are *Bicknell's Counterfeit Detector and Bank Note List* in Philadelphia, *Clark's New-England Bank Note List and Counterfeit Bill Detector* in Boston, *John Thompson's Bank Note and Commercial Reporter* in New York, and the *Connecticut Bank Note List and City of Hartford Monthly Advertiser.*

25. From 1782 to 1866, there were over 72,000 different notes produced by U.S. banks. See James Haxby, *Standard Catalog of Obsolete United States Bank Notes, 1782–1866* (Iola, WI: Krause Publications, 1983).

26. See Lawrence Ingrassia, "Exchequered Past, One Dollar is Worth One Dollar, but That Wasn't Always So," *Wall Street Journal,* January 13, 1998, pp. A1.

27. The currency was supposed to be backed by cotton.

28. E.M. Lerner, "Inflation in the Confederacy, 1861–65," in *Studies in the Quantity Theory of Money,* ed. M. Friedman (Chicago: University of Chicago Press, 1956), 164–175.

29. Greenbacks were printed only until 1863. After the Civil War, a large portion of the issued U.S. notes was retired, and in 1878, their issue was frozen at approximately $347 million. There are still greenback notes outstanding today, which are redeemable at face value in cash.

30. It was not until 1871 that the Supreme Court affirmed in a 5–4 vote that the federal government had the constitutional right to declare a currency legal tender. See *Legal Tender Cases (Knox v. Lee; Parker v. Davis),* 12 Wallace 457 (1871).

31. Ironically, the only debts for which they could *not* be used were for customs duties and for the payment of interest on public debt.

32. See Ingrassia, "Exchequered Past."

33. The creation of the Federal Reserve in 1913 added Federal Reserve notes to the list of assets qualifying as U.S. currency in circulation, but it was not until about 1935 that the Federal Reserve notes began to supplant the U.S. notes as the dominant currency. The decline in U.S. notes was due to the government's decision in 1935 not to issue any more bonds that could be used to back the U.S. notes.

34. At that time, gold coins constituted the largest component of the U.S. money supply. They were first issued in 1792, and in 1933 Congress withdrew them from circulation.

35. Silver coins were first issued in 1792, but in 1966, Congress decided to stop minting them. Minor coins are made of an amalgam of metals, which are worth less than the face value of the coins.

36. Gold certificates were backed 100% by gold and withdrawn from circulation in 1933.

37. Silver certificates were backed 100% by silver. Congress decided to stop printing them in 1963.

38. National banknotes have not been issued since 1935. When (and if) they are redeemed, they are not reissued.

39. U.S. notes were backed by government bonds that were placed on deposit with the Comptroller of the Currency.

40. Official acceptance of the gold standard occurred in 1900, but its legislation was passed during the early 1870s. The Gold Standard was one of William McKinley's presidential platforms, and his victory put the final dagger into the heart of U.S. bimetallism. The United States remained on the Gold Standard until 1933, when it was abolished due to the Great Depression. After 1933, gold coins were no longer minted and no longer circulated in the United States. Nevertheless, from 1933 to 1971, gold continued to back the U.S. dollar.

41. This reasoning was known as the "real bills doctrine," the fallacy of which would later become apparent.

42. Federal Reserve notes became legal tender in the United States in 1933.

43. Recognition must be given to at least one group of critics. Nobel Laureate Friedrich von Hayek and the Austrian School of Economic Thought have challenged the idea that money must be provided by the central government. They advocate "free banking" with the separate currencies of private banks competing against each other under an umbrella of government regulation. Hayek is critical not only of a uniform government money but also of central bank regulation, because, as he says, "History is largely a history of inflation, and usually of inflations engineered by governments and for the gain of governments." See Friedrich A. von Hayek, *Denationalisation of Money: An Analysis of the Theory and Practice of Concurrent Currencies* (London: Institute of Economic Affairs, 1976); and Kurt Schuler and Lawrence H. White, "Free Banking: History," in *The New Palgrave Dictionary of Money and Finance,* ed. Peter Newman, Murray Milgate, and John Eatwell, 198–199 (London: Macmillan Press, 1992).

44. Both the European Commission and the IFO Institute for Economic Research estimate that the annual savings from carrying out transactions in a common currency are as high as 1.0% of GDP. See Directorate General of the European Commission, "What Are the Main Economic Benefits of the Euro for Participating Member States?" in *Euro Essentials Changing over to the Euro: The Final Phase, Questions and Answers Using Quest.* Available: http://europa.eu.int/euro/quest/normal/frame.htm?language_nb = 5.

45. This section is based on the work of Robert Mundell. See Robert A. Mundell, "A Theory of Optimum Currency Areas," *American Economic Review* (September 1961): 657–665. Also see Michael A. Kouparitsas, "Is the United States an Optimal Currency Area?" *Chicago Fed Letter* 146 (October 1999): 1–3; and Peter B. Kenen, "The Theory of Optimum Currency Areas: An Eclectic View," in *Monetary Problems of the International Economy*, ed. Robert A. Mundell and Alexander K. Swoboda, 41–46 (Chicago: University of Chicago Press, 1969).

46. This section draws on Kouparitsas, "Is the United States an Optimal Currency Area?"; and Michael A. Kouparitsas, "Is the EMU a Viable Common Currency Area?" *Economic Perspectives of the Federal Reserve Bank of Chicago* Q4 (1999): 2–20.

47. G.A. Carlino and R. DeFina as well as M. Kouparitsas have used vector auto regressive statistical methods to determine if regions are subject to common shocks. See G.A. Carlino and R. DeFina, "The Differential Regional Effects of Monetary Policy," *Review of Economics and Statistics* 80 (Cambridge: November 1998): 572–587; and Kouparitsas, "Is the United States an Optimal Currency Area?"

48. See Kouparitsas, "Is the United States an Optimal Currency Area?"; and Kouparitsas, "Is the EMU a Viable Common Currency Area?"

49. Kouparitsas arrives at similar conclusions by using quarterly gross personal state income from 1969:Q1 to 1998:Q3, deflated by the national Consumer Price Index. His lowest correlation is 0.76 for the Southwest region, and his highest correlation is 0.99 for the Southeast region.

50. Kouparitsas, "Is the United States an Optimal Currency Area?"; and Kouparitsas, "Is the EMU a Viable Common Currency Area?"

51. The unionization in the private nonagricultural industries is now less than 10%, but among government employees, it is approximately 38%. Approximately 16.3 million U.S. workers currently belong to unions.

52. Barry Eichengreen, "One Money for Europe? Lessons of the United States Currency Union," *Economic Policy* 10 (April 1990): 118–166.

53. See Xavier Sala-I-Martin and Jeffrey Sachs, "Fiscal Federalism and Optimum Currency Areas: Evidence for Europe and the United States," in *Establishing a Central Bank: Issues in Europe and Lessons from the United States*, ed. Matthew Canzoneri, Vittorio Grilli, and Paul Masson (Cambridge: Cambridge University Press, 1992), 195 –220; and Jacques Mélitz and Fédéric Zumer, "Regional Redistribution and Stabilization by the Center in Canada, France, the UK, and the US," *Discussion Paper 1829*. University of Strathclyde, Glasgow, Scotland Centre for Economic Policy Research, December 1998.

54. The pessimistic (that is, $0.20) figure is substantially increased if we consider long-term rather than short-term adjustments.

55. U.S. Constitution, art. 1, sec. 8, cl. 3.

56. U.S. Constitution, art. 1, sec. 9, cl. 5.

57. U.S. Constitution, art. 1, sec. 9, cl. 6.

58. U.S. Constitution, art. 1, sec. 9, cl. 6.

59. U.S. Constitution, art. 1, sec. 10, cl. 1.

60. See J.A. Frankel and A.K. Rose, "The Endogeneity of the Optimum Currency Area Criteria," *Economic Journal* 108 (July 1958): 1009–1025.

61. Bureau of the Census, *Historical Statistics of the United States, Colonial Times to 1970* (New York: Basic Books, 1976); Bureau of Labor Statistics, *Employment and Earnings: January* (Washington, D.C.: U.S. Government Printing Office, 1983–2001); and Bureau of Labor Statistics, *Handbook of Labor Statistics: Bulletin 2070* (Washington, D.C.: U.S. Government Printing Office, December 1980).

62. From 1991 to 2001, Argentina used a currency board to peg the peso to the U.S. dollar. In late 2001 and early 2002, this link was broken.

63. Since 1993, Hong Kong has used a currency board to peg the Hong Kong dollar to the U.S. dollar.

64. Since 1994, Lithuania has used a currency board to peg the lita to the U.S. dollar.

65. Panama has had a currency board and used the dollar as its domestic currency since 1904.

66. Among these nations were Antigua and Barbuda, the Bahamas, Barbados, Belize, Djibouti, Dominica, Grenada, Liberia, the Maldives, the Marshall Islands, the Federal States of Micronesia, Netherlands Antilles, St. Kitts and Nevis, St. Lucia, St. Vincent and the Grenadines, and Suriname, although the Maldives had a managed float. See International Monetary Fund, *International Financial Statistics, Washington D.C.:* Publication Services, International Monetary Fund, December 2001) pp. 2–3 .

67. To be sure, there was a focus on varying levels of regional inflation and interest rates.

68. Austria, Russia, Prussia, and Great Britain were the major nations that met at the Congress of Vienna (1814–1815).

69. At this time, German states earned sizable revenue from coinage charges. The sacrifice of such revenues was, of course, a major obstacle to currency unification.

70. In 1818, the North German Customs Union was formed. In 1828, both the Central German Customs Union and the Southern German Customs Union were formed. In 1834, central Germany also formed a customs union called the Steuerverein (literal translation: tax union).

71. The Zollverein included most German principalities and free towns. The major exceptions were Austria and states in northwest Germany such as Hamburg, Lübeck, and Bremen.

72. Bordo and Jonung, *Lessons for EMU;* and Sartorius August von Waltershausen, *Deutsche Wirtschaftsgeschichte: 1815–1914* (Jena: G. Fischer Verlag, 1923), 176. See also Carl-Ludwig Holtfrerich, "Did Monetary Unification Precede or Follow Political Unification of Germany in the 19th Century?" *European Economic Review* 37 (1993): 518–524.

73. The exchange rate was thaler 1 = gulden 1.75 (or gulden 1 = thaler 0.5714).

74. After fixing the exchange ratio, arbitrage prevented the value of the thaler and the gulden from changing by more than the minting and transportation costs.

Germany's fixed exchange rate system was similar to post-1999 Euroland, when EMU members locked their currencies to each other with unvarying exchange rates.

75. Prussia was the industrial capital of Germany from which much of the nation's militarism and aggressiveness is thought to have originated. It comprised most of northern Germany, with Berlin as its capital.

76. In 1870, the Prussian bank was given effective control of the German money supply when the German federation prohibited the issuance of newly created state paper money and put limits on bank-issued paper notes.

77. The exchange rate was fixed at 1.5 Austrian gulden (florins) per thaler.

78. Only the minting of the special Vereinhandelsgoldmünze (literal translation: union trade gold coin) was permitted.

79. Legal tender status meant that the thaler had to be accepted as payment in settlement of debts. The one-thaler coin created by this Treaty became popular very rapidly.

80. It is a bit of an overstatement to say that the Treaty's handling of paper currency was visionary. The Treaty permitted the issuance of paper money but forbade members from granting legal tender status to any currency that was inconvertible. The Treaty addressed these pragmatic concerns, because Austria, a new member of the currency union, had issued inconvertible paper currency for almost a decade. See Carl-Ludwig Holtfrerich, "The Monetary Unification Process in Nineteenth-Century Germany: Relevance and Lessons for Europe Today," in *A European Central Bank,* ed. M. De Cecco and A. Giovani (Cambridge: Cambridge University Press, 1989), 224.

81. In 1862, Otto von Bismarck was appointed Premier of Prussia by King William I. Bismarck became head of the new German Republic and remained in office until 1890. He is said to be responsible for consciously igniting three wars, which resulted in German victories that united the northern and southern regions of Germany. In 1864, Bismarck's Northern Confederation Germany fought together with Austria against Denmark over Schleswig–Holstein. In 1866, the (seven-month) Austro–Prussian War was waged, resulting in large territorial gains for Prussia. Finally, in the Franco–Prussian War (1870–1871), Prussia thoroughly defeated Napoleon III and, again, reaped significant territorial gains. The outbreak of World War I can be traced directly from the imperialistic and militaristic spillover from the Franco–Prussian War. See infoplease.com, *History:* http://www.infoplease.com/ce6/world/A0860964.html. *Austro–Prussian War:* http://www.infoplease.com/ce6/history/A0805396.html.*Franco–Prussian War:* http://www.encyclopedia.com/articles/04695ResultsoftheWar.html.

82. The North German Federation was an alliance of 22 German states, located north of the Main River that had supported Prussia in the Austro–Prussian War.

83 England, for instance, was a major trading partner that was on the gold standard.

84 Silver was legal only for small denomination coins with an intrinsic value less than the face value. Silver thaler coins also remained legal tender.

85. Banks were given the alternative of either issuing notes, which could be used only in their regions, and operating only on a local basis or not issuing currency and conducting nationwide banking operations. Given the choice, the latter was the more profitable alternative.

86. Some economic historians date the true beginning of German monetary unification with the creation of the Reichsbank. See C.P. Kindleberger, *A Financial History of Western Europe* (London: George Allen and Unwin, 1981). For a different point of view see, Holtfrerich, "Did Monetary Unification Precede or Follow."

87. The paper Reichsmark gained legal tender status in 1909, and in 1948, it was replaced by the Deutschmark. The Reichsbank has since been replaced by the Bundesbank.

Chapter 6

Country Risk

INTRODUCTION

Before assessing the effect that currency unification has on a nation's asset prices, it will be helpful to review and explain country risk and the impact it has on the market yield of capital market investments. Country risk, an arcane measure that few people have heard of and even fewer fully understand, is a silent assassin that slashes trillions of dollars off the world's total financial wealth. It is a coldly calculated discount that the financial markets apply to assets in countries that have their own national currency or other risk factors, and it has a history of causing monetary instability in both developing and developed nations.

In this chapter, we will find that an investment's nominal yield is composed of seven major factors. Country risk is just one of those factors, but it is crucial to the decisions of international portfolio investors. Country risk is difficult to quantify, because it is a multidimensional variable that covers an amorphous range of highly interdependent causes and effects. Despite the difficulty, there is a conventional technique for quantifying country risk, and we will illustrate this technique. Some of the factors that most influence country risk are controlled directly by governments and central banks, but thrown into the mix is a much wider group of real and perceived variables over which the government has little control.

This chapter begins with a brief discussion of capital market yields and their major components. We will find that yields are composed of a hard-core base, called the "real, risk-free rate," and, upon this base, an assortment of six conceptually distinct risk premiums is layered. Of these layered risks, country risk will be highlighted along with the major factors that influence it. To further the arguments in this book, particular emphasis will be placed on the country risk from the perspective of international portfolio investors, but it should be kept in mind that risk premiums are the result of decisions by a complete range of economic actors, including importers, exporters, direct investors (for example, corporations establishing foreign subsidiaries), portfolio investors (for example, investors who place funds in money market and capital market instruments), and speculators.

It is important to keep in mind that our emphasis is on international portfolio investors, because different participants may perceive country risk differently and act according to their individual assessments and time horizons. Corporations that are interested in making foreign direct investments abroad might perceive country risk from a very long-term perspective, because they are interested in developing solid and lasting relationships with foreign countries—relationships on which new and expanded lines of business might be built. By contrast, portfolio investors, traders, and speculators are more likely to evaluate country risk from a shorter time perspective—often a time period that lasts only until the end of the investment's expected holding period or until collection (payment) of an accounts receivable (accounts payable). For them, the relevant time horizon is focused more narrowly on the duration and size of their expected cash flow exposures.

Not only do the perceptions of country risk differ among investors, traders, and speculators, but also there are differences in the steps they can take to protect themselves against this risk or cushion themselves against its impact. For example, a company opening operations in a foreign country can try to assure itself fair and equal treatment under the law by:

1. hiring local managers and many local workers,
2. tying worker compensation to the company's stock price or local subsidiary performance,
3. hedging revenues by borrowing in the local (host country) currency,
4. using transfer pricing strategies that minimize cash flow exposures,
5. controlling proprietary information or resources that are crucial to the operation of the foreign subsidiary,
6. forming joint ventures with local business partners,
7. pre-negotiating with the host government important, key details regarding finances and ground rules (for instance, profit repatriation rights, local content, local financing, local sourcing, and taxes),
8. strengthening their positions within the political process by forming lobby groups and supporting pro-business candidates for office,[1]
9. employing other operating strategies that would reduce the chances of the host country government interfering with company operations (for instance,

exporting a large portion of domestically produced goods and earning essential foreign exchange for the nation), and

10. insuring risks by means of one or more of the publicly and/or privately available insurance companies.[2]

Portfolio investors do not have such a wide range of operating remedies, but they do have access (as do corporations engaging in foreign direct investment), albeit limited, to redress through legal and arbitration proceedings. For instance, investors could try to seek a favorable legal judgment in the courts of the host country, but such redress might not be available, because of the government's sovereignty within its own borders. Furthermore, even if these suits could be served on the host government, the chances of a company winning are remote, because there is likely to be a large home country advantage for the government.

The likelihood of finding a legal remedy in courts outside the host country is also low. A fundamental principle of international law is the immunity of a state from the jurisdiction of another state's courts. As a result, companies are blocked, in most cases, from pursuing in the courts of foreign nations suits against host country governments. For instance, in the United States, the Act of State Doctrine prohibits U.S. courts from judging the legality of public acts of a recognized foreign sovereign when those acts are carried out within the territory of the foreign sovereign.

Sovereign immunity from the jurisdiction of foreign courts had almost no exceptions until the twentieth century, but because of the active involvement of governments in commercial activities, such as state trading, some exceptions have crept into the law. For instance, the Foreign Sovereign Immunities Act of 1976 (FSIA)[3] prohibits the U.S. courts from making decisions on state immunity and thereby limits the role that the executive branch can play in suits brought against foreign governments. At the same time, FSIA includes some exemptions that could open the door to company suits.[4] There are other possible avenues of redress, but, in every case, the prospect that a company could bring them to court, win the suit, and recover satisfactory compensation is small.[5]

Unfortunately for companies, there are no international courts in which they can adjudicate commercial claims. The International Court of Justice, which is the main judicial arm of the United Nations, was created for the purpose of arbitrating legal disputes between nations (states) and giving advisory opinions on legal questions.[6] Unless the company's claim could be melded into a national grievance, the International Court of Justice would not be the venue for such cases.

Arbitration is also a possibility, but to engage in such settlements, both parties have to agree to the process and agree to be bound by the decision.

One party in a dispute cannot force arbitration on another party.[7] The World Bank has established the International Center for Settlement of Investment Disputes (ICSID) to handle disputes over investment claims,[8] but the World Bank does not have the power to compel nations to abide by its verdicts.

Earning sufficient compensation to cover differentials in country risk is essential for rational investment decisions, and controlling this risk is also a must. In general, the easier it is for investors to switch quickly into and out of foreign investments, the greater is the possibility that real or imagined changes in country risk will cause capital flight and become a major source of concern to host country governments. As we have seen time and again over the post–World War II period, the combination of unfavorable changes in country risk and enormous volumes of short-term capital has inflicted a form of capital punishment on nations that has brought economies to their knees and resulted in the removal of powerful political and economic leaders.

A FEW WORDS ABOUT RISK PREMIUMS

If an asset could guarantee investors an increase in real purchasing power in the future (with no variability), then this rate of interest would be the equivalent of our real, risk-free rate yield. To the extent that such a fixed level of future purchasing is not (and cannot be) guaranteed, yield volatility gives rise to risk for which investors should be compensated. Local investors face a number of risks on domestic investments (such as inflation) that threatens to reduce their real purchasing power and taxes (subsidies) that alter future cash flows, as well as industry- and company-specific risks. Foreign investors face these same risks but also bear the exposures associated with exchange rate changes and the hazards of being a foreigner (that is, country risk). As a result, every dollar, euro, yen, or peso that foreign investors expect to earn must be discounted to accurately reflect the higher or lower risks associated with them. In short, they have a lower chance than local investors of being repaid in full, and therefore the expected value of their cash flows should be lower than it is for local investors.

Generically, there are two ways of weaving this uncertainty into a bond valuation or capital budgeting analysis. The first way is simply to reduce the expected cash flows by the probability of loss, and the second way is to account for risk by increasing the cost of capital (also known as the applicable discount rate). Let's use an example to explain these two approaches, starting with the reduced cash flow method. Suppose a domestic investor or company had a 10% cost of capital, and there was a 100% chance that its year-end earnings of $10 million would be paid and would be free from any government restrictions. The present value of these expected earnings would be $9.1 million.[9] By contrast, suppose the company earned this $10 million return in a foreign nation, and there was an 80% chance it could repatriate the entire amount but a 20% chance that the foreign government would impose restrictions that would permit the repatriation of only $5 million. As a result, the company's expected return would fall from $10 million for the domestic investment to $9 million for the foreign investment, and the present value of its expected return would fall from $9.1 million to $8.2 million.[10]

Rather than adjust the cash flows by the risk of government repatriation restrictions, a second alternative is to raise the cost of capital that is used to discount the cash flows. We saw in the last paragraph that the introduction of a repatriation risk reduced the present value of the expected cash flows from $9.1 million to $8.2 million. Had we kept the expected future cash flow at $10 million and simply raised the discount rate to 22.2%, we could have arrived at the same result, because a certain return of $10 million discounted by a risk-adjusted cost of capital equal to 22.2% yields a discounted present value equal to $8.2 million.[11] Therefore, ceteris paribus, one can say that the country risk premium (due to repatriation risk) was equal to 12.2%, which is the amount by which the cost of capital rose in the presence of repatriation risk.

THE MAJOR COMPONENTS OF NOMINAL YIELD

Exhibit 6.1 shows the seven major factors[12] that comprise the nominal yield, namely:

1. the real, risk-free rate of return,
2. the maturity premium,
3. the expected inflation and exchange rate premium,
4. the tax and subsidy premium,
5. the industry premium,
6. the credit premium, and
7. the country risk premium.

This section looks at each of these factors but focuses mainly on their connection to portfolio investments. It is important to remember that the returns on all assets and claims on wealth are arbitraged in the market and should move in tandem. As a result, the return on human capital (that is, education and knowledge), real estate (often called rent, which is the return on natural resources, land, and structures), capital goods (for example, production equipment), and financial assets (that is, corporate equities, homeowners' equity, debt, and cash) influence the average

Exhibit 6.1
Seven Major Components of a Borrower's Cost of Capital

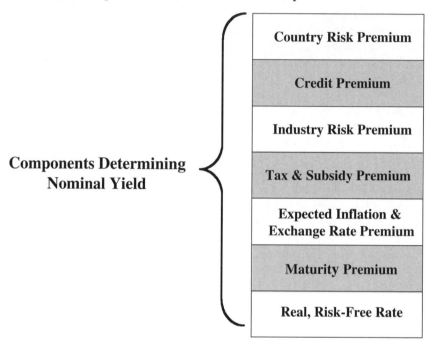

Components Determining
Nominal Yield

Country Risk Premium

Credit Premium

Industry Risk Premium

Tax & Subsidy Premium

Expected Inflation &
Exchange Rate Premium

Maturity Premium

Real, Risk-Free Rate

nominal investment yield.[13] Let's begin by reviewing the major factors
that influence nominal yield and then turn our attention to the country
risk premium.

The Real, Risk-Free Rate

The foundation of any nation's yield curve is its real, risk-free rate of
return. This return is called a "real" return, because it is adjusted for the
effects of expected inflation, and it is called "risk-free", because the borrower has no credit risk. Typically, government securities denominated in
domestic currency are considered risk free, because the government controls the machinery that creates the currency in which the securities are
denominated. The risk-free rate reflects society's time value of money,
and, as defined here, it is the foundation for all returns.[14] Therefore, it is
the same for every interest-earning asset in a nation, regardless of where
funds are invested.

Generally, the factors that most influence the real, risk-free rate are
slow-moving, long-term ones, which governments and central banks can

influence but do not control. Factors such as productivity, saving preferences (that is, society's time preference for consumption), demographic
factors, cultural trends, shifts in economic structure, and the level of international economic integration all influence the real, risk-free rate.

Productivity is important, because the productive abilities of a nation
define the range of feasible economic tradeoffs between current consumption and certain future consumption. The more productive a nation is, the
more current consumption is sacrificed when a nation invests in the future. To compensate for this current loss, the real, risk-free rate of return
must increase so that income earners are guaranteed future consumption
that is proportionately more than they could consume now.

Factors influencing productivity determine the *ability* of a nation to
trade off current consumption for future consumption, but society's saving rate determines its *willingness* to make such a tradeoff. The graying of
nations, such as the United States, Japan, and countries in Western Europe, is a good example of how demographics can change the saving
decision. A progressively aging population, such as the baby-boom generation, tends to save relatively less and, therefore, consumes relatively
more of its current income. Not only are increasingly more individuals re-
tiring—and therefore are no longer actively participating in the creation of
GDP (that is, a proxy for income)—but also, being in the second nine holes
of their lifetimes, they have less need to save. Many have their houses
fully (or nearly) paid off, and their children have completed (or will complete shortly) school. Under these conditions, one would expect the supply of saving to contract, and the real, risk-free rate of return to rise.
Simply put, the increased attractiveness of current consumption means
that it would take a higher real interest rate to make historic levels of saving worthwhile for these individuals.

Economic integration has the effect of improving participating nations'
productivity and simultaneously increasing their propensities to save. As
a result, economic integration has a double-barreled effect on the real,
risk-free rate of return. On the one hand, productivity improvements raise
the real, risk-free return, but on the other hand, increased saving propensities lower it. Therefore, the net effect is indeterminate.

Maturity

Typically, investments of different maturities have different yields. To
the extent that these markets are segmented and investors cannot or
will not switch freely from one maturity to another, yield differences
would not be arbitraged away. Consequently, an investment's maturity
could exert an independent influence on its rate of return. This non-ar-
bitraged rate differential would occur, for example, if individuals had a
natural preference for liquidity and borrowers had a natural preference

for long-term funds. Under these circumstances, the forces of supply and demand would force short-term rates down relative to long-term rates. Such a shift in rates would be reinforced by financial intermediaries that would be faced with persistent gaps between the maturity of their assets (long term) and liabilities (short term). To compensate for this risk, a maturity premium would be built into the yield structure.

The Inflation Premium and the Exchange Rate Premium

The inflation premium compensates investors for a decline in their real future purchasing power due to an expected increase in prices. Like the real, risk-free rate of return, the inflation premium is independent from any particular investment asset and, rather, depends on expected changes in the average price of all goods and services. This premium is not compensation for inflation uncertainty—such uncertainty is included under the *country risk* category—rather, it is a premium connected to the consensus view of future inflation.

To control inflation, central banks have to control their money supplies, and one of the most important lessons we have learned from monetary history is that the more independent a central bank is from the government, the greater are its chances of controlling inflation. Exhibit 6.2 shows the results of a frequently cited study that illustrates the direct relationship between central bank independence (that is, its ability to select policy objectives without government influence) and low inflation.[15] Independent central banks tend to focus more on achieving price stability than increasing GDP and reducing unemployment. Therefore, the level of central bank independence should be (and is) an important factor in determining the expected level of inflation (that is, inflation premium).[16]

Domestic borrowers and investors are concerned about the corrosive effects that inflation has on the real purchasing power of their principal and earnings. Foreign investors are more concerned about the deterioration in the exchange rate. In short, even if a nation has no inflation, a depreciation of its currency over the term of an investment could harm foreign investors. To compensate for this risk, a premium is attached to the real, risk-free rate.

The risk of inflation is a threat to domestic investors who expect to spend their funds at the end of the investment period. The risk of a fluctuating exchange rate is a threat to foreign investors who expect to convert their earnings into a different currency at the end of the investment period. Over a long period of time, the risk of inflation and the risk of a change in the exchange rate are almost one and the same. Higher inflation, which reduces the purchasing power of the domestic currency, causes the host country's exchange rate to fall, thereby reducing the purchasing

Exhibit 6.2
Central Bank Independence vs. Inflation

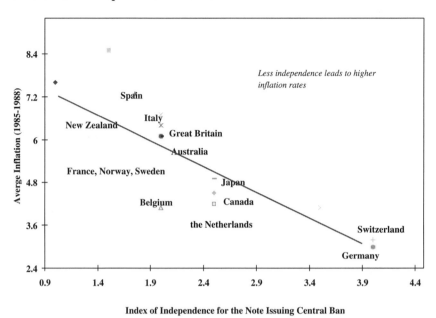

power for foreigner investors as well. The theory that posits that long-term changes in nations' inflation differential should be offset by changes in the exchange rate is called the "relative purchasing power parity theory" (PPP).

If risky assets are valued by the multicurrency capital asset pricing model (CAPM) and if PPP conditions hold, then the risk premium between nations should be equal. This means that, if a nation is in equilibrium, every asset's risk premium should be independent of both the currency in which it is denominated and the investor's base currency. Therefore, aggregate risk should depend only on the relative weights of the components; that is, the market's aggregate risk premium will be the weighted average of the constituent assets' premiums. We arrive at this conclusion, because, in equilibrium, cash returns in different nations on government securities should differ only by expected changes in exchange rates. As well, in equilibrium, PPP implies that expected exchange rate changes will equal the differential between nations' expected inflation rates. Therefore, arbitrage will ensure that the risk premiums among nations are equal.[17] If PPP were ensured over a long period of time, then the risk of inflation and exchange rate changes would offset one another for international investors.

Of course, the assumptions of CAPM and/or PPP can be violated. For instance, not all investors perceive the same market portfolio, construct efficient portfolios, have homogeneous expectations, fully anticipate rates of inflation, and have the same single-period investment time horizon. Moreover, problems could arise from investment indivisibility, taxes and transaction costs, and an inability to borrow and lend at the risk-free rate. Similarly, the PPP conditions could be violated. Percentage changes in exchange rates may not be equal to country inflation differentials, because many factors besides inflation rates influence exchange rates (for example, interest rates, GDP growth, expectations, and supply-side shocks). As a result, there may not be a single risk-free rate of interest, and covered investments could produce different returns.[18]

Inflationary expectations and exchange rate expectations are formed in two major ways. First, they are formed *adaptively* by taking a weighted average of the past inflation rates and projecting this weighted average into the future. Second, they are formed as a by-product of *rational* deductive reasoning based on the most recent news and perceptions of how this news will play out in the future. Over a long period of time, expectations should converge to reality, because it is hard to fool all the people all the time. It is hard even to fool some of the people all the time.

Tax and Subsidy Premium

Yields vary with the expectation that government taxes and/or subsidies will change over time. Because subsidies are typically given to individual companies and not entire market segments, they are not usually important factors determining the yield curve of a nation. By contrast, a country with a relatively large increase in its income taxes could prompt investors to reduce their exposures by investing elsewhere or offsetting these taxes with artificial costs (for instance, by borrowing in host-country currency and converting to another currency).

Industry Risk Premium

Like the tax and subsidy premium, the industry risk premium is an important factor for explaining interest differentials among investment assets, but it is not usually a central factor determining a nation's yield curve. Unlike the tax and subsidy premium, the industry risk premium is connected to the cash flows of businesses within a particular industry and how those cash flows change with the business cycle. If the industry's cash flows respond more than average to cyclical variations in economic activity (that is, it has a relatively high beta), then this risk premium should be built into the investor's discount rate.

It is highly possible for the credit risk of an entire industry to change due to broad systematic changes in the economy. As an example, new environmental protection laws (for example, requiring smokestack scrubbers), international turmoil (for example, wars, riots, and other civil disturbance), consumer resentment (for example, selling products to developing nations that have been banned at home), or FDA warnings (for example, against smoking or asbestos) could change the inherent risk premium attached to an industry.

Credit Risk Premium

The credit risk premium is the *private, commercial* risk associated with the expected inability or unwillingness of a borrower to meet debt service commitments. This risk is entirely dependent on the cash flows of the individual company. The riskier the company, the higher this cash flow risk will be and the higher the credit risk premium will be that is built into the rate of return.

It is important to remember that this credit premium is added onto the country risk and other risk premiums of a nation. A foreign company that issues securities may be very solvent, have excellent products, and have a dominant position in its local market. Logically, the company should be judged a very strong credit. Its bonds may be the local equivalent of bonds issued by Procter and Gamble or Kodak in the United States. Yet, these securities trade in the international markets at yields higher than U.S. junk bonds simply because of where the company is located. The company may find itself paying onerous rates of interest to borrow funds for prudent projects when its solvency and standing in the country where it is located seem sufficient to give it access to cheaper credit.

The reason this company's bond is riskier than the local government bond is because, in a crisis, the local government could print the money to pay back the government bond,[19] use its taxing power to pay it back, or exercise its international borrowing rights (for example, at the IMF) to gain needed liquidity. Meanwhile, the private company does not have these alternatives. Consequently, bond traders require a higher yield to be willing to buy the company bond. The term *sovereign cap* is often used to describe the tendency for company debt to have a lower credit rating than local government debt. This relationship is not a law—because there are many cases in which companies have issued bonds that are higher rated and lower yielding than local government bonds—but it is a rule of thumb in the financial markets.

Country Risk

Exhibit 6.3 shows the seven major components of a nominal yield and the factors that affect them. Of major importance to the analysis in this chapter is an understanding of the country risk premium and how it is measured. Country risk is a multifaceted metric that agglomerates all private and sovereign threats connected to country-specific changes in the economic, political, and social conditions of a nation. Most important is the systematic relationship between country risk and economic, political, and social activity. Because a large investor can diversify internationally, the losses in one region of the world could be offset by gains elsewhere. As a result of these offsetting cross correlations (that is, covariances), country risk for an internationally diversified portfolio investor may not be as large as the computed premium makes it first appear.

Country risk premiums are inversely related to the level of international capital market integration. If the international markets were fully integrated, investors would have portfolios that replicated the global weightings of global capital markets. There would be no biases toward or away from any industry, country, or region of the world. By contrast, if international capital markets were only partially integrated, perhaps due to governmental impediments that interfered with the free flow of capital, country risk premiums would rise to compensate investors for these risks. It has long been known that the portfolios of investors in many countries, such as the United States, are not internationally diversified and show a clear preference for domestic assets. That persistent preference is one reason why country risk premiums remain large. Finally, if international capital markets were fully segmented, the relationship among the yields in different countries would not (and could not) be arbitraged, and persistent differences among nations would prevail.

Country risk can be divided into two broad categories: factors influencing a nation's *willingness* to pay its debts and factors influencing its *ability* to pay its debts. A nation's willingness to pay is influenced by what we will call "political risk," and its ability to pay is mainly a function of its economic health (financial and real), debt management practices, and infrastructure (social environment, economic conditions, and human resource base). Let's discuss these risks and what causes them to change.

Political Risks

A country's political risk premium is determined by a variety of factors that do not always lend themselves to quantification. Among the most important factors are political stability, the regularity and fairness of the political process (for instance, elections), turnover of elected leaders, perceived and actual levels of corruption and bureaucracy, government

Exhibit 6.3
Components of Nominal Yields and the Factors Affecting Them

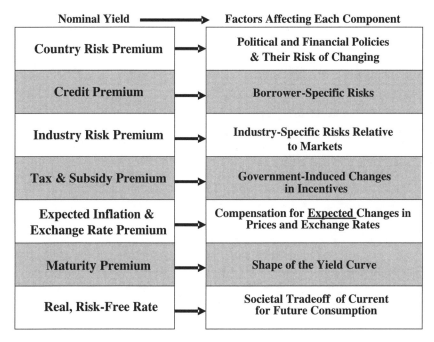

Nominal Yield	→	Factors Affecting Each Component
Country Risk Premium	→	Political and Financial Policies & Their Risk of Changing
Credit Premium	→	Borrower-Specific Risks
Industry Risk Premium	→	Industry-Specific Risks Relative to Markets
Tax & Subsidy Premium	→	Government-Induced Changes in Incentives
Expected Inflation & Exchange Rate Premium	→	Compensation for Expected Changes in Prices and Exchange Rates
Maturity Premium	→	Shape of the Yield Curve
Real, Risk-Free Rate	→	Societal Tradeoff of Current for Future Consumption

fractionalization, social fractionalization (for instance, ethnic, cultural, language, and religious), social conflicts and unrest (for instance, riots, widespread strikes, public demonstrations, coups d'etat), the government's willingness and ability to control civil unrest, distributional imbalances in income levels, xenophobia, nationalism, the level of socialism (for instance, threat of nationalization), and currency convertibility. In general, political risk is a national attribute, but there are cases in which it could be different for different industries. For example, the defense industry in any country is likely to be more protected and therefore have a higher country risk premium than an industry sector dealing in a freely traded international good (for instance, clothing).

During the last century, there have been dramatic examples of changes in the political climate that led to discrete, sizable revaluations of the country risk premium and a substantial deterioration of the value of international investment assets. Examples of major events that led to the revocation and nonperformance of contracts, expropriation, confiscation, terrorism, and, sometimes, murder on a massive scale were:

1. World War I.
2. The 1917 Bolshevik revolution.

3. Hitler and his Nazi regime's rise to power in the 1930s.

4. World War II.

5. The 1959 Cuban revolution.

6. The 1979 Iranian revolution, overthrow of the Shah of Iran, and official banning of Western goods. and

7. Ethnic-based civil wars during the 1990s in Yugoslavia, Bosnia, and Czechoslovakia.

Country risk premiums were also modified, albeit to a milder degree, by events such as:

1. the election of socialist governments (for example, the 1981 election of French Socialist François-Maurice Mitterand) and conservative governments (for example, the 1979 election of Margaret Thatcher in England);

2. nationwide labor strikes, such as those that occurred in Nicaragua (1978) and Poland (1980);

3. the political turmoil and social disorder in Mexico in 1994 owing to the assassination of two political luminaries,[20] formal allegations of political corruption leveled against high-ranking officials of the ruling party, the resignation of two high-profile government officials,[21] and armed uprisings by Chiapas rebels;

4. the economic and political turmoil in Argentina that caused, over a two-week period from late 2001 to early 2002, five presidential changes. The changes were the result of an extended, four-year period of economic stagnation from 1997 to 2001 and led to the ruin of largest and richest middle class in Latin America, as well as the temporary collapse of the Argentine economy.

Imbedded in the political risk premium is the existing state of political and socioeconomic conditions, but more importantly, this premium is influenced by the chances that these conditions could change quickly over the investment time horizon. Businesses look for fair and equal (nondiscriminatory) treatment under the law, and they will attach a higher premium to those countries where this certainty is in doubt.

Economic Risks

Taking a country's economic pulse is usually a rather routine matter of analyzing some standard economic statistics. By contrast, forecasting what the economic health will be in the future is much more difficult but, at the same time, much more relevant to the investment decision. Crucial to an accurate understanding is an ability to forecast domestic indicators, such as a country's real growth of GDP, inflation rate, the price of major commodities such as oil, copper, or coffee, unemployment rate, employment rate, labor costs/productivity, effective real exchange rate, developments that affect the communication/transportation infrastructure, and changes in the depth and breadth of the domestic money markets and capital markets. Added to these risks are broad changes in technology, consumer preferences, and market structure.

We know from a previous discussion that nominal interest rates are directly related to expected inflation, but the variability of expected inflation is captured in country risk. The larger the variability (that is, standard deviation) of expected inflation, the higher the chance that expectations will prove to be incorrect. As a result, this risk increases nominal rates. In the long term, inflation is a monetary phenomenon. If the central bank regulates the rate of money creation so that it closely approximates the long-term rate of increase in real output, average inflation should be close to zero, but in the short run, a multitude of factors can change it. Nevertheless, even with the most stable and conservative central banks, inflation can be volatile over short periods of time, and this volatility should be reflected in the risk premium. Of course, an unstable central bank would only serve to add to this risk premium.

International indicators of a country's economic health are also important, if not more so, for investors who are interested in monitoring a country's ability to repay international loans. The international indicators that are most often used to monitor a country's economic health are the three major accounts of the balance of payments (that is, current account, financial account, and official reserves account), as well as financial ratios that reflect national indebtedness, liquidity, leverage, and debt service. Among the most closely watched of these ratios are the proportion of external debt to GDP (indebtedness), external debt to exports, accrued debt service to exports (debt service ratio), accrued interest to exports (interest service ratio), exports to GDP, and external floating rate loans to total external loans. A country's past repayment performance in the international capital markets is also used as an indicator of both its willingness and its ability to repay in the future and the ease with which it might be able to reschedule the debt, if necessary. In general, the poorer a country's payment record and the worse its balance of payments ratios, the higher the country risk premium will be.

The willingness of a country to repay debts is often reflected in its fiscal, monetary, and political policies. Adjustments of these policies are frequently triggered by unfavorable changes in the measures of economic health or the country's balance of payments picture. Active fiscal and monetary policies are a natural reaction to unfavorable changes at the domestic and international levels. If they become severe enough at the international level, the country could resort to restrictions on currency convertibility, tariffs, quotas, and other nontariff barriers (for example, voluntary export agreements).

THE MARKET VALUE OF COUNTRY RISK

We mentioned previously in this chapter that many economic, political, and social variables influence country risk. Because of this, it is technically challenging to calculate past and current country premiums, and it is extremely difficult to predict what these premiums will be in the future. An example might help to show why. Suppose we were comparing the returns on U.S. and Indonesian Treasury bills. The United States had no inflation, and U.S. Treasury bills that paid $100 one year from now had prices of $95.24, earning investors a real, risk-free annual yield of 5%.[22] If, at the same time, Indonesian Treasury bills paid 1,000,000 Indonesian rupiahs (IDR) one year from now and had prices of IDR862,069, then investors in these securities would earn a return of 16%.[23] Under these conditions, why would anyone purchase U.S. Treasury bills?

We know from a previous discussion that seven factors influence each country's nominal yield: the real, risk-free rate, maturity premium, expected inflation premium and exchange rate premium, tax and subsidy premium, industry risk premium, credit risk premium, and country risk premium. Maturity would not be a source of difference between the U.S. and Indonesian yields, because both securities mature in one year. Similarly, there would be no industry risk premium or credit risk premium, because the borrowers are governments. Differentials between the country's tax/subsidy rates would be easy to separate, so let's assume they are identical. Therefore, the difference between the two government security rates would have to be due to differentials in three factors that are related to the real, risk-free rates, expected inflation/exchange rate premium, and country risk premium.

Exchange rate volatility plays an especially important role. Suppose the beginning exchange rate was IDR10,000 = $1, and the buyer who spent IDR862,069 for the Indonesian bill was a foreigner who had paid $86.20 to get the rupiahs to buy the security. One year later, this investor would receive IDR1,000,000 and would promptly sell them for dollars, or use them to buy another Indonesian bond. The investor's rate of return after one year would be 16% if the rupiah did not depreciate relative to the dollar, but it is highly likely that the rupiah would suffer some decline in value vis-à-vis the dollar. The key question for the investor is how much the decline will be. If the dollar value of the rupiah deteriorated so that the IDR1,000,000 were worth $95 instead of $100, then in one year, the dollar investor would earn a net return of $8.79 on an investment of $86.20, which is a 10.2% return and better than the return he would have earned on the U.S. Treasury bill.

By contrast, if the rupiah declined severely in value, the investor could suffer a loss. To see how bad the loss might be, suppose that the exchange rate weakened so that at the end of the year it took IDR20,000 to purchase one dollar. In that case, the IDR1,000,000 earned by the investor would be worth only $50. In other words, the investor would lose 42%, or $36.20, of the $86.20 investment.[24]

If the difference between the two government security rates is due to differentials in the three identified factors (that is, the real, risk-free rates, expected inflation/exchange rate premium, and country risk premium), then how does one divide the total risk premium among these three factors? In other words, how does one separate and identify the country risk premium? One way is to assume that the real, risk-free rates of return of each country are equal, because any differential should be arbitraged away by international investors.[25] Given this scenario, the real, international, risk-free rate of return would be 5% in both the United States and Indonesia. Therefore, if exchange rate volatility were melded into country risk so that the country risk premium became a broader but more observable economic variable, we could say that Indonesia's country risk was 11%. We know this is true, because a real, risk-free rate of 5% plus our newly defined (that is, expanded) country risk premium of 11% equals Indonesia's 16% nominal yield.

The 11% figure would change every day according to market participants' assessments of the differential between the two countries' country risk. If the international community felt that Indonesian bonds had become safer, they would offer to pay more than IDR862,069 for them, and if they felt that the bonds were becoming riskier, they would offer to pay less. The difference in yields between the U.S. Treasury security and the emerging country security might seem exaggerated, but, in fact, the differences are often much larger—for example, during the Argentine crisis in mid-2001, its country risk premium often exceeded 30%. When there are reports of violence or doubts about the financial system in an emerging country, nervous investors sell and the market prices of the emerging country bonds fall, often to distress prices. This scenario happens enough to make investors wary of the entire asset category, even during good times.

We can now analyze the effect currency unification could have on bond prices. Assume that the Indonesian government sold one million bonds for IDR862,069 each and the bonds immediately were traded in the secondary market. On a daily basis, the bonds would be bought and sold as investors moved funds into and out of investments in the normal course of business. The prices that buyers of the already issued bonds would be willing to pay would vary, and any new information would affect the prices that buyers would bid. If there were no new information that made the bonds look any more or less risky and if interest rates in other parts of the world did not vary, then after six months, the Indonesian bills should be trading at IDR931,035, which is halfway between the price of IDR862,069 they commanded when they were issued with a one-year maturity and the IDR1,000,000 they will be worth when they mature.

Of course, new information flows constantly to the market and affects the prices of the securities, so it is too much to hope that their daily price quotations would rise smoothly toward IDR1,000,000 as they approach redemption. Suppose the Indonesian currency and the Philippine currency merged and the monetary authorities of both countries ceded their power to a new central bank that was jointly controlled by Indonesia and the Philippines. Under the new monetary regime, inflation would still be possible, but any increase in the money supply would require more approvals than before, so it would be more difficult to orchestrate. Assume there were no restrictions on convertibility unless both countries agreed at the same time to put in restrictions. Bond investors everywhere would sit up and take notice. They would translate this bolt of positive economic news into purchase orders for Indonesian (and Philippine) securities, because two of the major risks of owning those bonds would have diminished. The prospects for lower inflation would attract Indonesian bond buyers, and foreign buyers would raise their bids because of the reduced threat of exchange controls and depreciation. As a result of the increased demand, security prices would rise.

The rise in price of Indonesian bonds would be large relative to their initial issue value. To see how much the rise could be, consider a more realistic example in which the average maturity of an Indonesian security was 10, 15, or 20 years rather than 1 year. If the 11% difference between U.S. and Indonesian yields were due totally to country risk, then the potential for financial wealth creation would be enormous, and this potential would be greater the longer the term to maturity of domestic debt. Table 6.1 shows the increase in the value of bonds (that is, wealth) for 10-, 15-, and 20-year maturities as country risk drops incrementally from 11% to 0%.

The lucky investors who bought the bonds at their rupiah issue price would immediately enjoy this gain, but there is more. The gains shown in Exhibit 6.1 are in rupiahs. For foreign investors, the gains could be even greater if the rise in foreign demand for Indonesian securities strengthened the dollar value of the rupiah. Foreign exchange dealers in Jakarta and across the world would react to the increase in demand for rupiah by raising its price. If the rupiah strengthened, foreign investors who bought Indonesian bonds before the positive news about currency unification would gain proportionately more than the amounts listed in Exhibit 6.1 because of the additional positive exchange rate effect. Like Indonesian nationals, foreign investors would derive economic benefits very rapidly.

Interrelations between Economic and Political Risks as well as Reality and Perceptions

There is no way to clearly separate economic and political risk, because changes in one cause changes in the other. Furthermore, the public reacts not only to the reality of new conditions but also to its perceptions of the new conditions and the discrepancy between national aspirations and the nation's ability to deliver on those aspirations. Many of the important economic and political risk factors that go into forming the country risk premium are quantifiable, but there is a huge subjective part that is also

Table 6.1
Percentage Increase in Prices for Securities of Various Maturities

Reduction in Country Risk Premium	Percentage Increase in Prices of Securities for 10-, 15-, and 20-year Maturities		
	10 years	15 years	20 years
1%	5.1%	5.9%	6.3%
2%	10.6%	12.4%	13.3%
3%	16.5%	19.6%	21.2%
4%	22.9%	27.5%	30.1%
5%	29.9%	36.3%	40.1%
6%	37.4%	46.1%	51.5%
7%	45.5%	57.0%	64.4%
8%	54.4%	69.2%	79.2%
9%	64.0%	82.8%	96.1%
10%	74.4%	98.0%	115.6%
11%	85.7%	115.1%	138.1%

important. These ratios have to be interpreted, and the ways they are interpreted reflect market perceptions, which can, at times, be rather mercurial and irrational. For instance, Mexico's budget deficit in 1994 was far lower than the average for all OECD (Organization for Economic Cooperation and Development) nations and well below the 3% Maastricht criterion for nations joining the 1999 European Monetary Union. Nevertheless, this deficit was perceived as being a problem, which fueled speculation against the peso that resulted in a severe peso depreciation, and precipitated an international contagion called the "tequila effect" that spread to other nations (for example, Brazil and Argentina).

Political Risk Measures, Financial Risk Measures, and Country Risk Measures

There are numerous public and private sources from which investors can obtain information on political, financial, and country risk. Among the most popular are Bank of America World Information Services, Business Environment Risk Intelligence (BERI) S.A., Economist Intelligence Unit (EIU), Institutional Investor, Moody's Investor Service, S.J. Rundt and Associates, Standard and Poor's Rating Group, Political Risk Services' *International Country Risk Guide* (ICRG), Control Risks Group, Coplin–O'Leary Rating System, Control Risks Information Services (CRIS), and World Markets Research Centre.[26]

CONCLUSION

Currency unification immediately reduces to zero the currency risk premium among member states, and if the supranational central bank is perceived as being more willing and able to control inflation, it should result in the reduction of currency risk between the currency union members and external nations. For countries that choose to converge their economies by going through the prolonged stages of economic integration (for example, free trade areas, customs unions, and common markets), many of the other factors that influence country risk can also be reduced. We feel that the same is true for nations that move directly toward currency unification, even without substantial economic integration. Cases in point are Argentina, Ecuador, El Salvador, and Panama. The problems that Argentina felt in 2001–2002 would have been far less and the long-term hopes for Argentina would have been far brighter if responsibility for monetary policy were taken totally out of domestic hands. A convergence toward the U.S. standard of living would begin. Likewise, the spillover contagion effects from the Argentina crisis would have been far more severe for nations such as Ecuador and Panama if they had not already abandoned their own currencies and adopted the U.S. dollar as their domestic currency.

NOTES

1. These activities usually have very low payoffs and a high probability of backfiring.

2. For instance, publicly sponsored insurance is offered in the United States by the Overseas Private Investment Corporation, in Canada by the Export Development Corporation, in Japan by the Ministry of International Trade and Industry, in Germany by Treuarbeit, in the United Kingdom by the Export Credit Guarantee Department, and by the World Bank through the Multilateral Investment Guarantee Agency. Private insurance is also offered by companies such as Lloyd's of London and AIG.

3. *Foreign Sovereign Immunities Act of 1976*, Pub. L. 94–583, 90 Stat. 2891, 28 U.S.C. Sec. 1330, 1332(a), 1391(f) and 1601–1611. Available: http://travel.state.gov/fsia.html.

4. FSIA states that a nation "is immune from the jurisdiction of the courts of another State, except with respect to claims arising out of activities of the kind that may be carried on by private persons." Under Section 1605(a)(3), action can be brought when the property taken is in violation of international law, and Section 1605(a)(6) allows action to be brought if it is to enforce an agreement made by the "foreign state with or for the benefit of a private party to submit to arbitration." See *Foreign Sovereign Immunities Act of 1976*.

5. One example of a possible avenue of redress for U.S. citizens is the *Alien Tort Claims Act* (ATCA). 28 U.S. Code § 1350. The ATCA gives U.S. federal courts jurisdiction over "any civil action by an alien for a tort only, committed in violation of

the law of nations or a treaty of the United States." Such a case was brought by Zimbabwe nationals seeking civil damages in the United States against Robert Mugabe for the organized acts of violence inflicted against them by his political party. It is important to note that, to win their cases, the plaintiffs would have to prove that these alleged acts of violence were either committed by state officials acting in that capacity or committed under the umbrella of the law. See Frederic L. Kirgis, "Alien Tort Claims Act Proceeding against Robert Mugabe," *American Society of International Law* (September 2000). Available: http://www.asil.org/insights/insigh50.htm#N_1_.

6. See International Court of Justice, *The Court at a Glance.* Available: http://www.icj-cij.org/icjwww/igeneralinformation/icjgnnot.html. Accessed October 29, 2001.

7. On November 4, 1979, the U.S. embassy in Tehran, Iran, was occupied by militant Iranian students who backed policies advocated by the Ayatollah Khomeini. For 444 days, the students held 52 U.S. citizens hostage, and on January 20, 1981—the day Ronald Regan was inaugurated—the hostages were released. January 20 also marks the beginning of the Iran–U.S. Claims Tribunal (located in The Hague, Netherlands), which was established for the purpose of handling claims of U.S. nationals against Iran and the claims of Iranian nationals against the United States. For such arbitration to take place, both the United States and Iran had to agree to the process (and they did).

8. The ICSID Convention never defined the word "investment," and for this reason, it has been able to handle a wide variety of cases. See Georges R. Delaume, "Economic Development and Sovereign Immunity," *American Journal International Law* 79, no. 319 (April 1985): 339.

9. $10 million/1.1 = $9.1 million.

10. Expected value = (80% x $10 million) + (20% x $5 million) = $9 million. Present value = $9 million/1.1 = $8.2 million.

11. $10 million/1.22 = $8.2 million.

12. For pedagogical reasons and since our focus will be on country risk, the presentation in this chapter will treat these seven components as being additive, but a good case could be made that some or all of them are multiplicative.

13. Derivatives are not included, because they are claims on claims of wealth. See Brian D. Singer and Kevin Terhaar, *Economic Foundations of Capital Market Returns*: The Research Foundation of the Institute of Chartered Financial Analysts: Charlottesville, VA, 1997).

14. In more formal terms, the risk-free rate equates society's marginal productive ability to trade off current consumption for future consumption (represented by the production possibility frontier) with its willingness to do so (represented by constant-satisfaction/indifference curves). See Singer and Terhaar, *Economic Foundations of Capital Market Returns*.

15. See Alberto Alesina and Lawrence H. Summers, "Central Bank Independence and Macroeconomic Performance: Some Comparative Evidence," *Journal of Money, Credit, and Banking.* 25, no. 2, (May 1993): 151- 162.

16. This independence could also decrease the risk premium by reducing the variation of inflation.

17. See Singer and Terhaar, *Economic Foundations of Capital Market Returns*.

18. Ibid.

19. This assumes that the government bond was denominated in local currency.

20. The victims were Mexican presidential candidate Luis Donaldo Colosio and Institutional Revolutionary Party official Jose Francisco Ruiz Massieu.

21. Special Investigator and Deputy Attorney General Mario Ruiz Massieu, and Interior Secretary Jorge Carpizo McGregor resigned.

22. $\$95.24 * (1 + 0.05) = \$100$.

23. IDR862,069 $(1 + 0.16)$ = IDR1,000,000.

24. $(\$50- \$86.20)/\$86.20 = -42\%$.

25. Actually, differences in the two countries' real, risk-free rates of return may vary, because real (that is, inflation-adjusted) capital in emerging countries is often scarce, causing interest rates to be higher than in developed nations. Also, emerging country governments often do not have enough revenue to cover current expenditures so they issue bonds to bridge the fiscal deficit. This huge increase in demand for loanable funds should cause the real, risk-free rate to rise.

26. See Stephanie Clifford and Matthew Maier, "Who's Who in Risk Management: Where to Find the Leading Risk Experts," *Business 2.0* (January 2002 Issue): Also see Steven A. Waller, *International Economics Links*. Available: http://www.flash.net/~stevew9/international.html.

Chapter 7

Hypothetical Examples of Wealth Creation in Asia and Latin America

INTRODUCTION

The American and European experiences with currency unions and the discussion of country risk pose the question whether there are groups of countries elsewhere in the world that are good candidates for currency unification. Asia and Latin America are geographical entities that are home to many nations and an almost equally large number of national currencies. Asia and Latin America each have regional identities but are diverse, and the individual national economies differ so much that their accomplishments in economic integration have fallen short of what Europe and America have accomplished.

This chapter stops short of giving scenarios of full economic integration for groups of Asian or Latin American countries. The potential gains and costs have been extensively discussed and the barriers remain high. The scenarios here focus on wealth creation that could result from currency unification for pairs or larger sets of countries in Asia and Latin America. These examples are tantalizing, because they would be beneficial and might also be politically feasible.

The scenarios in this chapter are all hypothetical. The discussion centers on financial calculations, because there are standard techniques that can compute how much financial wealth currency unification could deliver. The debate about currency regimes usually does not take these calculations of wealth changes into account and so does not reveal the wealth potential of currency unification.

To illustrate the potential gains, we create hypothetical groupings of countries and then apply estimation techniques to determine the dollar magnitude of the gains. The formulas are valid for valuing individual securities or income properties, but some readers may question whether our estimation technique gives the same precision when we apply it at the macro level. Our pricing formulas give the "fair" or "no-arbitrage" value of a bond or a common stock in a market with many investors, symmetric information, and enough liquidity. The reader will decide whether those conditions would prevail well enough for the formulas to work.

CURRENCY UNIFICATION IN ASIA

Introduction

Asia accounts for approximately 33% of the global landmass, 60% of the world population, almost 30% of global GDP, and more than half of all international reserve assets. Despite its size, increasingly well-educated workforce, and high saving rate, this region remains relatively poor, with an average per capita income that is only a fraction of the world average and an even more paltry fraction of the averages in Euroland and North America.

This is not to say that all Asian nations are below the international average. Japan's GDP remains second only to the United States, and some Asian nations have had sustained levels of growth that have almost defied the laws of economic gravity (for example, Japan prior to 1990, the Asian Tigers prior to 1997, South Asia, and China). Nevertheless, offsetting these islands of success there have been and continue to be a host of low-performing nations, and even among the nations that have experienced the most rapid growth, poverty persists, because the high growth has been on an extremely low base. Living standards in these nations have improved but not enough to push many residents above the poverty line.

For the most part, Asian nations (and particularly Korea, Japan, and China) have not been active participants in the global rush to form new regional blocs. It is not that integration has been totally off their radar screens, but relative to Europe and America, economic integration among the Asian nations has been anemic. For a variety of historical, economic, and cultural reasons, Asian nations have not been able to negotiate trade, investment, and exchange rate treaties that compare in scope and depth to agreements such as the European Coal and Steel Community, North American Free Trade Area, European Economic Community, or European Monetary Union. Nevertheless, we must remember never to say "never" when it comes to integration, because there is a handful of relatively new and ongoing experiments in this region that could sprout into more broadly based forms of integration. For example:

- The Association of Southeast Asian Nations (ASEAN)[1] Swap Arrangement began in 1977 as a way of providing short-term liquidity to nations experiencing balance of payments difficulties. These Asian-based swap funds were intended to supplement the existing sources of liquidity provided by the IMF. Initially, five ASEAN nations participated in the arrangement, but in 2000 (under the Chiang Mai Initiative), the agreement was extended to all ten ASEAN nations, and additional arrangements have been negotiated with China, Korea, and Japan. Longer term financing arrangements under the Regional Financing Agreement are currently being discussed;

- In 1985, seven South Asian countries[2] formed the South Asian Association of Regional Cooperation (SAARC), and since then, progress has been made toward integrating their economies. In 1995, the SAARC founded the South Asian Preferential Trading Agreement, and there is hope that in 2002 the South Asian Free Trade Association will begin.[3]

- The ASEAN Free Trade Area, with a domestic market totaling 500 million people, is scheduled to begin in 2002;

- At a regional summit meeting held in Brunei in November 2001, China and the ASEAN agreed to create, within ten years, a free trade area. This market could be as large as $1 trillion in size, could include close to 2 billion people, and could usher in a new era of economic growth and political stability for Asia. With China's admission in 2001 to the World Trade Organization, the benefits of such a union should be even larger than initially expected. The entry of Japan and Korea to the free trade area will be discussed at the 2002 summit in Cambodia.[4]

- Significant progress has been made between Japan and Korea on an investment treaty, which is expected to begin in 2002.[5]

One could rightly ask why the Asian nations have not already formed economic alliances equivalent to their Western counterparts. One of the major reasons is the huge difference in their levels of economic growth and development, as well as the perception that economic convergence is necessary for such agreements to be successful. Also, there is historical distrust and resentment among these nations (most of which is tied to the intense enmity by Korea and China toward Japan's imperialist past). Another major reason, which is perhaps less quantifiable and far from completely understood, is the Asian countries' tendency to view each other as opponents rather than partners in the economic, political, and cultural arenas. Consequently, economic integration has been and is expected to be slow and intermittent.

The recent success of the euro has prompted many Asian leaders to re-ask why Asian countries could not accomplish the same. Forming an Asian currency union is not a new idea. In fact, the Philippines and Hong Kong have already proposed the creation of an Asian Currency Unit (ACU), which conceptually and practically would mirror the European Currency Unit (ECU). Before such a currency union could be effected, some clear obstacles would have to be surmounted—the first of which is the perceived need for a significantly higher level of cyclical and structural coordination among the Asian nations. We should remember that, depending on how you count time, economic convergence among the Euroland nations took either six years (that is, between the 1993 Maastricht Treaty and 1999) or nearly 50 years (that is, between the 1951 formation of the European Coal and Steel Community and 1999); such time lines would be used as benchmarks for any Asian undertaking. As well, preconditions, such as were negotiated by the Maastricht Treaty for the Euroland nations, might have to be determined, and decades of adjustment might be required.[6]

Asian nations remain deeply divided over the costs and benefits of the alternative exchange rate systems, which range from the creation of a common currency to currency pegs, managed ("dirty") floats, and freely floating exchange rates. The lack of a dominant Asian currency hinders the development of an Asian currency union taking over the role of the dollar or the euro. Even though the yen would seem to be the most likely choice, it lacks a global presence in the trade, foreign exchange, and investment (that is, debt, equity, and direct investment) markets, and it has a diminutive presence as an international reserve currency. If we add to these obstacles the huge cultural differences and governmental dissimilarities among these nations, it becomes increasingly clear why economic and monetary integration have not flourished in Asia and why future progress may be slow in coming.

Regardless of the political, economic, and social prerequisites that inhibit the formation of an Asian currency union and regardless of whether a currency union becomes a priority (even in the long term) of these nations, it is worthwhile to examine the economic gains and losses that such a union could create. We know from previous chapters that the most obvious sources of gain come from:

1. the elimination of intra-union currency transaction costs and exchange risks among local currencies,
2. reduced exposure to external economic shocks,
3. improved price transparency,
4. deepening and broadening of the union's capital and money markets,
5. creation of an important international reserve currency, and
6. the ability to economize international reserves.

Our focus in the following sections will be on the wealth creation effects of such a currency union. What would the Asian nations sacrifice, if anything, by forming a union, and what would they gain? Let's begin the process of analyzing some possibilities.

Estimating the Costs and Benefits of an Asian Currency Area

The aggregate size of Asia and its total potential to create wealth can be put in perspective with a few simple computations. Asia's total population is approximately 3.5 billion, and the World Bank estimate for its average output per capita is approximately $3,000.[7] If the value of the average country's capital stock were between two and five times its annual output (as it usually is), the value of Asia's capital stock would be between $21 trillion and $52.5 trillion (which it is).[8] In mid-2001, the market value of all productive assets in Asia, including both securitized and unsecuritized assets, was between $6,000 and $15,000 of wealth per capita, which was within the range of two to five times annual income.

Suppose that Asia's average output per capita rose partway to the level of the industrial countries, for example, from $3,000 to $10,000 per capita. If the value of its capital stock rose in tandem (that is, maintaining a ratio between 2:1 and 5:1), it would grow to an amount ranging from $70 trillion to $165 trillion. That would be an increase of between $49 trillion and $112.5 trillion, which would be a total increase in the range of five to 12 times U.S. annual GDP and an increase of between $14,000 and $32,000 per capita. If Asia's average output per capita rose still further to $30,000, the value of its capital stock would then be much higher still—in the range of $210–$525 trillion, which would be an increase in the range of 20 to 50 times U.S. annual GDP and between $60,000 and $150,000 per capita.

You may be wondering why such figures are worth discussing when the linkages and amounts are so hypothetical. Part of the reason is to show how much wealth Asia could potentially create, compared to how little the region has created so far. Most analyses focus attention on annual output rather than wealth, especially financial wealth, and as a result, readers have become so accustomed to Asia's low average output rate that these diminutive figures have lost their power to shock. Estimates of the potential increase in wealth are many orders of magnitude greater than yearly output, but readers do not see these figures very frequently. It is for this reason that the enormity of foregone wealth should be put into perspective. Sheer size commands attention, especially when it as large as 50 times U.S. GDP. Such a huge figure opens the debate to a new panorama of possibilities. It provides an image of what could be—one that dwarfs the average person's ingrained perceptions of the realistic range of possibilities, and puts the spotlight on Asia's true economic potential.

There is another reason for computing and comparing actual wealth to potential wealth. Financial wealth can rise sooner and faster than income. When heavy flows of foreign portfolio investments raise the market prices of assets, these higher prices could spur consumption and capacity building. In times past, the sequence of events was thought to be that new investments in productive capacity stimulated consumption, setting in motion a rise in economic growth. Thereafter, the Keynesian multiplier and accelerator effects were set into motion, and the market prices of assets rose along with rising output. Today, the amount of financial wealth in the world and its mobility have become much more important than in the past. Increasingly, the world community, including the residents of Asian countries, holds its savings in many forms and shifts them from one currency to another as well as from one country to another. Not only has wealth become larger, but also its mobility has become more catalytic: When wealth rises, it has the potential to increase spending and create jobs.

A Hypothetical Scenario: Unifying Asian Currencies and Capital Markets

Historically, the force that served most to unify markets was specialization. In earlier times, transport costs, natural geographic barriers, political divisions, and tariffs posed huge obstacles to trade and integration. But the advantages of specialization and the reduction of transaction costs gradually overcame these barriers. Low-cost producers gained access to markets farther away, and market unification proceeded.

Economic integration typically began in the markets for goods and then spread to financial markets, but times have changed. Now the power of external shocks and worldwide macroeconomic pressures make a strong case for financial unification, whether or not goods markets have unified. There is nothing stopping countries from merging their currencies without first passing through the various stages of trade integration. The steps toward unification and convergence that historically have preceded currency unification are not as necessary as they used to be. For groups of Asian countries, the first and only step toward market unification could be currency unification. Since the 1997 Asian currency crisis, there has been a significantly stronger motivation for unifying Asian currencies than for integrating their product markets.

In this chapter, we present scenarios that analyze the effects of unifying selected Asian currencies without integrating their markets in other ways. These unification scenarios may seem hypothetical and preemptive, like building the top floor of a skyscraper without first building the foundation and the 50 floors beneath. We argue that the reduction of currency risk could be one of the most powerful forces pulling markets together. Financial wealth is now larger and more volatile than annual output. Any proposal for institutional change that would increase financial wealth and dampen its fluctuations deserves to be considered and then perhaps implemented.

The first unification scenario in this chapter begins with two Asian countries that have suffered currency instability. The initial step in our scenario is for these nations to unify their currencies in the same way the European countries unified to create the euro and with the intent to raise the market prices of their capital stocks. For reasons mentioned previously in this chapter, there is strong reason to believe that the hypothesized currency unification would add measurably to the stability of both currencies, lower nominal interest rates, and raise the market value of assets.

The proposed currency unification would not involve pegging the two countries' currencies to the dollar, the euro, or the yen. Instead the newly created currency would float relative to foreign currencies. This is a different exchange rate policy from the one that most Asian countries have used. During the heyday of the Tigers, the important exchange rate policy question for most Asian countries was whether to peg their currencies to the yen, dollar, or a European currency, and if they decided not to formally peg their currencies, how they could intervene so that their currency closely tracked one of the two major world currencies.[9]

Because the small, open Asian economies, in effect, managed their individual exchange rates relative to one of the two major currencies, they paid close attention to the exchange rate policies of their Asian counterparts in order to monitor their competitive export positions. These nations were careful to avoid "beggar-thy-neighbor" competitive devaluations, and their mode of competing for export markets was to emphasize quality, delivery terms, and product differentiation, as well as other product attributes and elements of the marketing mix. Because they thought of each other as competitors for foreign markets, they did not go to great lengths to coordinate their exchange rate policies.

Most Asian nations paid special attention to the relationship between the value of their currencies relative to both the yen and the currencies of their export markets. In short, they tried to set optimal exchange rates, where "optimal" aimed at ensuring that they had good competitive positions in their export industries. To a lesser extent, each small Asian country adjusted its exchange rate so that the burden of its foreign debt would not be too great. For example, a country, such as Thailand, might export to Japan but borrow in the U.S. dollar capital markets and money markets. Consequently, the ideal Thai exchange rate policy would be to depreciate against the yen and revalue against the dollar. That, of course, would require the dollar to depreciate against the yen faster than the baht's depreciation against the yen.[10]

In the scenario proposed here, each of the two Asian countries with large trade sectors would give up the autonomy of managing its own exchange rate. The countries would merge their two currencies and create a single central bank that would manage the new supranational currency. This is a policy that has not been widely discussed before and would be an unconventional step for two Asian countries that previously had not made other major efforts to unify their markets. Indeed, many readers would question whether two Asian countries would be willing to take such a step.

The idea would be hard to sell politically. Proposals to increase trade in goods and services among Asian countries have legitimacy, and, indeed, there are institutions working to achieve that aim. By contrast, calls to unify Asian currencies are relatively new, and there are few institutions seeking to achieve that objective. The Euroland nations achieved unification only after passing through many stages, the culmination of which was unifying their currencies and completing the unification of their capital markets. Intra-Asian trade barriers have not been significantly reduced, and only preliminary steps have been taken toward a monetary union.

Yet, currency unification has advantages that Asian countries can seize immediately; and it is the form of integration that is most feasible in this region, because it can raise the market prices of assets immediately and substantially. The usual first steps associated with unifying the markets for goods and services would probably not generate gains as large and as fast.

Three major groups would be harmed by the policy discussed here. Most affected would be the exporters and domestic producers in import-competing industries who benefit from the national exchange rate policies tailored to their needs. Both groups would find the terms of trade turning against them. They would lose market share or go out of business. Cheaper foreign goods would replace products from inefficient local producers in formerly protected markets. The economic victims of a currency union would be easy to identify, because they would clamor for redress and vote against the politicians who exposed them to the cold winds of competition.

A second group that would be harmed by a currency union would include those who lost access or suffered reduced access to financial capital at advantageous terms, perhaps because government-controlled banks could no longer lend to privileged borrowers at nonmarket rates. The third group of "victims" would be the local technocrats who set monetary policy in each country. Unless they were assimilated into the new central bank at the same (or higher) stature, these high-status individuals would very likely lose clout, because in an enlarged supervisory structure, the chance for any one individual or a few individuals to dominate policy for an extended period would be reduced.

One of the largest beneficiaries of currency unification would be the owners of financial assets denominated in the local currencies. When their assets were converted into the new, more stable supranational currency, the value of their holdings would rise instantly, and immediately thereafter, there would be positive, reverberating rounds of winners as the international investment community responded to the increased stability. These countries' risk profiles would be updated, the compensation needed to account for risk would fall, and funding could be obtained at a lower effective cost. Lower interest rates would echo forward by increasing consumption and investment spending, thereby increasing jobs. Moreover, domestic saving would increasingly be channeled back into the nation, thereby stimulating the further development of the local financial system, lowering the cost of capital, and inducing greater real investment spending. In short, the currency union would have the potential to create a virtuous circle of economic effects for the nations involved.

Adoption of currency union would be a profound policy reorientation for these nations. Previously, their economic missions were to produce and export, and their financial sectors and exchange rate policies served the needs of these sectors. But a policy of merging their currencies would turn these nations into financial wealth creators. The relative power of financial elites would rise, and pressure would rise for economic policy makers to maintain currency stability.

Asia could follow a pattern very much in line with the European Monetary Union, which began with a core group of countries and held open (and often encouraged) the possibility of others joining in the future. It is highly unlikely that Asian countries would merge their currencies into a single supranational currency. Nevertheless, even if the seeds started by a couple of nations germinated into a union of a few more, the benefits of a supranational currency could be enormous.

Of course, as the currency union grew, an inherent conflict might arise, because the benefits to new members might be relatively large in comparison to the existing members. Such was the case in 2001 when Greece gained entry to the European Monetary Union. The benefit to current EMU members from having Greece join Euroland were likely marginal in comparison to the benefits Greece derived from joining. Regardless, unifying Asian currencies in a sequence of steps would be plausible, as long as each incremental step brought at least some net benefit (even if it were a long-term strategic benefit) to both the union and the new member.

Unifying Two Asian Currencies

The main numerical illustration in this chapter shows how much financial value could come into existence when two countries unify their currencies. The new policy has to be compared to the policy it replaces and needs to create net gains. Assume the former policy was for each country to manage its exchange rate in such a way as to keep exports competitive without the cost of its foreign debt becoming excessively burdensome. To compare the two policies, the numerical illustration begins by computing how much wealth unifying the currencies could create. The increase is then capitalized and compared to GDP. For example, if the capitalized increase in wealth were 20%, then the benefits a nation would have to derive from having its own currency would have to be greater than 20% for the currency union to be rejected on economic grounds.

To proceed with the example, we must choose two Asian countries that might unify their currencies. In other analyses of this issue,[11] the pairs of countries proposed for such unification were chosen on the basis of classical, optimal currency area criteria, which were related to the real economy. In general, the test was whether the nations had economies that were at a sufficiently close level of development and cyclical coordination to merit the ultimate step of currency unification.

Choosing countries that are likely unification candidates on the basis of how their productive sectors fit together is a reasonable selection procedure if the two countries are going to go through the gauntlet of traditional economic integration stages (that is, preferential trading agreements, free trade area, customs union, and common market). Our example suggests a less thoroughgoing unification that would not involve having such an aim and not involve such an extended period of alignment. Our example is a marriage of convenience to achieve monetary stability only. As a result, the two countries we choose would not have to be matched with prerequisites that focus on real economic factors. The salient feature of the countries we choose is that their currencies and financial markets were categorized together in times of currency crisis. As a result, we focused on nations with country risk premiums that have been chronically high—especially since the 1997 Asian currency crisis.

Our example will use Indonesia and the Philippines, whose 1999 GDP figures were $119.5 billion and $78.0 billion, respectively.[12] How much would these two countries gain from abandoning their independent currencies, central banks, monetary policies, and exchange rate policies? Suppose Indonesia and the Philippines unified their currencies, delegated monetary policy to a supranational central bank, created a new currency called the "rupso," and thereafter denominated all domestic financial transactions in rupsos. As long as there was a low probability (perhaps due to severe costs) of disbanding the union, the arrangement would eliminate the risk that either national currency might devalue unilaterally and would have the likely effect of reducing both inflation and inflationary expectations. Let us compute what effect these changes might have on the value of the capital stock of each country. To the extent that the rupso was a more credible currency than either of its predecessors, the effect could be large.

An Estimation of the Benefits of a Currency Union

How much wealth would currency unification create? If the union and its independent central bank were able to lower country risk, then nominal interest rates could fall quickly, which would cause a rapid increase in wealth. Suppose the government debts of both Indonesia and the Philippines were composed of ten-year government bonds[13] denominated in local currency, were trading in the market at face value,[14] and had face values equal to 100% and 80% of GDP, respectively. Suppose further that companies in each country issued similarly structured bonds with face values equal to 25% of GDP. Given the recent turmoil in both countries, assume that the coupon rate on the government bonds of both countries was 16%, and the coupon rate for corporate bonds of both countries was 18%. If the ten-year U.S. Treasury bond yield were 5%, the country risk for Indonesia and the Philippines would be 11%,[15] and the added risk premium for the corporate bonds would be 2%.[16]

How much would currency unification reduce the country risk of these two countries? For countries such as Spain and Italy that joined the European Monetary Union in 1999, government bond yields fell by as much as 9%, but it took several years (1992–1999) for this to happen. In our example, assume the country risk declined immediately by 5%,[17] thereby reducing government bond yields to 11% and corporate bond yields to 13%. Given these conditions, there would be an immediate increase in the market values of the bonds (government and corporate) equal to approximately 34.5% of combined GDP, which would be equivalent to $68.1 billion.[18] This calculation covers only bonds and, thus, understates the total gain. A more complete estimate of the change in wealth would apply a gain of similar proportion to the rest of each country's capital stock (that is, productive assets that are not pledged to collateralize bonds). Because capital markets in both countries are underdeveloped and small, these assets could comprise the majority of the nation's capital base. To be conservative, we assume that unsecuritized assets are of the same magnitude as the securitized assets, represented here by government and corporate bonds. If the market value of the unsecuritized assets rose by the same proportion as the market value of the bonds, the gain would be an additional $54 billion.[19] The immediate windfall gain to owners of unsecuritized assets could be much larger than the gain to the holders of the bonds, because the unsecuritized assets may be a larger part of the total capital stock of the two countries.

This calculation shows the order of magnitude of gain that two Asian countries could quickly obtain if they unified their currencies. The figure is not precise and depends on how large and how fast the reduction in country risk could be accomplished. Nevertheless, the $68.1 billion immediate gain in bond valuation alone is approximately equivalent to a perpetual annual increase in GNP of 3.8%.[20] In other words, the annual benefits these countries could derive from having their own currencies, their own central bank, and the ability to conduct independent monetary policy would have to amount to more than 3.8% of GDP for the currency union not to make economic sense. If we were to add in the ancillary benefits, such as the benefits from reduced transaction costs, the chances would diminish even further for the advantages of an independent currency to be greater.

Our computation covers only Indonesian and Philippine bonds, and it is only a rough (albeit conservative) estimate of the true increase in wealth that would result from a currency union. At the center of the computation is a percentage increase in the market value of ten-year bonds, but it also gives an estimate of the price increases for unsecuritized income-producing assets. For example, apartment buildings and office buildings in both countries would become more valuable, because the future rents from those buildings would be more highly valued in the present.

A Third Asian Country Joins

To continue with the scenario of currency unification, suppose that Thailand joined the currency union with Indonesia and the Philippines. There would be two likely ways that Thailand would be allowed to enter. If the rewards to Indonesia and the Philippines were large enough, it could be done without imposing any conditions; in which case, Thailand would simply replace the baht with the rupso at a mutually agreeable exchange rate (for example, 24 baht per 1 rupso). Thailand's monetary policy would henceforth be set by a supranational central bank in which it might or might not have representation. In any case, the focus of the supranational central bank would be on the economic health of the union as a whole and not Thailand (or any particular country).

A second path to currency union membership would be for Indonesia and the Philippines to impose entry criteria on Thailand and to monitor, for some specified probation period, those criteria to ensure that they were met. A justification for such criteria could be to ensure that Thailand's economy was prepared for the cold shower it would receive as a member of the union. Another justification could be that these criteria were imposed to ensure that the rupso lost no international credibility when Thailand joined. Of course, after the merger, the rupso's credibility would depend solely on the discipline and professionalism of the supranational central bank, its power to resist political pressure from the three governments, and the credibility of the three countries to continue the union even when times were hard.

As a practical matter, it would probably not be feasible for Indonesia and the Philippines to crack the whip over Thailand and require the Thais to satisfy stringent criteria before letting the baht join. Some posturing might be worthwhile to bolster the rupso's credibility, but the value of having Thailand in the currency union would exceed quickly the gains that Indonesia and the Philippines might achieve by keeping Thailand out until it satisfied any strict criteria. The reason is that, as soon as Thailand joined, there would be a high likelihood that the country risk premium for both Indonesia and the Philippines would drop, thereby causing their nominal interest rates to fall and the value of their fixed income securities, stocks, and the capital infrastructure to rise.

Having a third country in the union would move the rupso a step closer to becoming a major currency. In addition, the broader and deeper rupso market would be less vulnerable to natural disasters and exogenous economic shocks. For instance, if a volcano erupted or a typhoon hit the Philippines, the peso would, no doubt, suffer; but, the effects on the rupso would be cushioned, because it is the currency of a broader economic area, much of which would not experience the hardship that was affecting the Philippines. Moreover, with a greater number of member nations, the newly created central bank would be less vulnerable to pressures from any one of the three governments. When only two countries merge their currencies, many of the old risks might remain, but when a third one joins the merger, the risks of inflation, devaluation, and currency controls are highly likely to drop even more.

To be sure, Thailand's joining the currency union would probably reduce its country risk more than the country risk of Indonesia or the Philippines, but even an incremental reduction in country risk for the two existing members could tilt the scales clearly in favor of opening the door to new members. Suppose, for example, that the risk premium for Thailand fell by 6% (that is, from 11% to 5%), which was larger than the 5% drop we assumed for Indonesia and the Philippines. As a result, government bonds yields fell from 16% to 10%, and corporate bonds fell from 18% to 12%. At the same time, assume the risk premium for the two original members fell by an additional 1%. If Thai government bonds and corporate bonds had average maturities of ten years, the drop in country risk would raise their values by 37% and 34%, respectively. Assuming that government bonds were 60% of GDP and corporate bonds were 25%, the increase would be equivalent to $37.1 billion, or 31% of Thailand's $121 billion GDP in 2000.[21] In addition to these gains, the market prices of unsecuritized assets in Thailand would rise for the same reason they rose in Indonesia and the Philippines.

If Thailand's joining the currency union reduced the country risk of Indonesian and Filipino assets, their prices would immediately rise to higher levels. The gains would be added to the ones that already occurred, and they would amount to an increase in the value of government bonds by a further 7.5% and corporate bonds by an additional 6.9%.[22] In total, this would be an increase of $17.1 billion.[23] The market prices of these nations' unsecuritized assets would also rise in tandem.

The Addition of Other Asian Countries to the Currency Union

According to our calculations, the economic benefits to Indonesia and the Philippines from forming a currency union easily exceeded the value that the two countries gained from having their own currency and their own independent exchange rate policy. When a third country joined, the marginal gains to the new entrant were larger than the current members, but the union generated additional windfall gains for current members as well. On that basis, it is reasonable to expect that a fourth, fifth, and sixth country might choose to join the currency union. Indeed, the currency union might generate enough force of attraction to unify the currencies of a large part of Asia, despite the marked differences among Asian economies.

We do not hold the utopian view that all the countries in Asia would be receptive to the force of attraction. The computations in this chapter demonstrate that the potential exists for Asian countries to create much more financial wealth than they have done until now. Nevertheless, from there it does not follow that they will feel any immediate urgency to take action.

The hypothetical currency union of Indonesia, the Philippines, and Thailand is only one permutation among many that could arise in Asia. Larger groupings of countries could join together, and there is no a priori reason why Indonesia, the Philippines, and Thailand would be together in a union that included other countries. An interesting question is whether Asia should logically have one, two, three, or more regional currency unions. That depends on fundamental economic dimensions, including the classic conditions for a currency area to be optimal, and it also depends on which alliances and trading arrangements can lead to monetary cooperation. We do not forecast whether India or China would find it advantageous to join such a currency union, and we do not forecast whether Asian countries will adopt the yen as their official currency.

Once a currency union is formed, we predict that it will exert force of attraction on countries that have not joined, and its force of attraction can operate in more ways than we have described so far. Unification's most obvious appeal is to owners of financial assets, because they would reap windfall gains, and the gains would be easy to forecast before they happen. But there are other ways that may prove more decisive. For example, the force of attraction can communicate its message via individual cross-border investment transactions. Investors in a country that has succeeded in lowering its country risk suddenly will be able to afford to pay more for assets in countries where the risk premium is still high. For example, a businessperson who lives in Manila might suddenly be able to borrow funds cheaply enough to buy an office building in Vietnam, paying slightly more than local buyers could afford to pay. When that happens, the business community in Vietnam may at first question whether the Filipino is making enough on the building in Vietnam to pay debt service. But when they realize that the Filipino is making a profit and will now compete with them for other office buildings that come on the market, they may lobby for policies that will lower the cost of capital in Vietnam.

Another way the force of attraction may exert influence is via real economic growth. When the risk premium drops, the real economy should react positively, creating both output and jobs. Once a country's risk premium declines, residents may find that they earn more by retaining their savings within the country. As well, borrowers will find themselves paying less to attract foreign portfolio investment, because the entire yield curve would fall as the cost of capital declined for local businesses. Soon after that, new investment projects, which would not have been profitable at a higher cost of capital, will be able to clear this hurdle and be approved and will begin to be implemented. Countries that have not joined the currency union will observe how member nations have benefited and will begin to view the idea of joining more favorably.

Conclusions For An Asian Currency Union

Asia is an immense, diverse, and, on average, poor region with clusters of countries that, in theory, could join their currencies to the mutual benefit of all. These clusters of countries are not necessarily organized along geographical lines or trade lines but rather by their country risk and vulnerability to external capital market shocks. In this chapter, we created a hypothetical example to compute the value that might be created if two or three Asian nations merged their currencies but without simultaneously merging their real economies. Neither changes in trade patterns nor the terms of trade effects and the familiar array of customs union issues were analyzed. The focus of our analysis was on the potential benefits that stem from an abandonment of the national currency and central bank in favor of a more stable supranational currency and central bank. We maintain that stalling currency unification until countries' economies are sufficiently coordinated sacrifices precious time and may be the wrong criterion to apply to all putative currency unions. The standard to which the traditional lines of integration must be held is the extent to which their benefits (oftentimes, very long-term benefits) are expected to offset the instantaneous benefits that could arise from an immediate unification of currencies. Our approach introduces the possibility that unions of convenience might be arranged, under which nations have no intention of integrating their real economies and only desire the stability that a supranational currency might provide. In this sense, one day we might see a nation, such as Switzerland, be asked by another nation, such as

Venezuela, to form a currency union, which would be as independent and as committed to price stability as the current Swiss National Bank.

The computations in this chapter show that unifying the currencies of two countries with high sovereign risk premiums would create financial wealth. In particular, the amount of financial wealth is so large as to pose the question whether the benefits of an independent currency could off-set it. Furthermore, this wealth creation increases as more countries join the union, until the currency risk component of country risk is elimi-nated. Unification scenarios that span larger groups of Asian countries would create yet more financial wealth. Since the computations for two countries and three countries illustrate our methodology, we do not ex-tend the examples to cover all of Asia—the total value of which would be enormous. We are aware of the many impediments to currency unifica-tion. Nevertheless, the potential gains are large enough to deserve seri-ous consideration.

CURRENCY UNIFICATION IN LATIN AMERICA

Introduction

The striking natural wealth of Latin America contrasts sharply with its chronically disappointing economic performance. A region with so many resource endowments and such pleasant, hardworking people should not be so poor and should not have such a chronic pattern of lurching from hope to disillusion. Explanations for this erratic performance sometimes lay blame on the region's monetary arrangements. Those arrangements may not be the prime cause of the malaise, but they do draw attention, and they inspire comments and suggestions. The monetary history of the Latin American region is a wild, surrealistic adventure, with villains, he-roes, and noble failures. It would be a suitable backdrop for a novel about grandiose conflicts and passions. By comparison, the convoluted U.S. story sounds straightforward.

The region's monetary history has been tumultuous for reasons that are entirely understandable. First, it has approximately 20 countries, each with a different history and each with a different present-day financial system. Some of these nations have been more stable than others, but all of them have had to face challenges and assaults, many of which have been too great for their currency regimes to withstand. Second, most of these countries have populations that are still young, with few holdings of local financial assets; therefore, the preference of the majority of the young vot-ers is for governments that put a relatively low priority on monetary sta-bility. As a result, the majority of all voters has often chosen governments that spend in excess of tax collections. Third, they are exposed to the ups and downs of world commodity prices and also are at the mercy of international capital inflows and outflows, so macroeconomic external shocks frequently destabilize their monetary arrangements.

All these reasons are well-known and are less important today than they were in the distant past, because a new pattern is spreading across the region that is creating the basis for these nations to abandon domestic currencies and adopt supranational money. There are many dimensions to the new pattern. Most obviously, the dependence on trade and the extent to which this trade is focused on primary products have declined to the point at which it no longer monopolizes the thinking of local opinion leaders. Latin American countries have made conscious efforts to reduce their dependence on traditional commodity exports (for instance, oil, coffee, sugar, bananas, copper), and many of them have succeeded. Local value added has expanded, and diversification has already become widespread. Another important dimension of this quest for currency stability has been the development of local financial infrastructures (for example, money markets and capital markets). Pension fund systems have taken root and now enjoy a growing constituency. Capital flight is still a reality, but it is no longer as chronic and widespread as it was in earlier years, because some countries have national pension systems that are succeeding in keeping local savings from fleeing. The preference for monetary stability, retaining local savings in each country, lowering the cost of capital, and raising bond and stock prices is gradually triumphing.

The differences among the Latin American countries are great, but in the minds of too many analysts, the similarities are still so strong that it is customary to group them into one generic entity, for which generic solutions to the "Latin American problem" are offered. In our view, the perception of similarities has lingered longer than the similarities themselves, and for this reason, monetary arrangements and economic solutions that do not address the subtle, but important, differences among these nations are likely to fail. Our analysis groups countries into clusters and proposes monetary coordination and unification schemes for each cluster. We consider clusters of countries to illustrate the potential gains from currency unification not because the countries have any special degree of intrinsic similarity. These clusters are along geographic lines (that is, a Pacific cluster and an Atlantic cluster), because the Andes and the Amazon Basin make a natural continental divide in South America. For each cluster, the costs and benefits of monetary unification are quantified, and the net benefits (or costs) are determined. We also consider the effects of creating one supranational currency for the entire Latin American region and quantify its net benefits (or costs). Finally, we analyze the consequences for the entire region if all local currencies were dropped, and the U.S. dollar, the yen, or the euro were adopted as the region's common monetary unit.

Contagion and Shared Destiny

It has been a harsh fact of life that Latin American countries are painted
with the same brush, but the effects of this stereotyping are not necessarily pernicious. There can be some potentially constructive effects, because
the stereotyping creates a sense of shared destiny. Latin American countries seem to be as aware of their relative economic positions within the region as they are of their absolute standards of living. Latin American
countries compare themselves to each other and consider each other's experiences and policies relative to their own. Clearly, the specter of contagion constantly hangs over Latin American policy makers, and it compels
each of them to be attuned to what policy makers in the neighboring countries are doing. Nevertheless, because of their closer mutual economic
identification, Latin American policy makers have long been accustomed
to thinking along these lines and have had to consider carefully the reactions of foreign portfolio investors. By contrast, Asian policy makers have
been able to rely on high local saving rates and accumulations of financial
wealth to insulate their economies from financial contagion; yet, after the
Asian crisis of 1997, even they have had to acknowledge that no emerging
country is immune to financial volatility.

Part of the reason for the relatively close identification of Latin American countries can be traced to similarities among their monetary histories.
Regrettably, periods of high inflation and significant currency depreciation have punctuated many of their pasts. Is it any wonder why residents
have developed a chronic preference for foreign exchange over local currency? From Tierra del Fuego to the Rio Grande, these populations have
had to endure sudden devaluations, currency controls, convertibility restrictions, and multiple exchange rates. Latin American governments
have struggled to encourage and retain local savings, as well as to attract
foreign investment. They have tried a wide range of clever schemes to accomplish these objectives; indeed, a vast array of monetary arrangements
has been on parade. A significant amount of effort and debate has gone
into devising these arrangements, and afterward one well-qualified tech-
nocrat after another has been appointed to manage them, but despite all of
the energy that has been exerted, the success of these monetary arrangements, particularly in the long run, appears to have been limited.

Abandoning National Currencies

Fatalism and skepticism about meaningful currency reform in Latin
America now prevail. Through the years, the number of reforms has been
approximately equal to the number of failures, and many experts now
favor dollarization, a policy that exists in two broad forms. In its definitive
form, dollarization requires the country's government and its central bank

to buy back all the local currency in circulation, legislatively prohibit the further issuance of local currency, and transform all existing local currency-denominated contracts into dollar-denominated contracts.

Panama, Ecuador, and El Salvador are current examples of nations that have dollarized their currencies in this almost irreversible form. Plainly, dollarization does not necessarily ensure these nations that monetary instability will be a thing of the past, but it does transfer control over stability to an independent and external monetary agent. The decision to put complete dollarization into effect bears strong similarity to the decision European countries faced when the idea of a unified European currency began to look probable. Some countries could opt out of the currency union and retain their monetary autonomy, or they could join and abandon it.

With complete dollarization, independent local monetary policy, the national unit of account, and country-specific exchange rates cease to exist. The local central bank may still have authority to regulate the operations of domestic banks—for example, by setting reserve requirements, operating the discount window, and holding reserves of foreign exchange—but the local central bank has much less influence than before, and its activities are relegated to a marginal role.

The second form of dollarization is exemplified by Argentina's once-celebrated fixed exchange rate system. This type of dollarization is not as absolute as the first form, because the local currency (the peso) continues to exist, but its emission is strictly limited. The Bank of Argentina committed itself to holding at least one dollar for each peso in circulation.[24] As was the case in the more complete form of dollarization, any country that adopts such a monetary standard concedes to the U.S. Federal Reserve aggregate control over the total supply of dollars in the extended U.S. dollar area. Changes in the local (in this case, Argentine) money supply are accomplished by a currency board, which has all the discretionary decision-making power of a flea on the back of a dog. For countries adopting such a system, changes in the money supply become rule-based and could be accomplished as easily (and as well) by a currency computer as the familiar currency board.

The monetary rule is simple. Specifically, the local currency money supply cannot increase (decrease) unless there is an inflow (outflow) of dollars to the central bank, which can be used to support an increase (a decrease) in the supply of local currency. Of course, inflation could still occur, but it would be of a different sort. For example, if the flow of dollars to Argentina was disproportionate to the aggregate increase in the money supply (for example, perhaps, because of an Argentine export boom), inflation could rise—similar to the way the inflation rate in Massachusetts could differ from the rate in Arizona. Inflation could also occur if Argentine residents borrowed dollars and spent them locally, bidding up prices.

The second form of dollarization offers an escape valve, which is not offered by the first, because the nation retains the ability to devalue its currency. The existence of a separate local currency preserves a nation's right either to change the conversion ratio between the local currency and the dollar or to alter the quantity of dollars needed to back each local currency unit in circulation. For instance, Argentina could (and did in 2002) discretionarily change its ratio of one peso per dollar to 1.40 pesos per dollar, and it could change the dollar backing each peso from one dollar per peso in circulation to any other amount of pesos in circulation.

Both the irreversible and the reversible forms of dollarization provoke intense debate. The key question that has to be answered is why a country would take such a drastic step. Either form of dollarization is an abandonment of monetary sovereignty that forces the nation to sacrifice seignorage revenues. Furthermore, the country delegates its monetary policy to the U.S. Federal Reserve whose mandate is to control inflation in the United States, not everywhere in the Americas.

To have a fuller appreciation for the sacrifice that a country would be making by adopting a supranational currency, put the discussion in terms of a country's ability to tax. Any government that wants to spend has three basic financing alternatives: It can acquire the needed funds by taxing, borrowing, or printing money. Taxing rarely appeals to government officials, because it so noticeably taps the wallets of taxpayers. The taxlike effects of borrowing are less visible and less direct, because they raise real interest rates and, thus, mostly borrowers are taxed. Voters often mistakenly blame banks for the rising rates, but banks are only responding to the conditions the government puppet masters create. Printing money to finance government spending is the third alternative, and it is too often the chosen means, because it is the least visible to the average voter. Using this source of funds to finance public expenditures avoids problems, such as trying to track down pesky tax dodgers who, like wet bars of soap, always seem to elude the taxman's grasp. By printing and spending, the government raises prices, and it is this inflation that acts as a tax on local residents. To the uninitiated, these price increases are caused by avaricious local merchants, but in reality, it is, again, the government pulling the strings.

If a nation is at or near full employment, financing public expenditures by creating money could be a zero-sum game—one in which the losses to one internal group are offset by the gains to another. The groups that benefit from these expenditures are those who gain from increased public expenditure, borrowers whose real debts are reduced by the increased inflation, and merchants who are able to raise their prices at rates above the average inflation rate. The losers are merchants in sectors that are not the recipients of public expenditures, creditors whose interest and principal are eroded by inflation, businesses whose competitive position requires them to absorb a portion of the general increase in prices, and other groups with weak bargaining power. Such inflation creates a type of economic civil war, in which success is measured by how much one group's income increases relative to another group's income, rather than by how the nation's absolute standard of living changes.

From the viewpoint of an outsider looking at magnitudes only, the decision to abolish the local currency turns on the question whether future prospects for currency stability are so discouraging as to constitute a compelling argument against continuing the issuance of a local currency. If so, the country's stock of productive capacity would be worth more and its output would be higher if the country dropped the local currency and adopted some alternative monetary arrangement. From the viewpoint of a person in the country, the decision is much more visceral and awakens deeper feelings of class identity, regional affiliations, and views of the country's mechanisms for distributing gains in wealth and income.

This section addresses whether Latin American countries should continue to issue national currencies. The analysis estimates the aggregate benefits a county derives from issuing its own currency. It does not attempt to estimate internal transfers of wealth or income or distinguish the beneficiaries from the victims or explain how to accomplish the transition from the existing currency regime to any of the alternatives.

Historical Context of Local Currency Issuance

During their colonial periods, the economic structure of Latin American colonies was similar to that of the North American colonies. For the mother country, trade was a strategic centerpiece of economic and foreign policy. Because it was such a profitable activity, there were strong reasons for keeping and defending the colonies. Cross-Atlantic trade consisted mainly of the colonies exporting raw materials and importing finished goods, with the mother country controlling the terms of trade, resulting in the mother country gaining on both the raw materials and finished goods sides of the transactions. Often, the colonies in the Americas were prohibited from manufacturing products that would compete with imports from the mother country.

Adventurers (for example, settlers and fortune seekers) who crossed the Atlantic from the mother countries knew before they left Europe that their chances of returning with a fortune were slim; but despite the low probability of success, the large potential rewards made the risk worthwhile. They went to the Americas knowing that, if they could export enough raw materials back to Europe, they would be able to return after 20 years as rich men. Not many succeeded, but enough did to keep the flow of adventurers coming. The successes of a few were the envy of many, and the failures were easy to rationalize or ignore, because so few returned. Spanish adventurers who succeeded were called "*indianos*" after they came back to Spain, because they had been to the Indies. They built mansions in their home provinces and married above their formerly humble station.

At the macroeconomic level in the Americas, the trade imbalance with the mother country manifested itself in a chronic scarcity of hard currency. The lack of hard currency became a theme in the Latin American colonies. When an export boom provided some relief, there was an opportunity. Local governments celebrated by building opera houses or monuments. The local elite celebrated by taking grand tours of Europe; but the booms did not last, and the locals had to deal once again with the chronic shortage of hard cash.

A number of plausible explanations exists for the large Latin American trade deficits. One is that the region's relatively fast growth rate increased its ability to purchase from abroad. The colonies imported manufactured goods, because imports were cheaper, and this pattern of trade continued, because the colonies lacked any competitive edge over their more developed trading partners in the production of capital-intensive goods.

A second equally valid explanation for the trade deficits was that the colonies were relatively attractive places to invest. These investment inflows were the natural economic counterpart (that is, they ultimately financed) the colonies' net import expenditures.

A third explanation for the trade deficits is that Latin America was a victim of economic rents extracted by the mother country from its possessions. Such extraction was accomplished by the mother country demanding too much for her manufactured exports and paying too little for imported raw materials. Under such conditions, colonies were in the same position as a coal miner working in a small town with a monopoly employer. They spent more than they earned and continually had to borrow from the company store.

Whichever explanation (or combination of explanations) is correct, the result was that trade deficits created severe currency shortages that forced the colonial locals to devise convenient means of payment to keep local commerce functioning smoothly. Necessity is the mother of invention, and locals used their full creative powers to circumvent the shortage. Finding practical solutions made both common sense and good business sense. As life became more settled, increasingly more Europeans chose to stay in the colonies, incomes began to rise, and the reason for creating formal and informal arrangements for issuing and controlling local currency became a higher priority.

Independence came to Latin American countries at approximately the same time as the formation of northern and southern monetary unions in Germany and the defeat of the Second National Bank in the United States. Latin American countries suddenly had an exciting panorama of economic prospects before them. They could diversify their economies, and they did. Manufacturing, which previously had been clandestine, came out of the shadows. In each country, there was suddenly the possibility of creating a national monetary authority.

Monetary autonomy became intertwined with the ideals of independence and freedom from foreign domination, and the benefit of having a local currency extended beyond the convenience of facilitating transactions with small denomination coins and bills. It became a practical necessity for countries that wanted to run fiscal deficits without having to cover the shortfall by borrowing abroad. An independent, national currency gave local governments the means to pay for outlays in excess of tax collections. During periods when prices of export commodities were low, it gave governments the power (or perhaps the illusion) of having a means to protect the local population from hardship and want. For those reasons, the desire to keep the currency issuance power has become deeply ingrained in the social contract of many Latin American countries.

During the nineteenth century and the early twentieth century, both Latin America and North America suffered numerous financial panics while they experimented with different currency regimes. But, the period between the Great Depression and the late 1980s witnessed a clear disjunction in the histories of these two regions. During that time, North America became a zone of relative financial tranquility, suffering from no severe and extended financial panics. By contrast, Latin America experienced numerous financial crises. During this time, the economies of many Latin America nations were punctuated with failure after failure as they established currency regime after currency regime.

What caused this chasm in financial histories between North America and Latin America? One explanation is the profound distaste that U.S. voters developed for financial crises once they realized the effect that such crises could have on *real* living conditions. U.S. voters elected leaders who were able to keep fiscal deficits relatively low and who appointed conservative central bank governors. Latin American voters may have felt a similar revulsion to financial panics, but because their populations were much younger, and because their level of wealth accumulation was lower, monetary stability never rose to a high level of priority for voters.

The monetary histories of Latin America and North America began to converge after Latin America suffered through the 1980s. The Latin American region called the 1980s the "Lost Decade" and compared it to the 1930s. For optimistic technocrats, it was a shattering experience, and they lost faith in their expertise and their remedies. As well, public patience faded as populations began to age and awareness spread that social security had to gain priority over sustaining current expenditures. The idea of dollarization began to gain adherents.

Value Creation from Local Currency Issuance

How can the costs and benefits of a common currency be quantified? We have chosen Peru as our representative country case study. Our analysis assumes that adopting an external currency would reduce Peru's monetary and fiscal policy flexibility and, therefore, result in a more volatile and slower growing GDP. Partly or wholly offsetting this loss would be the gains Peru would enjoy by having lower currency risk premiums and therefore lower nominal interest rates. These lower interest rates not only would increase the wealth of financial asset holders but also would help to stimulate spending and GDP growth.

The approach we took previously in this chapter to estimate the costs and benefits of an Asian currency union is different from the one we will use in this section. Our approach is to consider progressive stages of monetary reform that would reduce country risk. We begin with a single country and consider the effect that its country risk has on the market prices of its capital assets. We assume that when the country adopts a currency covering a wider region (that is, a supranational currency) its country risk diminishes. We consider a series of currency regimes and assume that the broader the union, the lower the country risk. After considering the effect on one of the unifying countries, we raise the level of aggregation and redo the calculations for clusters of Latin American countries. We then raise the level of aggregation once again—considering a supranational currency that includes all of Latin America—and we compute the effect of putting the entire region under the umbrella of a single supranational currency. We take this route to draw a parallel with Europe and the euro. Finally, we consider the effects of complete, irreversible Latin America dollarization.

Peru was chosen for this analysis, because it satisfies several conditions. First, the country has neither geographic nor commercial proximity to the United States nor is it overshadowed by its neighbors. Peru is in no way a satellite of Brazil. Even though it abuts Brazil, the Andes and the Amazon act as geographic buffers. Second, at the time this chapter was written, Peru was experiencing neither a boom nor a currency crisis, so its monetary affairs were not the subject of front-page debates in the world's financial newspapers. As a result, Peruvian security prices were within the range that had been typical for the previous ten years.[25] Third, Peru is large enough that experts and novices alike would plausibly argue that the country should have its own currency. Fourth, the nation does not depend on a single, dollar-denominated export; and finally, Peru has had relatively stable monetary affairs for more than ten years, which has made it an island of stability in a relatively turbulent Latin America sea. Peru did experience political turmoil in 2000, when President Alberto Fujimori tried to impose himself for a third term as president. This turmoil roiled the market prices of Peruvian government bonds, but it was less severe than the upheavals some other Latin American countries experienced. Nevertheless, in our view, these attributes make the choice of Peru as our representative nation a good one.

As of 1999, Peru had 25 million people, and its GDP at market exchange rates was equivalent to $60.3 billion.[26] In purchasing power parity terms, Peru's GDP was $110 billion.[27] The difference between these two measures shows that foreign exchange continues to command a premium and that non-traded goods and services, such as haircuts and carpentry, were cheaper in Peru than in the United States. For measuring the well-being of the Peruvian population, the latter measure is more meaningful, but for measuring the market value of capital assets, the former measure provides a more accurate reflection.

Peru's overall fiscal deficit in 1990 was 6.4% of GDP.[28] It would be difficult for a country to run a fiscal deficit of that magnitude without having a national currency. Local savers would have to buy newly issued government bonds, or the country would have to borrow abroad. To be sure, the government could also sell national assets (for example, privatize nationalized industries), but conventionally, the proceeds of such sales have been shown as offsetting government expenditure, so we take the published figure for Peru's fiscal deficit as net of any such inflows to government coffers. For these reasons, financing large budget deficits is greatly facilitated by having a national currency. Not only is such financing less vulnerable to the vagaries of international capital flows, but it also reduces the direct burden on domestic savers to finance budget deficits.

In the 1980s, Peru financed its fiscal deficit by creating and spending local currency and persuading local buyers to subscribe to new issues of local currency bonds. During most of the Lost Decade of the 1980s, foreign lenders refused to lend Peru adequate amounts to fund the desired levels of public expenditures. Spending that much in excess of what the government took in may have eased the suffering of some segments of Peru's economy during the Lost Decade, but the gains to these segments of the population were offset by losses to others, resulting in huge internal transfers of real income and wealth. The Peruvian economy suffered capital flight, brain drain, and stagnant growth. During the following decade, the country turned its back on fiscal deficits and rebuilt its international credit standing. By 1998, Peru's fiscal deficit was only 0.2% of GDP.[29]

Peru's inflation for the period 1980–1990 averaged 231.3% per year,[30] but the years following the Lost Decade saw a reversion to monetary stability along with fiscal prudence. Peru's experience in the 1980s was not the most extreme in Latin America: Argentina, Bolivia, Brazil, and Nicaragua all had higher rates of inflation,[31] which provides yet another reason for choosing Peru as our representative nation.

Estimating the Value of Local Currency Issuance

How does one quantify the value that a nation derives from issuing its own currency? Peru's experience indicates that the local population was willing to tolerate higher inflation and larger fiscal deficits when world (and especially Latin American) economic conditions were unfavorable. This does not mean they willingly bought Peruvian government bonds in the amount of 6.4% of GDP. It means they stood by while their local savings lost value, because there were higher priorities to occupy their attention. During better economic times, the Peruvian population was less likely to tolerate relatively high levels of inflation and relatively large fiscal deficits.

On the basis of Peru's experience, we assume that during normal times residents would allow the national government to have fiscal deficits in the amount of 2% of GDP. That is, local citizens would willingly buy newly issued government bonds in that amount, provided that the interest rates on those bonds more than offset expected inflation. During bad times, deficits as large as 4% of GDP would be supported but only for short periods of time. Finally, during good times, the population would insist that the government run fiscal deficits amounting to no more than 0.5% of GDP.

By contrast, populations would be less willing to tolerate budget deficits when a country adopted a supranational currency, and the reason is clear. The threat of bankruptcy would be at a minimum if the country borrowed in its own currency and had the legal authority to print and coin money. By contrast, default risk would increase when the country did not have its own currency and ran deficits in a supranational currency. We assume that during normal times the local population would support a fiscal deficit amounting to 1% of GDP; during bad times, the deficit could only be as large as 2% of GDP; and during good times the fiscal budget had to be balanced. These assumptions are summarized in Table 7.1.

Having set these parameters, the average difference in allowable fiscal deficits can be calculated. Assuming that one-third of the years in a decade are normal, one-third are bad, and one-third are good, the average tolerated fiscal deficit when a country has its own national currency is 2.2%.[32] When the country does not have its own national currency, the average tolerated fiscal deficit is 1%.[33] On average, therefore, given our indicated parameters, Peru's population would permit fiscal deficits to be 1.2% higher as a percentage of GDP when the nation had its own currency than when it did not.

What effects on income, employment, and well-being would this higher level of deficit spending have? To compute the effects, we take two approaches, the first of which places a higher value on retaining the power to issue local currency than the second. The first approach uses the Keynesian framework and assumes that any fiscal stimulus affects real GDP with a multiplier effect. The multiplier in a closed economy can be high, but Latin American economies are open, and there are many ways for pur-

Table 7.1
Budget Deficit Levels the Peruvian Population will Support Under Varying Economic Conditions *(% of GDP)*

Economic Climate	Assuming Peru has	
	Its Own Currency	A Supranational Currency
Good	0.5 %	0.0 %
Normal	2.0 %	1.0 %
Bad	4.0 %	2.0 %

chasing power to leak from the country's flow of funds before it has a chance to stimulate further rounds of local spending. For this reason, we tentatively assign a multiplier of 3.0 to any fiscal expenditure, which implies that GDP would be 3.6% higher if the country has its own currency.[34] Assuming that this higher level continued in perpetuity and if the discount rate were 15%, the present value of the added expenditures would be 24% of GDP.[35]

This valuation assumes that the Keynesian assumptions are applicable. In particular, it assumes that, in a typical year, private investment would not rise to fill the void (amounting to 1.2% of GDP) that was created by the government having to restrict its deficit. As a result, there would be idle resources unless the Peruvian government took the initiative to borrow from Peruvian savers in order to invest in projects that were profitable, socially beneficial, and self-liquidating in terms of tax revenue. It is further assumed that the Peruvian government chooses projects that do not compete with private initiative, so that when economic recovery occurs, private spending initiatives fill the void left by reduced government spending.

So far, we have calculated the gross benefit that Peru derives from having its own currency as equaling 24% of GDP. To this amount should be added the imputed insurance value that a currency provides its issuer against economic hardships during the bad years. We have estimated this insurance value as follows. By assumption, every third year is a bad one. During that year, a country with a local currency could have a fiscal deficit of 4% of GDP, while the country that does not have a local currency could only have a fiscal deficit of 2%. This difference is a rough gauge of the power a local currency has to cushion a country against economic hardship. Therefore, the capitalized value of the insurance is equal to 4.4% of GDP.[36] To complete the first computation of the capitalized value of retaining the power to issue local currency, we add this 4.4% of GDP insurance value to the gain 24% of GDP to get a gross gain of 28.4%.

The second approach for estimating the losses a country suffers from reduced fiscal flexibility assumes that the domestic capital markets are imperfect, and, therefore, financial resources may not flow to their most desired uses. Under these circumstances, justification could be given for the Peruvian government to issue bonds or sell guarantees to entrepreneurs if there were a combination of idle domestic resources, positive net present-value projects, and local entrepreneurs who were unable to get loans because of the capital market imperfections. This analysis assumes that the probability that this trilogy of ingredients (that is, profitable projects, idle resources, and frustrated entrepreneurs) will exist is 50% during a good year, 75% during a normal year, and 100% during a bad year.

These assumptions imply that Peruvian capital markets become less perfect the poorer the economic conditions. Justification for such assumptions can be supported on two grounds. First, during sluggish periods, the banks feel increasing pressure as the market value of their portfolios decline due to increasing defaults. As a result, entrepreneurs who are seeking funding for relatively risky and often unsecured projects may be unable to borrow from banks. Similarly, a part of the imperfection in Peruvian capital markets could be due to its vulnerability to financial panics from either internal shocks or from the contagion effects of foreign disturbances. Risk aversion is the foe of even the most creditworthy borrowers, but its cold touch is felt most directly by those debtors on the lowest rung of the credit ladder.

In this second framework, if we assume the same income multiplier (that is, 3.0) that was used in the first scenario, the expected annual benefit from the higher level of fiscal expenditure can be calculated. If the government could correct the capital market imperfections and fund worthwhile projects, the expected annual gain, as a percent of GDP, during good times, normal times, and bad times would be 0.75%, 4.50%, and 12.00%, respectively, and the overall expected annual gain would be 5.75% (see Table 7.2). Assuming that this gain was perpetual, its capitalized value would be 38.3%.[37] Note, though, that this result depends on the key assumption that Peruvian capital markets are too risk-averse or too imperfect to finance all profitable projects. This result also abstracts from the possibility that complete crowding out, international capital flight, or financial disintermediation would offset the government's attempts to borrow and lend.

If we were to add our estimation for the capitalized insurance value that a currency provides against economic hardship (that is, 4.4%) to the estimated gain from funding profitable projects, the gross gain would be (under these circumstances) equal to 42.7% of GDP.[38] If our two approaches to estimating the gain Peru derives from issuing its own currency are reasonable, then we can conclude that these gains lie somewhere between 28.4% of GDP and 42.7% of GDP.

Table 7.2
Gains if the Government Funded Profitable Projects that Would Not Be
Financed by Private, Domestic Capital Markets

1	2	3	4	2 x 3 x4
Economic Activity	Capital Market Imperfection Probability*	Income Multiplier	Allowable Deficit % of GDP	Gain % of GDP
Good	50%	3	0.5	0.75%
Normal	75%	3	2.0	4.50%
Bad	100%	3	4.0	12.00%
*Expected Value = (0.33 * 0.75) + (0.33 * 4.50) + (0.33 * 12.0) = 5.75% of GDP*				

*Probability of profitable but unfunded private projects

Value Creation from Abandoning Local Currency Issuance

What would Peru gain if it formally discontinued its policy of issuing local currency and instead adopted a supranational currency? This analysis considers only the first-order benefits and ignores ancillary benefits, such as efficiency gains from eliminating distortions caused by local monetary policies. Also, we ignore the stimulative effect that lowering real interest rates would have on economic growth. Even in the absence of these secondary benefits, the analysis will make clear that the benefits from adopting a supranational currency are overwhelming.

Computing the gains from adopting a supranational currency can be accomplished in three steps. First, the total annual payments to all owners of Peruvian capital stock are calculated. These payments include interest, dividends, rents, royalties, and lease payments. Second, the annual growth rate of these payments is estimated; and finally, a discount rate is defined in order to capitalize on the future stream of economic benefits.

Payments to all owners of Peru's capital stock in 1999 were approximately 22% of GDP.[39] This figure is an estimate, because the implicit rent on the housing stock was probably higher than the official figure.[40] There may also have been over-invoicing of imports and under-invoicing of exports, as well as unreported payments to friends and relatives outside the country who loaned money.

This analysis assumes that the annual growth rate of Peru's payments to capital stock owners is 2.5%. This 2.5% figure reflects Peru's average annual real growth rate of 5.4% for the period 1990–1999 and the mild recessionary rate of –0.3% for the period 1980–1990. The 2.5% figure is more moderate than the straight average during these two decades (that is,

2.6%), because Peru's 5.4% growth over the last decade of the 1990s included its recovery from the depressed Lost Decade.

To determine the appropriate discount rate, this analysis begins with Peru's prospective return on long-term sovereign bonds during the second half of 2001, which was about 11%. Of this 11%, approximately 7% were due to country risk. The 11% figure was then raised slightly, because the actual return on these sovereign bonds for the 12-month period ending October 26, 2001, was 33.74%.[41] The two yields are so different because of the major rise in Peruvian government bond prices during the 12-month period ending October 26, 2001, which was caused mainly by changes in expectations owing to political factors.

To see in simple terms what happened, suppose that there was a ten-year fixed-coupon Peruvian government bond with scheduled maturity in October 2009. Suppose also that the coupon rate on the bond was 10%. As of October 2001, if the market price of $100 face value of this bond were $94.75, its prospective yield for the remaining eight years of its life would be 11%. A year earlier, if the market price of $100 face value of this bond had been $78.32, then an investor who bought it at that time would have realized a 33.74% gain during the 12 months from October 2000 to October 2001.[42] The large price increase during that 12-month period is quite understandable, because at the beginning of that period, President Alberto Fujimori appeared to be on track to remain in power, despite his unpopularity with the voters and with investors. By the end of that period, Fujimori was in exile and Alejandro Toledo, the moderate, had beaten Alan Garcia, the populist, in a widely publicized election. As those events played out, market prices of Peruvian government bonds fluctuated and ended much higher than they began.

These conditions are what made the subsequent yield so much lower than the yield that investors earned in the preceding 12 months. Another way to understand the big difference between the ex post and ex ante yield is to consider that Peru's country risk declined during the 12 months prior to October 26, 2001. Also, the data indicate that the big rise in Peruvian government bond prices happened between October 2000 and December 2000. We know this because during the period from January 1, 2001 to October 26, 2001, the realized yield on Peruvian sovereign bonds was only 16.82%, which meant that market prices of these bonds were rising in 2001 but at slower rates than from October 2000 to December 2000.[43]

For determining the appropriate discount rate, there is another complicating factor: During 2001 the yields on U.S. Treasury bonds were declining. The falling yields on U.S. Treasury bonds were not caused entirely by prosperity and tranquility. They were caused (*inter alia*) by:

- Investors' concerns about a worldwide recession and the resulting "flight to safety" in the international capital markets;

- the September 11, 2001 attacks on the United States, which made investors wary of risky securities, in general, and Peruvian government securities, in particular;

- Argentina's foreign debt and fiscal crisis, which was in the news daily, and caused investors to fear buying emerging market bonds; and

- Peru's newly elected president Toledo's efforts to develop recognition outside Peru, which had not yet created for him a well-defined image as an economic policy maker.

For those reasons the applicable discount rate used to value Peru's capital stock is debatable. As of November 6, 2001, immediately after the U.S. Federal Reserve cut the target rate for federal funds to 2%, Peru's bellwether sovereign bond was priced to yield 10.93%. This is the lowest yield these bonds offered for many months, so for these calculations we make the following assumption. We assume that a rate of 12% is appropriate for the safer, more stable cash flows, and a rate of 16% is appropriate for the riskier cash flows. Also, for simplicity, we assume that half the cash flows are safe and half are risky. Consequently, we use 14% as the applicable discount rate. The valuation formula used in this analysis is:

$$\text{Market Value} = \frac{\text{Annual Cash Flow}}{\text{Applicable Discount Rate - Growth Rate}}$$

Combining the market valuation formula with the assumed parameters yields an estimated market value for Peru's income-producing assets equal to 191% of GDP.[44]

Effects if Peru Adopted a Supranational Regional Currency

Suppose that Peru changed its currency regime by joining a cluster of other South American countries that had created a supranational currency, and suppose further that this currency had greater stability than Peru's pre-union currency, causing country risk to decline, and with it, the nation's average discount rate to fall to 10%. The effect of the lower discount rate would be to increase the prices of Peru's income-producing properties. The new total market value of all these assets would be 293%.[45]

According to this calculation, if Peru moved from having a national currency to a regional currency, the market prices of capital assets would rise by an amount equal to 102% of GDP. This assumes that a large part of Peru's country risk consists of currency risk, and that abandoning its monetary sovereignty in favor of supranational monetary sovereignty would lower its country risk by the indicated amount. The hypothesized reduction may be greater than what would really happen, because country risk has other components, which we discussed in Chapter 6. Nevertheless, the hypothesized reduction is less than the total reduction in applicable discount rates achieved over the 1993–1999 period by the weaker-currency European countries that adopted the euro.

The increase in market prices of Peru's income-producing assets would happen quickly, and the owners of the assets would benefit from the windfall. It is not clear how much of the windfall would accrue indirectly to the Peruvians who do not own income-producing assets.

Effects if Peru Adopted a Supranational Latin Currency or a Supranational World Currency

Now suppose that Peru went one step further and adopted a newly created Latin American supranational currency that was even more stable than the hypothetical regional currency mentioned in the previous section. The applicable discount rate would fall further, for example to 8%, and the prices of Peru's income-producing properties would rise even further. The new figure for the total market value of all these assets would be 400% of GDP.[46]

Finally, suppose that Peru adopted the U.S. dollar as its national currency and bought back all the local currency that was in circulation. Suppose further that the adoption of the dollar lowered the country's risk premium and that its applicable discount rate fell to 5%. That extreme figure could only be reached if all the other components of Peru's country risk could be eliminated, so that investors perceived Peruvian assets as if they were long-term U.S. Treasury bonds. In that case, the prices of Peruvian income-producing assets would skyrocket. The new estimate for the total market value of all these assets would be 880% of GDP.[47] These figures for the market value of Peru's capital stock cover a very wide range, from 191% of GDP under the existing currency regime to 880% of GDP under a full, irreversible dollarization with other reforms included that would lower the risk of all Peruvian assets to that of a U.S. Treasury bill.

The range of benefits that Peru derives from retaining its currency printing powers ranges from 28.4% to 42.7% of GDP, but this gain is dwarfed by even the lowest gain (102%) the nation would derive from abdicating this right and adopting a supranational currency. To the extent that adopting supranational currencies allows Peru to reduce its country risk more, and more completely, and finally to eliminate it, the benefits explode exponentially (see Exhibit 7.1). Therefore, according to these calculations, it appears that Peru should immediately drop its national currency and adopt a regional or supra-regional currency, and if no regional or supra-regional currency were available, Peru should adopt the U.S. dollar, the euro, or the yen as its monetary unit.

Exhibit 7.1
Percentage Gains to Peru from Adopting a Supranational Currency

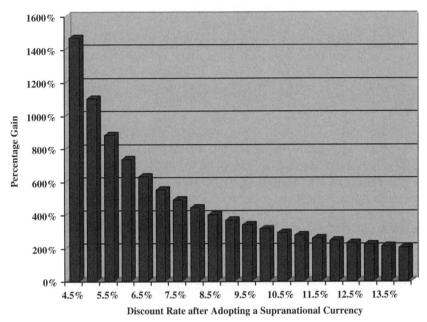

Is this result possible? Is the conclusion so simple? If so, why have so few countries taken this route and adopted a supranational currency? Let us examine the objections to a supranational currency and in the process see if the results are illusory, biased, or impractical.

The first objection to the adoption of a supranational currency is that the gain in asset prices would accrue solely to the owners of income-producing assets; that is, Peruvians with a dependence on wages would be left out. Although we believe that the economic benefits of the wealth effect will spread eventually to all strata of Peruvian society (albeit in varying degrees and at varying speeds), a short-term redistribution of wealth is highly likely. Nevertheless, government taxes and public transfers could go a long way toward evening out the playing field. The point is that the potential gains are so large that if there were a practical way for the winners to compensate the losers everyone could be, by vast dimensions, better off. Adoption of a national voucher system, for example, could be a means by which every Peruvian who did not own income-earning assets might be assigned part of the gain.

A second objection focuses on the belief that the huge net gains in asset prices that we have predicted will not materialize. Indeed, they might not rise immediately by amounts as large as 102% of GDP or more. Nevertheless, the likelihood that they would rise by more than 42.7% of GDP (that is, the higher of our two estimates of the value from retaining the power to issue local currency) is significant; and the longer the time frame, the better the odds.

A third objection is that foreign portfolio investment would have to flow toward Peru to make the asset prices increase. Local investors might bid up the prices of Peruvian assets by themselves, but their purchases would probably not be enough to raise prices to levels commensurate with Peru's lower country risk premium. Foreign portfolio investors would probably add some buying power to the upsurge, and this would have two effects that some observers may find objectionable. One is that part of the gains would be captured by foreign portfolio investors. The other is that, after the asset prices increased, Peru would be more vulnerable to the caprices of foreign portfolio investors who have little awareness or concern that their decisions to sell may cause hardship in Peru. These objections are well-known, and we do not dispute that they have some merit, but the magnitude of the foregone financial wealth convinces us that a currency union is worth seeking.

Regional Currencies in Latin America?

In the section on Asia, we postulated unifying the currencies of sets of Asian countries, beginning with two countries that both have high levels of country risk. The calculations showed that gains occur when two countries merge their currencies, and additional gains occur when a third country then merges its currency into the newly created supranational currency. In this section, we move directly from analyzing one country to postulating that clusters of countries cooperate to create supranational currencies.

The clusters that we have chosen are arbitrary. We do not imply that the countries in each cluster would really put into effect the currency unification we propose. Our clusters are for illustrative purposes only. We have ignored an existing agreement—the Andean Pact—and have also ignored several ongoing disputes between countries in South America. Our purpose is purely to illustrate the financial wealth that currency unification can create.

The clusters we have chosen are a Pacific cluster consisting of Chile, Peru, Bolivia, and Ecuador; and an Atlantic cluster consisting of Argentina, Brazil, Uruguay, and Paraguay. These two examples will illustrate the advantage of supranational currencies for regions that span less than an entire continent.

If four countries get together and create a supranational currency, they gain some of the wealth that comes from currency unification, while retaining some autonomy over monetary affairs. They would benefit from a large boost in market prices of capital assets for the reason we have asserted previously, namely, that, if the country risk premium for each of the four countries declines, asset prices would rise, and also currency unification would broaden the market for capital assets in each of the four countries. The market broadening would not necessarily happen overnight. At the margin, for example, portfolio investors might bid for assets in Bolivia after the currency unification, when they were unwilling to take that risk before. The countries include some, such as Argentina and Uruguay, that have an affinity for each other, and the currency unification would probably induce cross-border investment in those countries more quickly than it would in countries such as Chile and Ecuador, which are far apart geographically and have had few dealings with each other in the past.

With those caveats and points noted, we move to the calculation of how much wealth these currency unifications might create. For comparison with the Peruvian example, we use a beginning country risk premium for each country of 14%.[48] Then we assume, as with the Peruvian example, that unifying four national currencies would lower the country risk by 4%. In other words, we approximate the gain from unifying the four countries in each cluster by assuming that each country's applicable discount rate begins at the same high level and falls by 4% after the currency unification. This circumvents the problem of allocating the gains from the unification among the four countries.[49] It also circumvents another thorny computational issue: How much of each country's capital stock is relatively safe or relatively risky? In the computation for Peru, we assumed that the appropriate discount rate was 12% for assets with safe cash flows and 16% for risky cash flows, and we also assumed that half the assets were safe and half are risky. In the clusters we have chosen, that simplification may not be justified. There may be only a few assets with safe cash flows, and the remaining assets may display rising degrees of risk. There is no reason to believe that the portion of assets in each risk category would be the same in two countries. Consequently, we acknowledge that the simplification that we make might distort the result.[50]

Now that we have selected the discount rates, we need growth rates for the four countries in each cluster, as well as figures for the total payments to owners of each country's capital stock. The growth rates are forecasts that will continue for many years. For that reason, we have used 1% and 2%. For simplicity, we assumed that 25% of the GDP of each country is paid to the owners of capital. The reader can vary these inputs to see how much influence they have in the results. The figures we used are provided in Table 7.3.

To calculate the aggregate gain in market value of each cluster's capital stock, we compute the gain for each individual country and then add these gains. This estimate of the aggregate gain aims only to be a starting point for a discussion. The inputs to the calculations are data that are not equally accurate for all four countries in each cluster (see Tables 7.4 and 7.5). These simple results indicate strongly that, when four countries join their monetary affairs together and create a single currency, they create

Table 7.3
Assumed Growth Rates and Total Payments to Owners Each Country's
Capital Stock

Country	Annual Growth Rate*	GDP (billions)
Atlantic Cluster		
Argentina	1%	$281
Uruguay	1%	$18
Paraguay	2%	$7.7
Brazil	2%	$688
Pacific Cluster		
Chile	5%	$67
Peru	2%	$57
Bolivia	2%	$61
Ecuador	2%	$18

*All growth rates are our estimates. For GDP we used figures from the United Nations Development Program, http://www.undp.org/hdro/natinc.htm.

enormous potential value. This result is similar to the ones we arrived at for Asian countries.

The Pacific cluster includes Chile, a country with a high credit rating and a low risk premium. That makes the Pacific cluster similar to Europe, with Chile in the role played by Germany. The euro did not bring as much wealth benefit to Germany as it did to the countries in Europe with weaker credit ratings and higher risk premiums. In fact, there were many Germans who questioned whether Germany would benefit from the currency unification. They feared that the euro might be a weaker currency than the mark had been, and if events had worked out that way, the prices of German securities would have fallen. Chile would, for that reason, probably not join the Pacific cluster, unless it had a dominant position in it. Handing over monetary sovereignty to a supranational central bank makes sense only when the handover will quickly deliver a large increase in the market prices of financial assets or provide flow benefits of significant magnitude.

A Currency for All of Latin America

Europe moved rapidly from national currencies to a single currency for the entire region. Currency unification did not begin with two or three countries and then snowball, although there were inner and outer rings in

Table 7.4
Atlantic Cluster: Estimated Capital Stock Before and After Unification

Before Unification		
Value of Capital Stock	Portion GDP to capital owners * (GDP) / (Discount Rate - Growth Rate)	
Argentina	0.25*$281/(0.14- 0.01)	= $540 billion
Uruguay	0.25*$18/(0.14- 0.01)	= $35 billion.
Paraguay	0.25*$7.7/(0.14- 0.02)	= $16 billion.
Brazil	0.25*$688/(0.14- 0.02)	= $1,433 billion.
Total capital stock before unification		**$2,024 billion**
After Unification		
Value of Capital Stock	Portion GDP to capital owners * (GDP) / (Discount Rate - Growth Rate)	
Argentina	0.25*$281/(0.10- 0.01)	= $780 billion.
Uruguay	0.25*$18/(0.10- 0.01)	= $50 billion
Paraguay	0.25*$7.7/(0.10- 0.02)	= $21 billion
Brazil	0.25*$688/(0.10- 0.02)	= $1,911 billion.
Total capital stock after unification		**$2,762 trillion**
Summary		
Total After capital stock before unification		**$2,024 billion**
Total After capital stock after unification		**$2,762 billion**
Net Gain from Unification		$738 billion

the precursor monetary regimes. Then, when the unification happened, there were several European countries that chose to stay out, but their reluctance quickly looked quixotic and anachronistic. Already, one country that did not qualify to join at first—Greece—has aligned its economic affairs with the Maastricht standards and successfully joined the euro. In view of these facts, it is appropriate to ask whether Latin America might do the same as Europe and adopt its own currency.

As with the clusters in our examples, we postulate this pan-Latin currency as a thought experiment, not with the view that the Latin American countries are likely to take such a step. A pan-Latin unification is a higher level of monetary unification than the clusters and a step that is less extreme than the alternative of adopting the U.S. dollar, the euro, or the yen. We discuss this step in order to give attention to every possible level of monetary unification.

Table 7.5
Pacific Cluster: Estimated Capital Stock Before and After Unification

Before Unification		
Value of Capital Stock	Portion GDP to capital owners * (GDP) / (Discount Rate — Growth Rate)	
Chile	0.25*$67/(0.14- 0.05)	= $186 billion.
Peru	0.25*$57/(0.14- 0.02)	= $118 billion.
Bolivia	0.25*$61/(0.14- 0.02)	= $127 billion.
Ecuador	0.25*$18/(0.14- 0.02)	= $38 billion.
Total capital stock before unification		$469 billion
After Unification		
Value of Capital Stock	Portion GDP to capital owners * (GDP) / (Discount Rate - Growth Rate)	
Chile	0.25*$67/(0.10- 0.05)	= $335 billion.
Peru	0.25*$57/(0.10- 0.02)	= $178 billion
Bolivia	0.25*$61/(0.10 - 0.02)	= $191 billion
Ecuador	. . 0.25*$18/(0.10- 0.02)	= $56 billion..
Total capital stock after unification		$760 billion.
Summary		
Total After capital stock before unification		**$469 billion**
Total After capital stock after unification		**$760 billion**
Net Gain from Unification		$291 billion

A pan-Latin American currency has two points in its favor. One is that Latin Americans would control it, so they would not be delegating all monetary autonomy to a policy-making body outside the region. The other is that it would be a bulwark against contagion. The Latin American countries would create a regional central bank, similar to the European Central Bank, and the regional central bank would gather together a large pool of foreign exchange. It would also obtain lines of credit and would stand ready to use its financial clout to rescue a member country that found itself in a temporary liquidity crisis.

A temporary liquidity crisis in one country could not trigger a chain re-action of devaluations, because the whole Latin American region would have only one currency. So a crisis in one country would have less effect in neighboring countries, because its impact would be diffused over the entire region. The single pan-Latin currency would weaken slightly, but the sheer size of the region would buffer the effect. The crisis would probably pass without causing major dislocations or triggering a crisis in another Latin American country.

That is not the only reason why the pan-Latin regime would provide protection against contagion. There is reason to believe that the Latin American central bank would be more ready to use its reserves in defense of a member country than a supranational lending entity, such as the International Monetary Fund or World Bank. In the recent past, the U.S. Treasury has arranged a bailout for Mexico but declined to arrange a bailout for Argentina. The Latin American central bank, if it had existed, would probably have responded to pressure by trying to help both countries. This could deter contagion, but it might also increase moral hazard. Which outcome would dominate would depend on how much authority the Latin American central bank was able to exercise in each country to keep local banks from taking excessive risks. The Latin American central bank could serve as a watchdog, the way the IMF does now, and its intervention might be more palatable than visits from the IMF.

The Latin American central bank would have to obtain a full mandate from all the countries in the region. Then, it would have to exercise authority and establish its credibility as the supreme arbiter of monetary affairs for the entire region. It would have to be proactive and highly visible at all times, not only when there was a crisis. To be successful in lowering the region's high levels of country risk, it would need to perform roles that go beyond the usual central bank functions. It would need to monitor the member countries' fiscal affairs, refuse to bail out countries with deficits outside the guidelines, and oversee compliance with capital adequacy standards at the region's banks, insurance companies, investment banks, stock brokerage firms, and mutual fund management companies. If it could successfully carry out these responsibilities, it might replicate the success of Europe's monetary and financial market regulatory institutions.

How much could the Latin American central bank lower the region's average country risk? The answer will not come forth until such an entity is created, but we need a numerical estimate to do computations similar to those we have done for the single country and for the clusters. We have argued that a currency that spans a larger economic zone will be more stable than a currency that spans a smaller zone. For that reason, we assume that the pan-Latin currency's risk premium would be lower than the premium for a cluster of four Latin American countries but higher than the premium for the U.S. dollar, the yen, or the euro. The number we use in these computations is a premium of 4%. Table 7.6 sets out the assumptions we have used in this section.

Using these figures, we compute the amount of wealth the Latin American currency unification would create, but there are two more figures we

Table 7.6
Discount Rates Assumed for Implied Risk Premiums

Zone	Sovereign	Non-sovereign	Average	Risk Premium above U.S. Sovereign Rate
Peru	12%	16%	14%	10%
Cluster	8%	12%	10%	6%
Pan Latin	6%	10%	8%	4%
US	4%	Not applicable	4%	0%

need. One is the percent of the region's GDP that is paid to owners of the capital stock. We use 25% for that figure. The other is the average future growth rate of the region's economies, which we assume is 2%.

The total GDP of the Latin American countries for the year 1999 was $1,955 billion. Using the single-country discount rate of 14%, using 25% as the portion of GDP paid to the owners of the capital stock, and using 2% as the annual growth rate, we arrive at the figure for the dollar value of the capital stock prior to currency unification equal to $4,072 billion:

$$\$1,955 \text{ billion} * 0.25/(0.14 - 0.02) = \$4,072 \text{ billion.}$$

Next, we compute the value of the capital stock after Latin American countries have joined to form clusters. The risk premium falls, and the value of the capital stock rises to

$$\$1,955 \text{ billion} * 0.25/(0.10 - 0.02) = \$6,109 \text{ billion.}$$

That is an increase slightly in excess of $2 trillion.

Next, we compute the value of the capital stock after Latin American countries have created a pan-Latin currency and a Latin American central bank. This reduces the risk premium further, and the value of the capital stock rises to $8,145 billion:

$$\$1,955 \text{ billion} * 0.25/(0.08 - 0.02) = \$8,145 \text{ billion.}$$

This is a further increase in excess of $2 trillion, which is a figure that is double the status quo ante. The total increase in market prices of capital assets in this calculation is more than $4 trillion. To express this increase in per capita terms, the population of Latin America and the Caribbean at mid-1999 was 509 million, so the increase would be $8,002 per capita:

$$(\$8,145 \text{ billion} - \$4,072 \text{ billion})/509 \text{ million} = \$8,002 \text{ per capita.}$$

This is more than twice the annual per capita income of the region, which at that time was $3,841.

To complete the calculations, we next compute the value of the capital stock assuming all the countries of the region were able to drop their country risk premiums to zero. To provide an extreme contrast with the status quo ante, we assume further that the countries of the region would take additional steps needed to lower country risk. They would encourage all issuers of securities to buy credit enhancements, insurance policies, and hedging instruments to push down the risk premium that market participants would attach to the securities they issue. The countries would also make any modifications to their legal, political, and economic systems that might be needed to protect investors against losses from fraud, insider trading, and abusive corporate governance. The credit enhancements and insurance policies would cost money, so we subtract 2% of GDP to pay for them. Consequently, we use 23% of GDP as the net amount that would be available to pay to the owners of the capital stock. Those payments would be safe, so we use 4%—the U.S. Treasury security rate—to discount them. This gives the result

$$\$1,955 \text{ billion} * 0.23/(0.04 - 0.02) = \$22,485 \text{ billion.}$$

This result is more than five times greater than the figure for the status quo ante. It is a first approximation to the theoretical maximum market value that the existing capital stock of Latin America could attain. The theoretical maximum figure could also be higher, because the $22,485 billion figure does not include the value of untapped petroleum and mineral deposits; it only takes into account the value of annual output. The figure also does not take into account the potential output of Latin America. It only values existing capital assets on the basis of existing output.

If the annual per capita output would rise to a first-world level, for example to $30,000 per year, and if the amount of capital equipment each worker used would approach the first-world level, then the region's GDP could be

$$\$30,000 \text{ per capita} * 509 \text{ million people} = \$15,270 \text{ billion.}$$

If 44% of that were paid to owners of the capital stock, as it is in the United States, and if the applicable discount rate were 4% and the annual growth rate were 2%, the market value of the capital stock could reach

$$\$15,270 \text{ billion} * 0.44/(0.04 - 0.02) = \$335,940 \text{ billion.}$$

This extreme figure is more than five times the highest estimate for the dollar value of the U.S. capital stock. It assumes that all the productive potential would be developed to first-world levels, and the risky cash flows would be transformed at no cost into absolutely safe cash flows. It is also almost two orders of magnitude larger than the beginning market value of Latin America's capital stock before currency unification and before the effect of other measures that would enhance the market value of those assets. To quote this figure in per capita terms, it is \$660,000 for every man, woman, and child in Latin America.

Should Latin America Dollarize?

The message of these calculations is that, when countries cede their monetary sovereignty and merge their national currencies into a supranational currency, they create value. The value they create is immense compared to any measure of the value the country was getting from retaining its monetary sovereignty. Moreover, the computations indicate that larger increases in value occur when the supranational currency spans a larger economic zone. To carry this argument as far as it can go, the conclusion would appear to be that Latin American countries should abandon all their national currencies and adopt a world-level supranational currency. There is no such world currency at this time, except perhaps for IMF Special Drawing Rights (SDR), which meet some of the technical specifications but are known only to experts and exist only as a bookkeeping abstraction in the IMF.

To limit the choice of a world currency to one that already exists, only the dollar, the yen, and the euro are possibilities. The dollar has been the choice for Panama, Ecuador, and El Salvador. In 2001, Argentina has floated the idea of backing its local currency with the euro and the dollar in the proportion of 50–50. The market received the suggestion badly, because it was seen as a ploy to devalue the local currency. That is the only time that a Latin American country has proposed adopting the euro as the backing for its national currency. So far, there has not been a proposal to adopt the euro as a national currency, but the euro has only existed for a short time, so it may become a candidate to replace national currencies later. The yen is the strongest of the major world currencies, in terms of its track record relative to the other two currencies over the past 30 years since the breakup of the Bretton Woods agreement. The ten-year government bond yield for the yen is also the lowest. It follows that a country that drops its national currency and adopts the yen should experience a massive rally in the market prices of its capital assets.

For a country in Latin America, adopting the yen would be a more extreme choice than adopting the U.S. dollar. It would signal that the country's top priority was not to facilitate trade in goods and services but to raise the market prices of its capital assets. An argument for adopting the dollar has been that most Latin countries' trade transactions are with the United States or are denominated in dollars. So, the main argument for dollarization is to simplify transactions in the goods sector and to shield merchants from currency risk. The effect of dollarization on market prices of capital assets has been a secondary argument in favor of dollarization.

A proposal to adopt the yen would put the priority squarely on raising the market prices of capital assets. Merchants would still have to deal with currency risk—in this case the yen versus the dollar. Nevertheless, the increase in the market prices of capital assets would be much larger if market participants believed that the yen would remain strong relative to the dollar and the euro, and so the magnitudes would justify giving serious consideration to the idea of adopting the yen.

Although the calculations come out massively in favor of abandoning local currency and adopting a currency that is perceived as stronger, we do not presume to make the choice for sovereign countries. We offer our calculations for their consideration and remark that our calculations depend on assumptions and data that are subject to error. Having stated those caveats, we note that the magnitudes are so great that they justify a top-level review of alternative currency regimes, with emphasis on lowering country risk.

CONCLUSION

This chapter is full of large magnitudes. Several hundred trillion dollars of potential wealth is more than most people can imagine and is also an order of magnitude greater than the dollar value of annual world output. In a debate about economic policy alternatives, the usual range is billions or tens of billions of dollars. Nevertheless, the Asian and Latin American zones are so large and their potential is so enormous that magnitudes in the trillions are plausible.

The examples here start with a two-country, "marriage-of-convenience" currency unification and then go on to more grandiose schemes spanning larger groupings of countries, finally reaching an entire region. All the examples show immediate gains, well in excess of the gains the countries currently obtain from keeping their individual national currencies. This result indicates that there is no need to enlist a critical minimum number of countries in order for currency union to be successful. As soon as two countries announce credible plans to merge their currencies, gains should begin to accrue. This result comes directly from the reduction in country risk and emerges clearly from standard, well-known, and often-used financial formulas.

NOTES

1. ASEAN was formed in 1967 as a front against communism. Current members are Brunei, Cambodia, Indonesia, Laos, Myanmar, the Philippines, Singapore, Thailand, and Vietnam.

2. Bangladesh, Bhutan, India, the Maldives, Nepal, Pakistan, and Sri Lanka.

3. As India and Pakistan move substantial military forces toward their 1,100-mile border and saber rattling becomes increasingly more aggressive (January

2002), the chance of a free trade agreement coming to fruition is increasingly re-mote. These nations' relatively recent nuclear testing controversy, the military takeover of Pakistan, Islamic terrorist attacks on India's parliament, and a running dispute over Kashmir have slowed progress on the economic integration front. It is fair to say that the SAARC will be unable to start a free trade area or make sig-nificant advancement in other areas without the participation of its two largest members.

4. Negotiations will focus on agriculture, information technology, human re-sources, and development of the Mekong River Basin.

5. The treaty is expected to commence in 2002 and will be the first such treaty negotiated between or among East Asian nations. It would entitle Korean and Japanese residents to national treatment in most sectors of the counterpart coun-try, as well as the unrestricted right to move funds internationally and freedom from nontariff barriers, such as restrictions on local content and technology trans-fers. Because of their widely differing stages of development, Japanese invest-ments in Korea are expected to be most greatly affected by the treaty.

6. It has been suggested that if the euro can be used as a guide, an adjust-ment period of 50 years or more may be needed. See the speeches of Governor Buenaventura in *Archive: Some Thoughts on the Prospects for Asian Economic Co-operation*, presented at the First International Conference on Asian Political Parties, Manila (Philippines) Hotel, September 19, 2000. Available: http://www.bsp.gov.ph/archive/Speeches_2000/SomeThoughts.htm.

7. For 1999, the per capita GNP of low- and middle-income countries in East Asia and the Pacific was $1,000; for Central Asia, it was $2,150; and for South Asia it was $440. World Bank, *World Development Report: 2000/2001, Attacking Poverty* (Washington, D.C.: International Bank for Reconstruction and Development and Oxford University Press, 2001), 275.

8. Ibid. The World Bank gave the 2000 dollar values of stock markets in low- and middle-income countries of Asia as follows: East Asia and the Pacific was $955,379 million; Europe and Central Asia was $265,209 million; South Asia was $194,475 million; and Japan was $4,546,937 million. The rest of the quoted figures is the authors' estimate.

9. Barry Eichengreen, with Tamim Bayoumi, "Is Asia an Optimum Currency Area? Can It Become One? Regional, Global, and Historical Perspectives on Asian Monetary Relations," CIDER Working Paper C96–081, December 1996. Available from the CIDER website. Revised version published in Stefan Collignon, Jean Pisani-Ferry, and Yung Chul Park, eds., *Exchange Rate Policies in Emerging Asian Countries* (Routledge: London: 1999), 6–7.

10. Ibid., 10–13.

11. Ibid. Among the pairs suggested by Eichengreen were Singapore–Malaysia and Hong Kong–Taiwan. He chose these pairs, because they were expected to re-spond similarly to external supply shocks and, in general, would track each other more closely than other pairs.

12. World Bank, *World Development Report*, 274–275.

13. This simplification is so fewer calculations will be needed to illustrate the gains.

14. This simplification is so the coupon rates correspond to the yields.

15. $16\% - 5\% = 11\%$.

16. $18\% - 16\% = 2\%$.

17. That simplifies the calculation but does not distort the result, as long as the maturities of the bonds are as we have assumed.

18. This estimate assumes that Philippine government debt and corporate debt are 80% and 25% of GNP , respectively. A decline in the nominal yield on Philippine government debt from 16% to 11% would create capital gains of 30%, which would be equal to 24% of GNP (that is, 80% x 30%). A decline in the nominal yield on Philippine corporate debt from 18% to 13% would create capital gains of 27.5%, which would be equal to 6.9% of GNP (that is, 25% x 27.5%). Therefore, the total gain in Philippine wealth would be $24.1 billion, which is 30.9% of the nation's $78 billion GNP. For Indonesia, this estimate assumes that government debt and corporate debt are 100% and 25% of GNP, respectively. A decline in the nominal yield on Indonesian government debt from 16% to 11% would create capital gains of 30%, which would be equal to 30% of GNP (that is, 100% x 30%). A decline in the nominal yield on Indonesian corporate debt from 18% to 13% would create capital gains of 27.5%, which would be equal to 6.9% of GNP (that is, 25% x 27.5%). Therefore, the total gain in Indonesian wealth would be $44.0 billion, which is 36.9% of the nation's $119.5 billion GNP. Combined, the total increase in wealth for the Philippines and Indonesia would be $68.1 billion (that is, $24.1 billion + $ 44 billion), which is 34.5% of the combined nations' GNP.

19. The $54 billion figure is derived by applying the 27.5% revaluation of corporate bonds to the unsecuritized capital stock, which was assumed to be 100% of combined GDP (that is, ($78 billion + $119.5 billion) * 27.5%).

20. The capitalized value of an X% gain in GNP when interest yields are 11% would be equal to [X% x ($119.5 + 78)]/11%. A capitalized gain of 3.8% is approximately equivalent to $68.1 billion.

21. This estimate assumes that Thailand's government debt and corporate debt are 60% and 25% of GNP, respectively. A decline in the nominal yield on Thailand's government debt from 16% to 10% would create capital gains of 37%, which would be equal to 22.2% of GNP (that is, 60% x 37%). A decline in the nominal yield on Thailand's corporate debt from 18% to 12% would create capital gains of 34%, which would be equal to 8.5% of GNP (that is, 25% x 34%). Thailand's GNP in 2000 was $121 billion. Therefore, the total gain in Thailand's wealth would be $37.1 billion, which is 31% of the nation's $121 billion GNP.

22. Capital gains on Indonesian government debt would rise by an additional 7.5%, and corporate debt would rise in value by an additional 6.9%. As Indonesia's government debt and corporate debt are assumed to be 100% and 25% of GNP, respectively, the total capital gains would be $11.03 billion, which is 9.23% of Indonesia's $119.5 billion GNP. Capital gains on the Philippines' government debt would rise by an additional 7.5%, and corporate debt would rise in value by an ad-

ditional 6.9%. As government debt and corporate debt in the Philippines are assumed to be 80% and 25% of GNP, respectively, the total capital gains would be
$6.03 billion, which is 7.73% of the Philippines' $78 billion GNP.

   23. $11.03 billion + $6.03 billion = $17.1 billion.

   24. More technically, at least one U.S. dollar backed each peso of Argentina's
monetary base.

   25. Peru's index of common stock prices stood at 137.3 as of November 2, 2001.
It was at 100 on June 1, 1993, so it had gone up only 37.3% in eight and one-half
years. That performance is tepid but typical of emerging markets for that period.
Barrons (November 5, 2001): MW10.

   26. World Bank, *World Development Report*, 275.

   27. Ibid.

   28. Ibid., 295.

   29. Ibid., 301.

   30. Ibid., 301.

   31. Ibid., 294–295.

   32. $(1/3 * 2\%) + (1/3 * 4\%) + (1/3 * 0.5\%) = 2.2\%$.

   33. $(1/3 * 1\%) + (1/3 * 2\%) + (1/3 * 0\%) = 1.00\%$.

   34. Note that $1.2\% * 3.0 = 3.6\%$.

   35. Value = (Annual benefit/Applicable discount rate) = $(3.6/0.15) = 24\%$

   36. Perpetuity value of insurance against hardship = (Difference in allowable
fiscal deficit x Probability of occurrence)/ Interest rate) = $[(4\% –2\%) \times 33\%]/15\%$
= 4.4% of GNP

   37. Value = (5.75% of GNP/15%) = 38.3% of GNP.

   38. 38.3% of GNP + 4.4% of GNP = 42.7% of GNP.

   39. This figure is developed from U.N. Development Program data. Available:
http://www.undp.org/hdro/natinc.htm.

   40. Hernando de Soto, *The Mystery of Capital: Why Capitalism Triumphs in the
West and Fails Elsewhere* (New York: Basic Books, 2000), 6.

   41. *Barrons* (October 29, 2001): MW60.

   42. Note that $(94.75 + 10- 78.32)/78.32 = 0.3374$. An investor's gain consists of
coupon income of $10 plus the price appreciation.

   43. *Barrons*.

   44. Market Value = [22% of GNP/(14% – 2.5%)] = 191% of GNP.

   45. New Market Value = [22% of GNP/(10% – 2.5%)] = 293% of GNP.

   46. New Market Value = [22% of GNP/(8% – 2.5%)] = 400% of GNP.

   47. New Market Value = [22% of GNP/(5% – 2.5%)] = 880% of GNP.

   48. This figure is different from the market rates for some of these countries at
the time this is written. We use this rate so that the reader can easily compare how
much wealth a cluster of countries can create compared to the amount a single
country can create.

   49. In the case of Chile, the gains could be negative. Our hypothetical Pacific
cluster includes Chile and three other countries with much higher country risks.
At the time this was written, Chile's country risk was around 200 basis points,

whereas the other countries in South America had much higher country risk premiums, ranging from 700 basis points to 5,000 for Argentina. Consequently, if Chile joined the proposed Pacific cluster, its country risk might rise. That would mean that owners of Chilean assets would lose. They could take cold comfort in knowing that their losses would be more than matched by gains in Peru, Bolivia, and Ecuador.

50. To express this point in terms of the Capital Asset Pricing Model, we are assuming that the security market line in each country has the same slope and intercepts the Y axis at the same place. This assumption is very unlikely to be valid for the countries in the two proposed clusters.

Chapter 8

Wealth Trajectories and Spillover Effects

INTRODUCTION

Currency unions eliminate the exchange rate premiums among member nations, and they also have the potential to reduce substantially this risk premium relative to nonmember nations. As a result, enormous and immediate financial benefits can be created for the unifying nations, and these benefits spill over into the real sectors to provide higher standards of living and better paying jobs for domestic residents.

The premise of this book is that a chain reaction of beneficial effects is set off when a nation, by any means, reduces its country risk. Adopting a stable foreign currency or creating an enduring currency union is an instantaneous way to reduce country risk, to stimulate economic growth, and to deliver a massive increase in a nation's wealth. In this chapter, we focus on the direct and indirect wealth effects of a currency union, and we intend to show that the gains it delivers to a nation not only grow exponentially with the reduction in risk but also are delivered virtually overnight. The nation benefits not only from this direct increase in wealth but also from the reinforcing wealth spillover effects that have roots in the currency risk reduction.

The reasoning is as follows. If a country reduces its international risk premium, domestic nominal interest rates fall, causing the price of fixed income securities to rise and the nation's financial wealth to grow. If this rise in wealth were small and/or grew at a snail's pace, then we might marginalize it and devote our attention to the traditional lines of economic thinking that focus on how declining interest rates raise GDP by stimulating business investment, personal consumption, and net export expenditures. There is nothing wrong with this line of reasoning, but we feel it is too narrow. Focusing only on flow variables, such as consumption, investment, and net exports, undervalues the true benefits of a currency union, because flow variables do not measure the benefits that emanate from increased wealth. By putting the proper weight on these wealth-related benefits and their positive wealth spillover effects, a much stronger case can be made for a currency union.

Currency unions and dams are alike in the sense that both are human-made and intended to improve a community's well-being. Whether they actually accomplish this goal depends on how the structures are managed and maintained. Dams create large common pools in which fish can swim freely. Within broad ranges, increases or decreases in the water level behind a dam or turbulences at the water's surface have little or no effect on the tranquility of life underneath, but they can have a large impact on the surroundings. A ruptured or overflowing dam can wreak havoc on downstream communities.

Bringing this analogy into an economic policy area, a currency union creates a large common currency pool for nations to freely transact business. Currency risk among nations within a currency union is the same regardless of changes in the size of the union's money supply or the level of international economic turbulence, but these variables can very much affect member nations' economic relations with nonmember nations. A currency union has the potential to reduce currency risk and create a more tranquil economic life for member nations relative to the outside world, but whether it accomplishes this goal depends on the policies of the supranational monetary (and, if it exists, fiscal) authority.

All other things remaining the same, the chances that a currency union will reduce member nations' currency risk premiums relative to nonmember countries are usually much higher than the chances for the same country alone. A larger-size currency area means that, for any given change in demand or supply, exchange rate fluctuations should be smaller because of the increased trading volumes. Greater stability is also derived from the netting effect that occurs when bad news in one country is offset by good news in other regions. Moreover, currency unions permit central banks to benefit from scale economies in their reserve assets. The reserves needed to protect a currency from capital flight or speculation do not increase proportionately with the rate of GDP growth.[1] As a result, the ability and resources of a currency union's central bank to handle exchange rate crises, financial panics, and other disruptions that can paralyze financial markets and strangle real economic activity are far greater than the ability and resources of a noncentralized central bank.

Of course, the immediate, direct effects of a currency union are financial. The first sign of a successful currency union could well be the rise in prices of securitized financial assets. Only afterward would the prices of unsecuritized, income-producing properties (such as real estate) rise, and only after that would the real GDP and jobs be created.

This chapter develops three models. The first—the Wealth Spillover Model—links changes in financial wealth to changes in consumption and GDP. This model puts a magnifying glass to the linkages between the financial and real sectors when a currency union is formed. Model parameters are set and conclusions about the net benefits of a currency union are drawn. What makes this portion of the analysis especially interesting is its flexibility. Our model can be accessed via the Internet, allowing readers to change the parameters we use and to specify the strength of the links. With this flexibility, readers can experiment with the effects of changing asset prices, determine breakeven points, and conduct sensitivity analysis using parameters of their own choice. Readers can also use the model to analyze *feed-forward* effects, which involve economic changes due to self-reinforcing momentum and the interplay with a nation's workforce and installed productive capacity.

The second model—the Currency Stability Model—examines whether a country's foreign exchange reserves are adequate in the face of rising levels of securitization around the world. Because an income-producing property can be worth more once it is securitized, securitization has the potential to both create wealth and raise a nation's level of instability. The owners of securitized assets must find buyers, and depending on the market liquidity and the size of the turbulence, price movements can be quite dramatic.

Even in very liquid capital markets, where securitized (and nonsecuritized) wealth can be converted into cash, exchange rate convertibility is another potential source of instability facing asset holders. Once sold, an owner's financial capital is locked in the country where it is located, unless the domestic currency can be sold for a foreign one. As the world's capital assets become more securitized and as the securities are held in actively managed portfolios, owners feel increasingly able to move their capital at a moment's notice. Consequently, the stability of any given currency becomes more tenuous as the magnitudes rise. Financial asset owners feel empowered, because even long-term assets can be dumped at the first sign of trouble. There is less need for fatalistic, long-term views. As a result of this investor/speculator empowerment, central banks become increasingly overmatched. The Currency Stability Model provides a framework for analyzing the increasing vulnerability facing nations, and it allows the reader to vary our inputs and parameters if they would like to determine for themselves how likely a foreign exchange crisis could be.

The third model—World Financial Fluctuations—shows the vulnerability of a small country's currency to outflows of portfolio investment when the country's financial assets grow at a substantially slower rate than the growth of the world's financial assets and when the currency remains convertible for capital market transactions. As the world pool of financial assets grows, random fluctuations in demand for the small country's currency become larger, and these random fluctuations can overwhelm the small country's reserves.

The three models developed in this chapter scrutinize the trade-offs among wealth creation, GDP growth, increased consumption, and increased international financial instability that nations face when they form a currency union. The issues in this chapter are the modern variant of a theme, which has been in economic literature for more than a century, of whether money is neutral. In that controversy, if money is neutral, as some economists contend,[2] then monetary policy does not matter in the long run, because the prices of goods and services adjust to the varying levels of liquidity, causing accurate incentive transmission and optimal decision making. Another relevant theme is whether there is a "wealth effect" and, if so, what its magnitude is and how it affects central bankers' ability to manage currencies.

The effects of wealth creation and destruction were not central concerns in earlier eras, because changes in ownership and magnitude were so small. For instance, even though land was a major part of any feudal lord's wealth, fluctuations in its value had little or no effect on the lord's consumption. It was not so much because he was already rich, but rather, because there was no market for the land. Most feudal lords inherited the property and were expected to pass it on to the next generation. A lord would no sooner sell his land than the governor of Massachusetts would sell a portion of Boston.[3]

As a result, fluctuations in the hypothetical market value of land had little or no effect on the consumption patterns of the feudal lords. Landowners lived on their rents, and the peasants lived on their production after taxes. There were currency crises, but they took a simpler form and affected the macroeconomy via the feudal lord's access to credit. The lord's extravagances and misfortunes took their toll on the peasants, who had no easy way of escaping the burden. In those bygone days, most international transactions and sovereign loans were settled in gold, and cross-border capital flows were mainly in the form of direct investments.

Today, questions relating to the connection between wealth and income have moved to center stage. National and international capital movements affect the day-to-day lives of anyone who borrows, invests, or consumes. In short, they affect all of us either directly or indirectly, and understanding how financial wealth propagates has become one of the most important contemporary economic issues facing nations. Because of the huge up-front costs of establishing a currency union, there is almost no going back once it is formed. For that reason, it is important to examine, a priori, whether the union can bring improvements in the economic well-being of a large cross section of a nation's population.

The traditional goal of macroeconomic policy has been to keep employment and output at or close to their maximum potential levels, while at the same time keeping inflation under control. At a minimum, good macroeconomic policy should create better economic circumstances than would have resulted from the natural corrective fluctuations that ordinarily stabilize capitalist economies. Even though monetary policy makers have not officially accepted it or acknowledged that they are trying to achieve it, a more recent objective appears to be raising the market prices of existing assets. When asset prices rise, voters develop a vested interest in keeping them high. In past eras, the prices of all assets in a country could fall during recessions in response to changes in the country's investment climate and in response to capital outflows. Declining asset prices often caused hardship, but people felt powerless to prevent the declines or to arrest them once they began. Asset prices were thought to be out of the direct control or target range of economic policy. Now, voters expect the value of their houses and retirement accounts to appreciate or, at least, to stay the same. Asset prices now matter too much to be allowed to fluctuate violently. Voters want the rise in asset prices to be steady and enduring. Policy makers are under pressure to deliver steady increases in asset prices. Traditionally, both monetary and fiscal authorities have been most comfortable trying to promote changes in the flow variables, such as GDP and inflation. Now, stock variables, such as the aggregate size of pension funds, are sharing increasingly more of the attention.

In the first century after the Industrial Revolution, when the major tenets of classical economics were set forth, employment and wages fluctuated in response to only a few controllable prime causes, and those were what economists studied. Productivity, scale economies, and process innovation were the drivers of growth. In the classical economists' scheme, rising market prices of capital assets did not cause growth. Asset prices fluctuated passively and were not prime movers of economic activity. Their rise and fall were symptomatic, not causal.

Land rents rose if the price of grain rose, and the value of coal mines rose due to increased demand or technological improvements, such as the steam engine. In the classical period, there was little mention of a cycle of prosperity that began with asset inflation. Instead, several notorious incidents in capitalism's early days gave a bad name to all booms fueled by increases in asset prices.

Asset booms, starting as far back as the "South Sea bubble" and the "tulip panic," always ended badly.[4] Booms were destined to fail, because they rested on faulty foundations. Typically, asset prices would rise to unsustainable heights and then swiftly crash down with devastating consequences. Such bursts of euphoria were called "manias" and "collective delusions." Writers lumped asset booms with other cases of mass hysteria, thereby discrediting them. In the official histories of these sudden expansions, the deluded speculators always got their comeuppance and the chastisement they deserved. The instant millionaires went from riches to rags and then had to struggle for years to get back to the humdrum lives they had cast aside in their frenzy to join the speculative delirium.[5]

In the current millennium, asset prices have risen but not in a uniform or coordinated fashion. Wealth has appeared in the net worth statements of the middle classes, as if by magic, but the new wealth seems fragile and vulnerable, less substantial than the underlying productive assets that collateralize stocks and bonds. Yet, asset prices can obviously rise more, particularly in countries that have not adopted policies that facilitate such increases. In short, more wealth can materialize for those same people and for others who have not yet enjoyed windfall gains.

There are two broad objections to asset-price–driven growth. The first is a visceral aversion many people have to the arbitrary relative redistribution of wealth toward financial asset holders and away from both wage earners and landowners. Critics believe that these gains are illegitimate and that speculation is not work, because it adds nothing tangible to what already exists. They argue that it has no real or lasting value; speculation is a distraction from the real business of an economy, and the people who pay so much attention to the prices of capital assets are misguided. To such critics, the mere buying and selling of capital assets should not earn the returns they have over the past 20 years. The second objection is that asset-price–driven growth is unstable. A country that pursues such a policy may get onto a steeply rising trajectory, but then it is exposed to inevitable collapses that will follow the boom periods.

The three models in this chapter put these two negative characterizations of asset-price–driven growth under the microscope. We observe that the annual rate of increase of security issues has greatly exceeded the growth rate of output, so the ratio of financial wealth to flow variables has been inexorably rising, and a secular worldwide asset boom is underway. For that reason, the positive wealth creation effects of a currency union should be judged jointly with the negative effects of increased vulnerability. Recent experience has already shown that rising wealth can propel economies upward much more quickly than rising productivity. Economists use the terminology *wealth effect* for the change in an individual's consumption when wealth rises by $1. Few doubt that the effect exists. Rather, the debate centers on the magnitude of the wealth effect. Will an increase by $1 in a person's wealth raise consumption expenditures by 4 cents or only by 1 cent? These few cents can make a huge difference.

News of fluctuating asset prices already fills the front pages of mainstream newspapers, but financial intermediation has characteristically been viewed as the handmaiden of value creation in the real economy. Now we find that such intermediation can have its own direct real effect on value. As a result, allocating saving to investment projects continues to be a critically important task but no longer for the same narrow reasons. For example, investing in new factories can now be less profitable than packaging car loans and mortgages, but these new securities can give rise to increased speculative activity.

Wealth is the prime mover in the economic growth process that we put forward in this book. We feel that currency unification not only creates an increase of wealth but also stimulates international capital flows, and the combination of effects raises real economic growth for the unifying countries. Both rising wealth and growing trade call forth increases in spending and, hence, stimulate productive activity. This is a controversial assertion, and the models permit readers to experiment with our parameters and combinations of inputs in order to scrutinize the validity of our belief, which is that wealth effects are catalytic and the gains from higher asset prices can be enduring. In our view, asset prices do not oscillate above and below a long-run, unchanging average. Instead, the average is rising.

THE WEALTH SPILLOVER MODELS

To better understand the effect that changes in wealth have on economic growth, we have developed three variants of the wealth spillover model (WSM) in order to determine whether a currency union will increase both the GDP growth rate and the rate of financial wealth accumulation of a member nation. Version 1 is the "straw man" and the basis for comparison. It considers the effect that annual random shocks have on the GDP of an economy facing international capital flows that passively adjust to trade imbalances (that is, rather than to favorable or unfavorable random shocks to an economy). Version 2 analyzes the effects that currency risk reduction has on a nation after it joins a currency union. Like Version 1, it assumes that international capital flows respond passively to trade imbalances. Finally, Version 3 analyzes the effect of both currency union and the international investment community responding to the annual random shock to the real economy.

Each of the subsequent WSMs starts with the same set of inputs and simulates for 50 consecutive, one-year periods the effects of the annual random shocks. Special attention is paid to the changing value of common stocks and bonds and the interplay between these changing values and variations in real GDP and consumption.

To open the analysis to wider debate, we have posted our model on a website (http://faculty.babson.edu/wealth-by-association), which allows readers to change the assumed parameters according to their own specifications. In this book, we have used our best judgment to define the parameters, but by accessing our website, readers are free to experiment with these assumptions and determine how much, if at all, the results would differ under alternative assumptions.

Our hypothetical country begins with real annual output of 1,000. Consumption, gross private domestic investment, and net exports are assumed initially to equal 90%, 10%, and 0% of GDP, respectively.[6] Incremental variations in income are assumed to have a composition of 90% consumption and 10% investment, but consumption is also affected by changes in wealth. As a result, the rate of consumption each year could be greater than or less than 90% of income. When aggregate demand exceeds domestic output, the model assumes that imports rise to meet demand. If domestic output exceeds aggregate demand, exports are assumed to take up the slack. These changes in net exports are, in turn, financed by equal and opposite international capital flows. Current account surpluses cause capital outflows, and current account deficits cause inflows.

Each year, the economy is affected by a random shock that varies between 7% and –3% of GDP, and therefore, it has an expected value of +2%. The random shocks affect financial wealth (that is, stock and bond prices) in multiple ways. As a result, the nation's GDP growth is highly dependent on whether these wealth-induced effects reinforce or weaken the impact that the annual random shock has on GDP. Because our focus is on real changes in GDP, our analysis does not model inflation. The effects of monetary policy and the role of financial intermediaries are also not modeled in the analysis.

In the beginning, the nation's securitized wealth (that is, common stocks and bonds) is assumed to be worth 100% of the value of its GDP, and it is evenly split between stocks and bonds. Changes in wealth also are assumed to be split evenly between stocks and bonds. Our analysis posits that wealth and consumption are directly related, and we model five avenues by which changes in wealth or changes in the wealth-to-GDP ratio can vary and influence consumption. The first two effects are caused by the annual random shock; the third is stimulated by changes in the level of saving, which occurs passively due to changes in income. The fourth source is by means of changes in currency risk and induced capital inflows. The fifth linkage is via the wealth-to-GDP ratio. A brief explanation will make these sources clearer.

Two Random-Shock–Induced Changes in Wealth

Consider first the two effects, which are assumed to be activated by an annual random shock to the economy (that is, real GDP growth rate). Changes in the random shock are assumed to have a direct effect on the value of the nation's financial wealth. For every 1% change in the random shock, there is assumed to be a 0.5% change in the value of the nation's existing wealth. The market prices of common stocks and bonds rise (fall), because the same random events that change real GDP also make local savers view these securities more (less) favorably. Moreover, these same random events change international investment expectations, which in turn would affect the value of financial wealth. Our model as-

sumes that the these random shocks change international capital flows by
the same percent as they change real GDP and that every 1% change in
such capital flows causes a 0.5% change in the value of the nation's stocks
and bonds.

Income (Saving)-Induced Changes in Wealth

Changes in wealth are stimulated not only by the annual random
shocks but also by changes in GDP, which cause increases in saving and
the accumulation of financial assets by consumers. This treatment of saving and its direct link to investment and human well-being are classical in
nature. All domestic saving is assumed to be channeled into common
stocks and bonds.

Risk-Induced Changes in Wealth

Variations in currency risk also influence investor perceptions and,
therefore, change the value of financial assets, consumption, and GDP. If a
currency union can reduce a nation's foreign exchange risk, the diminu-
tion of this risk reduces nominal interest rates and raises the value of both
shares and fixed-income securities, which together comprise financial
wealth. In this model, we assume that currency risk falls linearly by 0.1%
for each of the 50 years. We chose to reduce risk incrementally over a 50-
year period, because it coincides with the approximate 50-year period
over which the European Union transformed itself from the European
Coal and Steel Community (1951) to a full currency union (1999/2001).
Had we chosen a shorter period with more dramatic reductions in currency risk, as occurred in the six-year period between the 1993 ratification
of the Maastricht Treaty and the 1999 creation of the euro, our conclusions
would be even more stunning.

Changes in Consumption due to Changes in the
Wealth-to-GDP Ratio

The changes in a nation's wealth trigger changes in its consumption,
and in the wealth spillover model, the linkage from wealth to consumption is crucial. Most of us would agree that if we inherited (or otherwise
came into) a nest egg of financial securities, this source of purchasing
power would influence our willingness and ability to consume out of annual income. The analysis in this chapter begins with a financial wealth-
to-GDP ratio of 1.0 and assumes that as the level of wealth grows in
relationship to GDP consumers spend increasingly greater portions of
their income. As a result, within broad ranges, if the random shock and the
annual reduction in currency risk result in a net increase above various

threshold levels in the wealth-to-GDP ratio, then the marginal consumption rate rises.

In our model, consumers spend an additional 1% of their incomes when the wealth-to-GDP ratio is between one and two. They spend an additional 2% of their incomes when the wealth-to-GDP ratio is equal to or above two, but below three; they spend an additional 3% of their incomes when the ratio is equal to or above three, but below four; and finally, an additional 4% of consumers' incomes are spent when the ratio rises above four.[7] At higher levels of financial wealth relative to income, individuals are assumed *not* to spend larger portions of their incomes.

Feed-Forward Effects

Changes in wealth are assumed to have feed-forward (or knock-on) effects that affect personal consumption expenditures by 4% during the first year following the increase, by 2% in the following year, and have no effects thereafter. That is, a $100 increase in wealth this year will increase an individual's consumption by an additional $4 next year and an additional $2 in the following year.

We chose this simple structure of forward linkages, because we think it is realistic for some industrial countries with aging populations, and because a more complex structure of forward linkages would add unnecessary complexity to the model.

How the Model Works

Our complete WSM works as follows. Each year (or time period), a positively biased random shock causes a change in the country's real GDP, financial wealth, and/or flows of international investments. The combination of these effects causes changes in consumption, real GDP growth, and the level of financial wealth, which in turn feed back to influence each other. If personal consumption plus gross private domestic investment expenditures exceed production income, our model assumes that the shortfall is met by changes in imports.[8] At the beginning of each subsequent year, new random shocks affect an economy that has already benefited from or been harmed by the random shock of the previous year. After these effects have all been taken into consideration, the ending value for our hypothetical nation's common stocks and bonds could be higher or lower than it was at the beginning of the period.

Causes and effects in the model occur sequentially. For example, the random shock occurs, followed by iterative adjustments by domestic investors, consumers, and international investors. The end result of this ordered adjustment is a substantial revaluation of common stocks and bonds. As a result, the model posits a scenario in which, for example, purchases of newly issued securities raise stock and bond values, but random events are capable of offsetting or exacerbating the change. Because the model is open for experimentation, readers who question the assumptions made in the analysis are free to vary the parameters and study the causal links to determine how the conclusions might change.

One of the most interesting questions that the WSM addresses is how much added consumption comes from the effect of inflows of portfolio investment. Inflows of portfolio investment raise the market prices of financial assets and thus induce and support higher levels of consumption. Our model shows that a country that succeeds in lowering currency risk and attracting international investment inflows can dramatically increase its standard of living, but the price it pays for the increase is less stability in its growth. We did not design the WSM to give this result. The result comes inevitably from the volatility of asset prices. In the WSM, market prices of common stocks and bonds fluctuate more than GDP, because the market value of common stocks and bonds rises and supports higher levels of consumption, but the rise is volatile, and so the growth rate of consumption is unstable.

Two results came as a surprise. First, the biggest difference in consumption came from the currency union, not from inflows of foreign investment. In one scenario, for example, the currency union raised the average annual growth rate of consumption from 4.4% to 6.6%. Adding the effect of foreign investment inflows only increased average annual consumption by 0.002%. Second, the big jump in volatility happened along with the currency union. Adding the effect of foreign investment inflows did not raise volatility very much at all. Before developing the model we thought that both the currency union and the inflows of foreign investment would raise the growth rate of consumption and the volatility of the growth rate. We did not have an opinion about which of the two would cause more growth and which would cause more instability.

Version 1: Closed Economy Affected by Annual Random Shocks

Version 1 analyzes a pre-currency union economy, which is affected each year by a positively biased random shock that changes both GDP and the value of existing financial wealth but which has *no direct effect* on international trade or international capital flows. Changes in wealth then spill over to affect consumption expenditures and GDP growth. Exhibit 8.1 provides an overview of all the wealth and other effects in Version 1, and Table 8.1 lists the assumptions behind this model.

The simulation results of this base case show that GDP in our pre-currency union country grows, on average, by 4.4%, which is a bit more than twice the expected growth of the direct effect the random variable has on

Exhibit 8.1
Wealth Spillover Version 1 (Base Case: Effects of an Annual Random Shock in a Closed Economy)

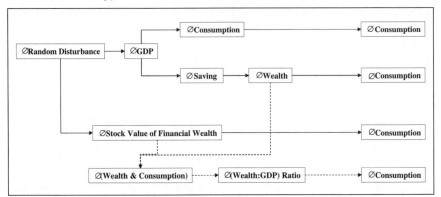

GDP. Equally important, growth in GDP ranges from a low of about –0.5% to a high of 10.5%, with approximately 95% of the years without recession. Under these conditions, wealth grows at an average annual rate of approximately 6.0%, with yearly rates ranging from approximately 5% to 10.5%. In no year does the value of wealth decline.

Version 2: Open Economy with Annual Random Shocks and Reduced Currency Risk

Version 2 analyzes a country after a currency union has been formed. Not only is this economy affected by the annual random shock, but also it is affected simultaneously by an annual 0.1% reduction in currency risk. Our assumption is that the country risk declines from 6.0% to 1.0% over the 50-year time horizon. The wealth creating effects of the annual reductions in country risk can be either reinforced or weakened by the annual random shock. The combination of declining currency risk and a positively biased random shock introduce a steady upward drift in securities prices (see Exhibit 8.2 in which the shaded boxes show the newly considered effects and see also Table 8.2).

Simulation results of our post-currency union economy show that GDP growth rates range from approximately 6.5% to 7.0%, which is over 2% more than the pre-union growth rate. This difference may seem small, but it is not. An economy growing at 5% will double its GDP every 15 years. By contrast, an economy growing at 7% will double its GDP every ten years—a 50% improvement. Over a 50-year period, the GDP of the faster growing economy (7%) will be over 250% greater than the slower growing one. Like the pre-union economy, recessions are virtually nonexistent in Version 2; wealth grows at approximately 9%, a full 3% higher than the pre-currency union economy. In no year does the value of wealth decline.

Table 8.1
Assumptions of the Wealth Spillover Version #1

Initial annual output (i.e., GDP)	1,000
Initial sovereign interest rate	11%
Saving rate (as % of GDP)	10%
Consumption rate (as % GDP)	90%
Inflation rate	0%
Source of change	Positively-biased, annual random shock with mean of +2%
Change in consumption per dollar change in wealth (a.k.a., feed-forward effects)	Year t + 1 = 4%
	Year t + 2 = 2%
Annual change in risk premium	None
Change in international capital flows due to random shock	None
Change in stock and bond prices due to change in international capital flows	None
Monetary and fiscal policies	None
Change in financial assets are distributed	50% in stocks
	50% in bonds
Additional consumption due to the Wealth-to-GDP ratio	If 1 ≤ Wealth-to-GDP ratio< 2 = 1%
	If 2 ≤ Wealth-to-GDP ratio< 3 = 2%
	If 3 ≤ Wealth-to-GDP ratio< 4 = 3%
	If Wealth-to-GDP ratio ≥ 4 = 4%
Number of periods in simulation	50

Version 3: Open Economy with Annual Random Shocks, Reduced Currency Risk, and International Capital Flows

Version 3 builds on the post-currency union analysis in Version 2. As was the case with Version 2, the economy is affected simultaneously by an annual random shock and a 0.1% reduction in currency risk, but in

Exhibit 8.2
Wealth Spillover Version 2 (Effects of Annual Random Shock & Currency Union in a Closed Economy)

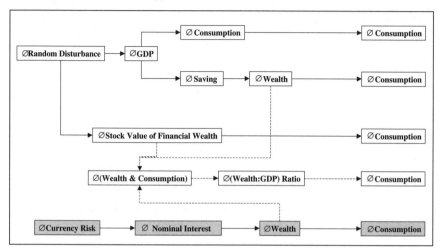

Version 3, the annual random shock also affects international capital flows. A positive shock attracts international capital, and a negative shock not only reduces it but also encourages capital flight (see Exhibit 8.3 in which the shaded boxes show the newly considered effects and see also Table 8.3).

As a result, annual international capital flows may be positive or negative, depending on the size and direction of the random shock. On average, they should be positive with the same 2% mean as the random shock. We feel comfortable with this assumption, because it is our belief that most countries that are prime candidates for currency unions have considerable untapped potential. A 2% positive growth bias may well be erring on the conservative side of this locked-up potential. As a result of these international capital flows, changes in the value of a member country's wealth are amplified and so too are changes in economic growth. The average annual inflows or outflows of foreign portfolio investment are not very large compared to the existing value of financial assets each year, but they have a dynamic effect on the market value of local common stocks and bonds. That effect, in turn, stimulates consumption.

To keep the country's wealth from exploding or collapsing, the model does not assume any serial correlation among the random disturbances. Rather, each year's random disturbance is generated so as to be independent of other disturbances. This may be a conservative assumption, because international portfolio investors remember the past. Nevertheless, using simple independent random shocks avoids introducing a complicated self-reinforcing process that would otherwise mask the wealth effects generated in the wealth spillover model.

Table 8.2
Assumptions of the Wealth Spillover Version #2

Initial annual output (i.e., GDP)	1,000
Initial sovereign interest rate	11%
Saving rate (as % of GDP)	10%
Consumption rate (as % GDP)	90%
Inflation rate	0%
Source of change	Positively-biased, annual random shock with mean of +2%
	Declining annual risk premium of 0.1%
Change in consumption per dollar change in wealth (a.k.a., feed-forward effects)	Year t + 1 = 4%
	Year t + 2 = 2%
Annual change in risk premium	None
Change in international capital flows due to random shock	None
Change in stock and bond prices due to change in international capital flows	None
Monetary and fiscal policies	None
Change in financial assets are distributed	50% in stocks
	50% in bonds
Additional consumption due to the Wealth-to-GDP ratio	If 1 ≤ Wealth-to-GDP ratio< 2 = 1%
	If 2 ≤ Wealth-to-GDP ratio< 3 = 2%
	If 3 ≤ Wealth-to-GDP ratio< 4 = 3%
	If Wealth-to-GDP ratio ≥ 4 = 4%
Number of periods in simulation	50

Version 3 gives results that are scarcely different from Version 2. The reasons are that the expected inflows of portfolio investment are small relative to the value of securities in the national market, and we do not attribute any special power or synergistic impact to the capital inflows.

Exhibit 8.3
Wealth Spillover Version 3 (Effects of Annual Random Shock & Currency)

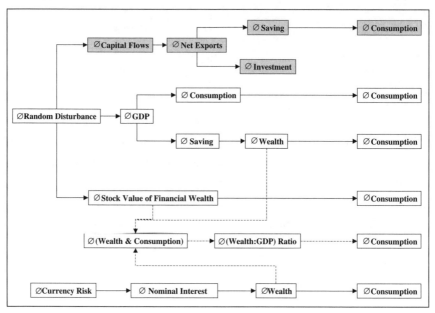

In the specification, we assumed that $1 of international portfolio investment inflows added only $0.50 to the value of common stocks and $0.50 to the value of bonds. Meanwhile, the market prices of stocks and bonds rose because of the steady decline in country risk. For those reasons, Version 3 gives only a slightly higher growth rate of consumption than Version 2, and the volatility of the growth rate in Version 3 is also only marginally higher than Version 2.

Discussion of Results

Version 1 of the WSM shows that the annual growth rate of consumption can exceed the average annual growth rate of GDP due to the effect of rising wealth on spending. Stock and bond prices drift erratically upward in response to the positively biased random disturbances, and savers hold more and more wealth each year. As individuals' wealth rises and they grow older, they consume more of it. Because they consume imports in growing amounts, their consumption can grow faster than local production.

Version 2 of the WSM adds the powerful stimulus of steady decreases in country risk. When a country joins a currency union and its securities become safer, the owners of the country's securities benefit from a sustained rally in the prices of the securities they hold. Foreign portfolio investors do not participate proactively in the rally in Version 2; instead, they buy

Table 8.3
Assumptions of the Wealth Spillover Version #3

Initial annual output (i.e., GDP)	1,000
Initial sovereign interest rate	11%
Saving rate (as % of GDP)	10%
Consumption rate (as % GDP)	90%
Inflation rate	0%
Source of change	Positively-biased, annual random shock with mean of +2%
	Declining annual risk premium of 0.1%
Change in Consumption per Dollar Change in Wealth (a.k.a., feed-forward effects)	Year t + 1 = 4%
	Year t + 2 = 2%
Annual change in risk premium	None
Change in international capital flows due to random shock	1% change in random shock causes 1% change in international capital flows.
Change in stock and bond prices due to change in international capital flows	1% change in international capital flows causes 0.5% change in stock prices
	1% change in international capital flows causes 0.5% change in bond prices
Monetary and fiscal policies	None
Change in financial assets are distributed	50% in stocks
	50% in bonds
Additional consumption due to the Wealth-to-GDP ratio	If 1 ≤ Wealth-to-GDP ratio< 2 = 1%
	If 2 ≤ Wealth-to-GDP ratio< 3 = 2%
	If 3 ≤ Wealth-to-GDP ratio< 4 = 3%
	If Wealth-to-GDP ratio ≥ 4 = 4%
Number of periods in simulation	50%

the country's securities only in the amounts needed to offset the country's current account deficit (in this case, trade deficit). The value of a country's securities goes up, because the lower risk premium causes investors to bid up their prices. The citizens of the country reach threshold levels of wealth sooner than they did in Version 1, and they consume their wealth earlier in the 50-year time frame the model covers. Their consumption grows faster, and their wealth also grows faster.

Version 3 of the WSM shows that including international capital flows that react to an annual random shock has a very small effect in comparison to the annual buying and selling that locals are doing. We do not attribute any special clout or impact to these flows, and we set the key parameters low. The reader may wish to make them larger. For example, a 1% increase in capital inflows only increases common stock prices by 0.5%, with bond prices increasing by the same amount. Also, there is no serial correlation in the random inflows and outflows. Each year there is a positive bias in favor of an inflow, but the bias does not increase the year after an inflow. So there is no bandwagon or herding effect. Instead, local buyers dominate the market. For this reason, inflows and outflows have virtually no effect over the 50-year periods on the average GDP growth rate, its volatility, the average growth rate of consumption, or the rate of capital accumulation.

The results of the WSM depend on the wealth effect and on the upward drift in asset values. Both are required for there to be a large sustained increase in consumption. Part of the increase comes from the upward bias in securities prices and another part comes from the secular reduction in the risk premium. These combine to give investors the benefit of an average annual improvement in the value of their holdings, with some exceptionally good years and few bad years. These results show that feed-forward effects do not have to extend more than two periods. The WSM's assumptions about investor behavior are simple. Holders of financial assets spend more if their holdings went up in the two immediately prior periods. The reader may wish to incorporate more complex feel-forward linkages, implying more sophisticated assumptions about investor behavior.

With the parameters that we used, the main result is that, if a country can both lower its risk premium and attract foreign portfolio investment, its consumers can enjoy a steep rise in their standard of living. In reality, any country that can do one of those two can at the same time hope to achieve the other. In that happy case, with the beginning parameters, WSM Version 3 shows that annual consumption can grow as fast as 6.5% to 7.0%. At such a rate, the level of domestic consumption could double in only 11 years and triple in 17 years.

It is interesting to note that the factor having the largest impact on the wealth effect is the change in common stock and bond prices as a multiple of the annual output. Local parameters, which local authorities can hope to influence directly (for instance, the ratio of the market

Table 8.4
Summary of Average Annual Real Growth of Consumption

Condition	Result
With no wealth effects	Straw man Version
With an upward bias in securities prices only	4.0 — 5.0%
With the multiple rising and country risk declining	6.5% - 7.0%
With inflows of foreign portfolio investment	6.5% - 7.0%

value of common-stocks-to-GDP and bonds-to-GDP, as well as the country risk premium), have an even larger effect than the change in asset prices. There is a powerful implication for developing nations. If a country can lower its risk premium, domestic consumers could enjoy a steep rise in their standard of living. (Table 8.4 summarizes the results of this section.)

Caveats about the Wealth Spillover Model

The Wealth Spillover Model raises some interesting questions that we put forward explicitly here. Our model shows that currency unification will increase wealth, but some readers may question whether rising wealth will pull up income and employment with it. We show it does, subject to the parameters in our model. Raising the value of assets that already exist is an attractive notion and certainly will appeal to owners of assets; but, employment and output are the metrics that tell if an economic policy is a success. The prime movers we have discussed here are purely financial, and their immediate and direct impact would be on the prices of financial assets, then on the prices of unsecuritized assets, and then on consumption, employment, and income. But will there be further knock-on effects that will spur job creation and increases in output? People need jobs that will pay them enough to live. An economic policy that does not create enough employment and fails to deliver an adequate quality of life has not performed adequately even if it generates wealth.

The WSM assumes that, when desired aggregate demand increases faster than output, any shortage of goods and services is met by an increase in imports. During this period, income grows to meet demand, and it is this new level of income that is affected by the next random shock. The reverse would be true if desired demand were less than output. In short, the model uses the conservative assumption that the Keynesian multiplier is equal to one. We wrote the model that way to err on the conservative side and to keep the basic tenets of the model simple. As a result, excess demand (or supply) has a direct effect on the nation's unemployment rate and level of well-being

Another point that the WSM raises is stability. Currency unification, according to the arguments we advance in this book, improves the stability of the currencies that previously were independent. To the extent that this is true, currency unification can be a defense against exchange rate crises, financial panics, and other disruptions that shatter financial markets and choke real economic activity. As the total amount of financial assets in the world grows, each individual currency becomes more vulnerable to sudden changes in investor psychology. The financial assets and foreign exchange reserves of any single country will be a smaller portion of the world total. Most countries, including those that are able to securitize their capital stock rapidly, will be vulnerable to currency crises. Each single country will have to build up its foreign exchange reserves at a fast enough pace to keep up with the growth of world financial assets. When two currencies unify, they gain strength against speculative raids and panics. The unified currency spans a larger area; thus, if there is bad news, the news is less likely to make the entire area look bad to investors. The foreign exchange reserves of the two countries are more likely to be sufficient to satisfy the demands the bad news will cause.

The WSM assumes that there will be no serial correlation among the yearly random shocks. That is, the initial random event at the beginning of each year is an observation from a uniform distribution ranging from +7% to –3%. The instability does grow over the 50-year period, but the cause is endogenous. The wealth-to-GDP ratio rises, and wealth is more volatile than GDP, so the instability increases for that reason. The reader may argue that we describe a 50-year growth trajectory that would not be achieved, because there would be currency crises, recessions, and depressions along the way.

Another question is, Does the wealth spillover model exaggerate how powerful the effects on the real economy can be? There are several features of this model that make its results come out so strongly. Perhaps most important, the process we used for generating random disturbances does not give many long periods of depressed securities prices. Every year is an independent event, and every year the model has a bias in favor of a positive disturbance in the prices of common stocks and bonds. Also in Version 3, every year there is a random amount of portfolio investment flowing in or out of the country, with a bias in favor of an inflow. These biases correspond to reality for some countries but not for others. Some countries have experienced long bear markets in common stocks and bonds and have experienced chronic outflows of portfolio investment.

An additional important driver is the assumption about the size and persistence of the wealth effect. A skeptic may question that, or may want to replace the simple assumption with a more complicated one. A young, risk-tolerant person, for example, may consume more from a windfall increase in her wealth than an old, risk-averse person would.

The WSM makes the assumption that countries can attract inflows of portfolio investment every year. It assumes that they may fail and suffer outflows from time to time, but they will recover and on average retain their ability to attract portfolio investment. This is obviously not true for all countries. There will always be some countries that are chronically unable to attract portfolio investment. The model also assumes that, in most years, countries will be able to retain all their citizens' annual savings; even though we know this is not true for all countries. What the WSM implicitly assumes is that there will always be countries growing slower than their saving rates would justify. These are the countries that chronically experience capital flight. They lose some of their national saving, and in that fashion, unwillingly support the higher growth rate of countries that successfully retain local savings and attract portfolio investment.

The WSM makes the market values of common stocks and bonds the prime mover in the country's economy. If security prices rise, consumption increases. In that sense, it assumes that the main influence government policy has on the economy is by influencing investor sentiment. This may seem simplistic, because there are many other ways government policy can work, but to people living in countries with open capital markets, the assumption seems much more reasonable.

We made another important simplification regarding the country's balance of payments in Versions 1 and 2. When the local population's holdings of financial assets grew, and it wanted to consume some of its wealth, people sold securities or borrowed. Foreigners bought the securities, thus providing the local population with the means to purchase imports. These capital inflows were the source of financing current account deficits over an extended period of time. In the Wealth Spillover Model, imports were the pressure relief valve for excess domestic spending.

THE CURRENCY STABILITY MODEL

Now we come to the second of the three models we developed. Every year increasing volumes of financial capital flow cross national borders to earn higher returns and diversify investor portfolios. Many countries are wary of this trend. Even though increased foreign portfolio investment may raise a nation's economic growth, it may also expose the country's currency to speculative attacks. The currency stability model (CSM), which is developed in this section, analyzes whether a country that joins a currency union will have foreign exchange reserves adequate to satisfy the demands of a growing foreign investment sector. The analysis moves from a yearly evaluation of changes in GDP, consumption, and wealth to daily changes in capital flows and international reserves.

The CSM begins with a single country holding foreign exchange reserves that are barely adequate to meet the demands placed on them. Then, as the time periods come one after another, there are crises, because the demand for foreign exchange sometimes exceeds the country's holdings. The crises happen for two reasons. First, the country's beginning holdings of foreign exchange are only three times larger than the standard deviation of the daily fluctuation in the demand for foreign exchange. So, even though the chances are less than 1%, from time to time, the country's foreign exchange reserves would run out due to random shocks to the economy. Second, whenever there is bad news, it predisposes the country to outflows for the subsequent days. If there is an outflow on Day 1, that outflow predisposes another one on Day 2, and so on until Day 6. The feed-forward mechanism negatively biases the subsequent random events. We have set the feed-forward parameters in the 0.2 to 0.6 range, meaning that if the random event on Day 1 were negative (for example, −1.00), then the random event on Day 2 would be biased downward by 0.2 to 0.6.[9] This assumption generates a series of daily flows that can be downward biased. The downward bias makes it likely that, after several periods, foreign exchange reserves will be exhausted.

In the CSM, there is one random event for each of the 100 days simulated. These random events take away foreign exchange reserves or add them. Consequently, the country's holdings of foreign exchange reserves fluctuate randomly from day to day. As was the case in the wealth spillover model, these random events are positively biased, so the country's holdings of foreign exchange should drift upward but the country's holdings do not always meander happily upward, because they are susceptible to streaks of downward bias. The bad effects of earlier unfavorable random events spill over to affect later periods. This feed-forward or forward propagation makes the country's currency much more vulnerable to crises than its initial holdings of foreign exchange and the standard deviation of daily demands would indicate.

The CSM creates a scenario showing what happens when two economically identical countries unify their currencies, merge their central banks, and pool their foreign exchange holdings. After the currency unification, the daily random events are the same as before. The feed-forward effects are also the same. What is different is that crises occur far less frequently, if at all. The unified central bank's combined foreign exchange holdings are twice as great, and, due to the offsetting cross correlations, its begin-ning holdings of foreign exchange are now six times the standard devia-tion of the daily demands for foreign exchange. For that reason the random daily fluctuations in demand for foreign exchange rarely exceed the unified central bank's holdings. The feed-forward mechanism creates some downward moves in the unified central bank's foreign exchange holdings, but these are very unlikely to become severe enough to exhaust the central bank's reserve holdings.

To generate a crisis, we used a simple process for creating random daily disturbances that has limited self-reinforcing negative effects to simulate short losing streaks.[10] When the initial random event is negative, it feeds for-ward and biases downward the subsequent random events for the next five periods. We used a simple mechanism to make bad news echo forward.

If the initial event is an inflow, we do not bias upward the next five events. Foreign exchange sometimes piles into a country day after day, but we are not focusing on that phenomenon. Instead, we are modeling a sim-ple type of downward bias that lingers for a few days after an initial neg-ative event.

The CSM does not have self-reinforcing downward spirals. Each pe-riod's random event starts with a positive bias. If previous random events were strongly negative, the feed-forward linkages may turn an inflow into an outflow, but the next period's random event still starts with a positive bias. There is no dynamic modification of parameters. If there are two or three bad events in a span of five periods, the effects of these will not snowball, because there are no endogenous modifications of the model parameters. Instead, each negative event biases downward the next five events, but not the sixth.

This process for generating a series of outflows and inflows does not need to be complicated to generate currency crises. Furthermore, with the assumed strength of the feed-forward parameters, the CSM generates an alarming number of crises during each 100-period scenario. The CSM does not include any herding behavior by speculators and does not take account of any learning or strategy on the part of the central bank. The process is mechanistic, and for that reason it illustrates how vulnerable in-dividual national currencies are to currency crises. With the magnitudes we used, a currency crisis can happen by chance, whether the country has done anything to "deserve" the crisis or not.

What is impressive is the frequency of currency crises before the two countries unify their currencies. A currency crisis in Period 1 is very un-likely, because the initial random event would have to be so significantly negative. Currency crises come after several periods, when there has been a series of negative events or a few uncharacteristically large negative events within a short span of time. The negative events provoke large enough outflows to drain all the central bank's foreign exchange—and that is our definition of a crisis.

Since a currency crisis is highly unlikely in Period 1, there are really only 99 periods when a crisis could occur, and the remarkable result is that, for a single country, six or seven times among 99 periods there will be a crisis. The parameters of the CSM cause the crises to be as frequent as they are. The feed-forward linkages are strong, and the central bank's beginning holdings of foreign exchange are low relative to the size of the random demands on reserves. With different parameters the frequency of currency crises drops sharply.

Despite the model's simplicity, the result is striking. Central banks have to hold substantial reserves and cannot release foreign exchange even when the amount looks large enough to provide adequate protection. A few bad events can cause demand to spike and empty the central bank's coffers.

There is a solution to this discouraging state of affairs. Suppose there was another country of the same size, with its own currency and its own central bank and the same amount of foreign exchange reserves. If the two countries merged their currencies and pooled their foreign exchange reserves, the frequency of crises would drop. The random events continue, the negative events happen, and the feed-forward effects aggravate the impact of two or more negative events in a short span of time, but the pooled foreign exchange reserves prove sufficient to meet the demand.

On the one hand, this result is nothing more than a proposition of elementary statistics. Pooling the two countries' foreign exchange reserves will drastically reduce the number of crises, unless the random demands on the pooled reserves become twice as large. William Baumol noted this point with his cash inventory model: When a firm's sales double, it does not need to hold twice as much cash. Its cash holdings only need to increase by the square root of two, or 1.41 times, to give the same level of protection against running out of cash.[11] On the other hand, the result is a powerful argument both against national currencies and in favor of supranational currencies. As the worldwide aggregate value of securities rises, the need for currencies that can withstand crises increases. A small, prudently managed country used to be able to have its own national currency, without worrying that a random event would provoke a currency crisis. Now, capital is so mobile and so large relative to reserves that crises are more frequent.

The CSM generates crises entirely by chance. The magnitudes of the random outflows and the simple feed-forward linkages are the only drivers in the model. There are no speculators, no herding or bandwagon behavior, and no points in time when the currency is especially vulnerable because of economic or political conditions. There is no learning, no bluffing, and no conspiracies. Every time period can be the beginning of the end. In that sense, the CSM depicts crises as routine outcomes—this is to be expected in a monetary regime that has a glaring structural defect: a predisposition to fail.

In the CSM, unifying one national currency with another with the same attributes remedies the predisposition to fail. In our specification, this is because the random demands on them do not get any larger. Our implicit assumption is that the size of the random events is an attribute of the world economy and not an induced response to bad news coming from either country itself. In other words, the CSM assumes that a country does not do anything to provoke outflows of foreign exchange. Investors may place funds elsewhere, because they do not like what is happening in one country, but they may also place them elsewhere for reasons that have nothing to do with anything that is happening in the country that experiences the outflow.

For that reason, our view is that it would not be enough for the two countries to agree to pool their reserves. The agreement would have to be absolutely binding to be credible. For example, the two countries would have to hand their reserves over to a third party or an independent central bank and give irrevocable, published instructions about how to use the reserves to defend both currencies. If both national currencies were merged into one supranational currency and both central banks ceded their reserves and their authority to a supranational central bank, market participants would be sure that the reserves had irrevocably been pooled.

THE WORLD FINANCIAL FLUCTUATIONS MODEL

The dollar value of world financial assets has risen rapidly in recent years. There has also been an increase in the percentage of world financial assets held in aggressively managed portfolios. At the same time, the foreign exchange holdings of most central banks have, in the aggregate, not kept pace with private markets. These facts have put world financial stability in jeopardy, and they have cast an especially dark shadow on the national currencies of small countries with fixed exchange rate regimes. The outlook is especially serious for a small country with a fixed exchange rate system whose national financial assets grow more slowly than the world total. The small country's total capital market may be less than 0.5% of world financial assets. The small country may be managing its affairs prudently and may still face a growing risk of capital outflows. The outflows may stem from contagion or from an unfortunate permutation of world macroeconomic events.

The third model that we present—the world financial fluctuations model (WFFM)—depicts a future in which there is a growing likelihood that any individual country will face a currency crisis, purely as a result of random capital flows in world financial markets. The hypothetical country in the WFFM is vulnerable to a currency crisis for several reasons. First, the world pool of financial assets grows twice as fast as the financial assets in the country's capital market. Second, the portion of total world financial assets held in aggressively managed portfolios rises. The aggressive managers attempt to place funds in countries that, in their opinions, are going to do well, and they liquidate financial assets in countries that are going to do badly. They try to cut their losses and get out of bad situations before things get worse, but they all hear at once the same news announcements. Consequently, they often act en masse, and the results are a mass exodus from and entry to the same capital markets. Third, they ceaselessly shift assets from their home market to markets abroad and bring them back again in response to slight differences in perceived advantage. These attributes of world capital markets appear in simple form in the WFFM, and together they create wild fluctuations in capital flows.

The WFFM computes scenarios for the next 100 days. It computes how large each daily random inflow or outflow is compared to a country's foreign exchange reserves. It notes each time that a random outflow is larger than the country's foreign exchange reserves. It also generates extremely unstable trajectories for the financial wealth of a small country with its own national currency and a rate of creation of financial assets that is only half the world average. The source of the volatility is capital rushing in and out, bringing moments of giddy prosperity followed by times of illiquidity and economic paralysis.

The violent fluctuations come from two sources that are in addition to the sources incorporated in the currency stability model. First, the country's financial assets grow slower than world financial assets, so the size of its capital market gradually becomes smaller than the day-to-day random disturbances in the world capital market. Second, the portion of world financial assets that is aggressively managed keeps rising.

As with the other two models, the reader can change the parameters and introduce more complex feed-forward mechanisms. The parameters and simple mechanisms that we used are surprisingly effective given their simplicity. They show how fragile world financial stability is and how vulnerable national currencies are becoming.

THE TOBIN TAX AND THE TEQUILA INCENTIVE

The currency stability and world wealth fluctuations models both support the idea that the world financial system needs a line of defense against excessive capital flows. Both models are simple, because they do not include speculators or traders with any skill or foresight. The currency crises happen entirely because of the magnitudes of random fluctuations. The only rule built into these models that aggravates the instability is an elementary feed-forward propagation. If a country suffers a damaging random fluctuation in a given period, the random fluctuation in the following period(s) becomes less positively biased, and if the negative random fluctuation is bad enough, the random fluctuation in the following period (s) can become negatively biased. After a few periods, the negative event no longer casts a shadow on the country's finances, and the bias in favor of capital inflows reasserts itself. Because of the magnitudes, the reversion to inflows may not have enough strength to produce stability if the pool of short-term capital outside any individual country grows so large that its random ebb and flow is capable of draining all the reserves from its central bank. Any fixed exchange rate country, whose central bank reserves are not growing at least as rapidly as the world financial markets, will face a rising probability of a currency crisis.

The picture, then, is one of national currencies sheltered from the storms of the world market by walls that are less and less adequate to defend them. Each currency's main defense is its central bank's reserves, which are augmented by credit and reserve pooling agreements.

The currency stability model shows that if two economically identical countries merge their central bank reserves, both gain protection against random outflows. The random outflows still occur, but it is less likely that any given outflow will be large enough to drain the merged reserves. This is one of the main arguments for unifying currencies. Speculators do not seek pyrrhic victories, so they pick on weak foes and easy victims. They assess whether a currency is overvalued and compute how much buying they will have to overcome to force a devaluation and, if the central bank has too much ammunition, the speculators do not attack.

Several themes run through the debate over the tug-of-war between central banks and speculators. The first theme is that the central banks hold the moral high ground, because they serve the greater good. They are the stewards of monetary stability, and they establish and defend the stable conditions in which commerce can flourish. The speculators are viewed as opportunists who fill their own pockets by assaulting the stability on which ordinary people depend. The second theme is that sovereign countries should have enough latitude to conduct their fiscal and monetary affairs as they see fit, without suffering hit-and-run attacks from speculators. The third theme is that the world financial system needs to be made more stable. If that can be accomplished, the cost of sheltering central banks from speculative attacks will be lower.

If the initial three themes set the parameters of the debate, schemes to reform the world financial system center on how to restrain the speculators. The phenomenon of contagion adds a new dimension to the debate. When the battle was between an individual central bank and a horde of currency speculators, the central bank was the beleaguered hero. Now, the central bank can be a worse sinner than the speculators. The act of a sovereign government can have severe repercussions on the rest of the world. When contagion and the damage it causes are taken into account, the whole nature of the debate shifts. Suddenly there are no saints and no devils. When contagion is taken into account, there can be millions of losers and only a few winners, so schemes to reform the world financial system shift their focus, and the question then becomes how to keep countries from having currency crises.

These two diagnoses lead to different prescriptions. If what the world needs is to restrain the speculators, a tax on cross-border financial transactions, sometimes called a "Tobin tax," is an appealing remedy. If what the world needs is to reward governments for prudence and penalize them for profligacy, then a different remedy is indicated. We propose such a remedy here, and we call it a *tequila incentive*.

The tequila incentive is named after Mexico's infamous 1994 "tequila" devaluation, which triggered a worldwide panic affecting many emerging markets. The losses that Mexico's action inflicted on other emerging countries and on portfolio investors in industrial countries were much greater than any possible advantage that Mexico's policy makers might have hoped to gain from the devaluation. Mexico suffered for the mistake it made. The country struggled through a deep recession lasting from 1995 to 1996. That may seem like punishment enough, but Mexico never reimbursed victims outside Mexico for the losses its actions inflicted on them. The scheme that we propose would internalize some of the outsiders' losses and tilt the policy makers' incentives so that they consider the externalities of their actions.

Our proposal is to reward countries for lowering the risk premium that market participants assign to their sovereign bonds. We also propose rewarding countries when their credit ratings improve. The amount of the reward would be linked to the country's GDP. For example, if the country improved its risk premium from 10% to 9% (that is, from 1,000 basis points to 900 basis points), the reward would be 0.1% of GDP. This amount would be paid in Special Drawing Rights to the nation's account at the IMF. The IMF could make this payment without taxing anybody and without raising the quotas of its members.

The tequila incentive would work in tandem with a "tequila penalty." We propose penalizing countries when the risk premium that market participants assign to their sovereign bonds is raised. The penalty would be of the same magnitude as the reward. For a 1% worsening of the country's risk premium, the penalty would be 0.1% of GDP. This amount would be recorded against the country's account at the IMF as a debt owed to the fund.

This scheme might seem harsh, because countries do not control how they are perceived in financial markets. Market participants may have biases and may treat inaccurate information as if it were reliable. A country may be working very hard to improve its financial affairs and may get no recognition in financial markets. So the proposed tequila incentive and tequila penalty may do nothing more than aggravate the capricious whims of uninformed, uncaring international portfolio investors.

To make the scheme fairer, we propose using averages over periods of time. To set the beginning risk premium for each country, we propose using the average risk premium for the preceding two years, with the best five days and the worst five days excluded. Then, to determine if a country's risk premium is improving or worsening, we propose using moving averages of the most recent 60 trading days. We also would exclude the three best days and the three worst days from the 60-day moving average. Finally, we propose delaying the release of funds from the tequila incentive for three months after they are earned. This is to keep the tequila incentive funds from generating a self-reinforcing improvement in a country's risk premium.

The tequila penalty is, in our opinion, a necessary concomitant of the tequila incentive. It is true that the penalty would fall on countries that are already feeling "Mr. Market's" wrath. It is also true that the poorest countries would be vulnerable to it. They are often dependent on a single export commodity, so if its price fell, their sovereign bonds would likely fall. They would also be vulnerable to weather disasters, external shocks, and internal institutional breakdowns.

Nevertheless, in our opinion the tequila penalty should be assessed. When a country defaults on its sovereign bonds or dispossesses foreign portfolio investors, the cost would be felt all around the world. Dozens of countries and millions of investors would suffer losses and would take comfort in knowing that the offending country would pay some part of the loss; but that is not the only reason for assessing the penalty. The scheme we propose would work better than one that gave rewards only for improvement. Speculators would be watching carefully, so there should be penalties for laxity too. If a country caused turmoil in the world financial markets and did not then face a penalty, the scheme we propose would not be as effective. The tequila incentive by itself will help make the world financial system more stable, but in our opinion it would work better in tandem with the tequila penalty. Even though the tequila penalty would not directly compensate the contagion victims (that is, residents of other nations who are harmed by the spillover effects), it would provide an incentive for more prudent behavior and thereby would provide at least some source of relief.

Still, it may seem cruel to assess the tequila penalty. If the country is destitute or if the country's sovereign risk rating worsened through no fault of its own, assessing the penalty may seem like kicking someone who is already down, but in cases like that, the penalty does not make the country's situation much worse. It already owes much more than it can pay, and the country can include the new amount in its application for debt relief. At the same time, assessing the penalty and treating it as a liability that the country will have to pay may alter the outcome of some policy decisions and push the country's policies in the direction of prudence. The effect of announcing the penalty will signal that the world is serious about bolstering world financial stability and may deter other unsound policy decisions.

This scheme of incentives and penalties does not completely remedy the growing instability of the world financial system. Currency unification will improve stability, at least for a time, by eliminating currencies that speculators would have been able to target one by one. After currency unification, speculators would have fewer targets to aim for, and the targets would be better funded. This scheme does not constitute a substitute for a Tobin tax. Instead it builds stability in a way that complements actions that governments, central banks, and multilateral agencies may take to discourage cross-border speculation.

IMPLICATIONS AND CONCLUSION

The three simple models described here convey a message that is both encouraging and discouraging. The wealth spillover model shows that countries can increase consumption very rapidly if they are successful attracting their own citizens' savings and attracting foreign portfolio investment. The currency stability and world financial fluctuations models show that the world financial system is already predisposed to crises, and is rapidly becoming more so. The results of these models come from their specification and the parameters we used. In total, the three models constitute an argument for countries to unify their currencies, and they show reasons for currency unification that were not powerful in the past but have now become compelling as world financial wealth grows.

In addition to calling for currency unification, we propose two additional mechanisms to shore up world financial stability: the tequila incentive and the tequila penalty, to internalize the costs of contagion. Countries that were able to improve their credit ratings or sovereign risk premiums would receive financial rewards in their accounts at the IMF; by contrast, if countries experienced deteriorating credit ratings or their sovereign risk premiums worsened, they would incur financial penalties.

NOTES

1. William Baumol, "The Transaction Demand for Cash: An Inventory Theoretic Approach," *Quarterly Journal of Economics*, 1952.

2. Mark Blaug, Walter Eltis, Denis O'Brien, Don Patinkin, Robert Skidelsky, and Geoffrey E. Wood, *The Quantity Theory of Money: From Locke to Keynes and Friedman* (Brookfield, Vt.: Edward Elgar, 1995).

3. See Robert L. Heilbroner, *The Worldly Philosophers: The Lives, Times, and Ideas of the Great Economic Thinkers* (New York: Touchstone, 1999), 27–30.

4. John Kenneth Galbraith, *Money: Whence It Came and Where It Went* (Boston: Houghton Mifflin, 1975).

5. "It is far better to be nouveau riche, than never to have been rich at all"— Anonymous.

6. Government spending is treated as a part of consumption, so we can abstract from fiscal policy.

7. There is another wealth effect, which acts via changes in securitization, that we could have added to the wealth spillover model. We assume that the unifying country does not actively try to increase the level of securitization. Securitizing financial assets would increase their value and create another means by which consumption and GDP could grow. We assume a 10% saving rate, and an expected average real growth rate of 2%, but the country's securitization ratio does rise passively. If securitization were a national goal, the ratio of securitized-to-nonsecuritized wealth would rise even more, thereby increasing GDP. We believe that if a country encouraged securitization both global investment inflows and economic growth would be higher. We did not introduce systematic changes in securitization to our WSM, because the importance of the wealth effect is apparent even without any reinforcing influences, and its introduction would only complicate the analysis. Nevertheless, the model shows numerous avenues that policy makers might pursue in their attempt to improve living standards.

8. International capital flows, then, must occur in the opposite direction to finance the deficit or to invest the surplus.

9. If the initial random event is an outflow, the model represents it as a negative number, and then 0.2 to 0.6 times that negative number is added to each of the next five random events. Readers are free to access the currency stability model at http://faculty.babson.edu/wealth-by-association and to experiment with the parameters.

10. There are no symmetric winning streaks in this model.

11. William Baumol, "The Transaction Demand for Cash," op. cit.

Chapter 9

Implications and Conclusion

The implications of the analysis we have set forth in this book are clear: If two currencies are going to unify, risk tolerant investors should buy securities denominated in the currency of the country with the higher pre-union yield and buy them according to a timetable, beginning when the currency unification is a rumor and continuing until the date when the unification enters into effect. Then, they should sell the securities after the union is formed to risk-averse investors, who by that time would be buying, and wait to repeat the process when a third currency joins the union. If a third currency is going to join the union, risk-tolerant investors should buy securities denominated in both the third currency and the new unified currency. After the third currency is certain to join the union, risk-tolerant investors, again, should sell all the securities denominated in the unified currency and wait for a fourth currency to join.

Buying should be disciplined and steady. Investors should seek to acquire the securities at prices below their trend value (that is, buy the dips with confidence). They should constantly reassess whether the monetary convergence is on track and, as long as it continues to move toward full implementation, continue to accumulate securities.

Opportunities to accumulate securities will come prior to ministerial-level meetings when the press will question whether the ministers are going to balk at taking the next step toward unification. There will be nervous sellers before and during the meeting. The ministers will announce their irreconcilable differences, and then set them aside and take the next step toward currency unification.

There will be additional opportunities to accumulate securities as the dates of national referenda on the subject of currency union draw near. As long as the end result is inevitable, investors can follow the old Wall Street rule of thumb: "Buy on the rumor and sell on the news." Opinion polls before the vote will often show more opposition to currency union than really exists. Once they are in the voters' booths, it is unlikely the electorate will set aside their pocketbooks for nationalistic sentiments. If they vote against unifying their currency with another, the matter will come up again. If they vote in favor, the decision will stand.

The rally in European securities prior to January 1999 is only a foretaste of a similar bull market that could occur in Asian bonds and stocks if a group of Asian countries decided to unify its currencies. Windfall gains in the range of billions or trillions of dollars can accrue to owners of securities and also to owners of unsecuritized properties. The stimulus to output and employment could also be significant. The exact trajectory and magnitude of this potential Asian rally and the concomitant growth surge depend on which countries unify their currencies and what timetable they follow as they do it.

Future rallies will probably be more erratic than the European one was, because market participants now know the milestones: the terrain is familiar, so they will pay for the value of convergence earlier, and frequently they will overpay for the amount of convergence that has occurred to that point. For that reason, more of the total gain may happen earlier as investors bid up the prices of securities denominated in weak currencies, and future rallies will be more likely to get ahead of themselves as investors enthusiastically pay for a glowing future before the crucial political consensus has come into place. Governments may fall if they allow investors to believe there is going to be a monetary unification and then delay it.

A centerpiece of the long history of commercial and economic progress has been the evolution of the many monetary conventions that link countries and societies. Survival of the fittest has dictated the way currency regimes, payment mechanisms, and trading systems have evolved. Experts are now aware that currency regimes can be as important as production processes in determining whether there will be prosperity or privation. Indeed, choosing what to produce and how to produce it now seems easier than choosing the correct design for a nation's monetary and payments regime. More than ever before, policy makers are playing a high-stakes game, with "Mr. International Market" constantly scrutinizing their every move. We are now at a point at which serious questions are being raised concerning the need for independent, national currencies, but such has always been the case.

The main point in this book is that enormous amounts of financial wealth can be created or destroyed when countries make choices about having national currencies. They can continue having national currencies, choose to merge their national currencies into supranational currencies, or adopt an internationally-recognized currency such as the dollar, euro, or the yen. This decision, which most countries took implicitly or avoided in the past, is now a much more conscious, well-publicized decision.

The sovereign has always had the right to issue currency, and part of the reason for doing so was to gain by decreeing that issued coins commanded more purchasing power than their gold or silver content would merit. That way, the sovereign could mint coins at a profit, and subjects would not complain, as long as the issuer was careful to avoid blatant debasement. If the sovereign was successful at coinage management, the stimulus to commerce would more than compensate for the debasement, and the polity would benefit. In modern times, a variant of the same view has been widely accepted: A nation can gain from having its own currency, provided that it manages its monetary affairs well.

This book challenges that view and submits it to a detailed examination. The matter is much more complicated than it used to be. The simple nostrum that it suffices for a country to manage its currency "prudently" is now questionable. A country may no longer benefit from having its own currency even if it carefully obeys the rules of monetary management. There are magnitudes that have shifted and players that have gained importance, and these changes have put the wisdom of having national currencies in doubt. The most important of these changes are listed below:

- Financial assets now greatly exceed annual output in value. Also, their market prices fluctuate much more than the price and volume of annual output. These two facts combine to set a new criterion for economic policies: To be beneficial, a policy should raise or maintain the market prices of the financial assets. A policy that lowers the market prices of financial assets runs a severe risk of doing more harm than good. This criterion is novel, and it adds a new dimension to many standard economic policies. If a country is in a recession, for example, one of the standard remedies used to be to devalue the currency. There is an extensive literature on when and why this remedy will help. This new criterion adds another element to the analysis of this time-honored policy: It cautions that devaluation may not help. As well, there is another standard remedy that now should be reexamined: If a country was having a fiscal deficit and high unemployment, the knee-jerk remedy was to increase the money supply and ease credit conditions. Again, the new criterion indicates that this remedy may stimulate the level of production and employment, but if it sets off a wave of inflationary expectations that increases nominal interest rates and reduces the value of financial assets, these losses could nullify any benefits.

- Financial markets are not only larger than goods markets, but also they are growing at a much faster rate. Policies that aim only at the goods and services market may be self-defeating, because they ignore the much larger and more responsive financial markets. A new criterion, again, applies: A policy will produce substantial benefits if it encourages capital to remain in the country, and it provides incentives for inflows of foreign capital. Capital inflows help maintain and increase the market prices of a country's financial assets.

Portfolio investors already exist in mass, and their number and financial power are growing. These investors are mostly middle-class savers whose investment decisions are far from professional but nevertheless are influenced by breaking news. They may not pay very much attention to the day-to-day fluctuations in the dollar value of their holdings, but they do respond to changes in perceived risk and return. This new group holds enormous financial power that is neither organized in any formal way nor focused toward any particular goal except wealth maximization. Nevertheless, the group's massive accumulation of financial assets has increased to the point at which it is an economic force to be reckoned with, if for no other reason than the momentum it can generate by slight changes in the composition of its portfolios. These investors have already grown large enough for us to reconsider traditional economic power relationships, and this power is going to continue to increase over the decades to come.

- The costs of trading financial assets are dropping, and the number of people who have on-line securities trading accounts is growing.

- The holdings of central banks are not growing as fast as the aggregate amount of financial assets in the world. Consequently, they are already increasingly overmatched and becoming less able to defend national currencies from speculative attacks.

- The frequency of currency crises is increasing, and their relative magnitudes make national currencies less stable than they used to be. There do not need to be cabals of speculators conniving to sabotage national currencies for personal gain. Many national currencies are already unstable enough to fall into crisis without any provocation.

These new magnitudes and trends do not justify the conclusions that national currencies are always unwise, and the world should move toward a common currency. Many nations still derive net benefits from an independent currency, and at the time this book was written, there was neither a discernible rush to create supranational currencies other than the euro nor countries casting aside their national monetary units in favor of internationally recognized currencies, such as the dollar or the euro. Instead, the few cases in which dollarization (for example, Ecuador and El Salvador) and euroization (for example, East Timor) have occurred are associated with turmoil, armed conflict, or natural disaster. In most countries, the electorate is a long way from being convinced that the national currency should pass into history.

With regard to optimal currency zones, the question used to be whether a single country was too large—southern Italy or Appalachia were textbook examples of regions that might have benefited if they could have devalued vis-à-vis Northern Italy or the rest of the United States. Now the scope has grown: Can the euro zone profitably expand to cover Central Europe? Can Mercosur be saved by a supranational currency for Argentina, Brazil, Paraguay, and Uruguay?

The motivation for European convergence was to forestall a third world war, but at every juncture until currency unification, the gains were immediate and the sacrifices less painful than skeptics feared. The currency unification was painful, because the 12 countries held themselves to very strict criteria, to ensure that their new currency would be strong. The gains they obtained from being strict with each other, according to our calculation, outweighed the cost they imposed on themselves.

The path the United States took to currency unification (1787–1864) and the path Germany took (1814–1873) had many parallels. Each seemed to follow its own course, but they both responded to similar pressures and arrived at similar resolutions at very similar times. The deciding trade-off was the value of local sovereignty over the need for a medium of exchange that would hold its value over a larger geographic area and over longer periods of time. When trade was mostly local, distances were short, and settlement was rapid. Financial assets did not have enough aggregate value to hold much sway when set alongside the need to deal with the day-to-day vagaries that affected ordinary local commerce. Weather conditions, factory output, and food prices in local markets took precedence. When canals and railroads expanded the trading area and lengthened the time it took to settle transactions, the balance swung the other way, and local sovereignty had to defer to the needs of long-distance trade within the country.

The world financial economy may be reaching a similar watershed, and the balance may be swinging in favor of currency unification and supranational currencies. They are remedies for country risk. Instead of treating country risk as an inevitable cost that countries have to bear, we advocate trying to lower country risk in ways that have not been attempted very often. The scenarios that we compute show how much a country would gain from lowering country risk and indicate that the effort would be worthwhile even at a fraction of the gains we predict. Clearly, the benefits would accrue first to owners of financial assets—and perhaps a short-term political redistribution of this wealth should be considered—but at the same time, there would be spillover effects that would help to stimulate growth of consumption and employment.

So far there has been no systematic attempt to implement a currency regime with the objective of raising the market prices of existing assets. The objective has always been expressed in other terms, such as stimulating output, employment, and exports. Flow variables have been the target until now. The effect that a currency regime will have on the market prices of existing financial assets and, in general, on the value of the capital stock has always been mentioned only in passing or officially ignored. We propose and discuss the idea that when a nation is choosing a currency regime, it should consider the effect the regime will have on the value of the nation's capital stock.

We have shown that policies that change the value of nation's capital stock have reinforcing effects on flow variables, such as output, employment, and exports. We showed these effects in favorable cases, but the same computational techniques also illustrate that, if these policies actively or passively change wealth in an undesired manner, the consequences could cause the nation to fall short of its macroeconomic goals. Our calculations estimate how much the market prices of existing bonds and common stocks would rise if a new currency regime succeeded in lowering country risk. There was no need to prepare an estimate of how much financial wealth could be lost when country risk increases—there have been enough real examples recently.

Currency regimes used to be an arcane topic, off the main agenda of academic debate but always able to engage a few scholars in long-simmering controversies. Now, currency regimes are on the front pages and on evening news broadcasts. Rioters stormed the presidential palace in Ecuador, and in Argentina, crowds in the street vented their frustrations for weeks. Ordinary citizens everywhere have seen key truths about the monetary underpinnings of today's complex economies: Barter does not work as well as money, and money does not work when too many people doubt its value. The tight linkage between the monetary economy and the real economy has also been laid bare. In economist David Ricardo's time, it was valid to assume that prices and wages would fall when hard currency flowed out of a country. His self-correcting mechanism for trade surpluses and deficits is one of the pillars of classical economics. He described how "adjustment" happened in his day, when not as many people depended on stable monetary conditions and financial institutions. Nowadays, "adjustment" is much more wide ranging and can be much more protracted. Devaluation or a default might set off a full-blown financial crisis that would put millions of people out of work.

We have described a world financial system that has an alarming vulnerability to currency crises. We have shown how the currency unions can deliver wealth, consumption, and employment well in excess of what they have done until now. The magnitudes that we compute are very large and many may question whether improvements in monetary stability of the sort we describe can deliver such large increases in wealth and prosperity. The magnitudes may be controversial, but the main point is harder to assail. The remedy we propose will improve stability, forestall currency crises, and deliver new wealth and employment.

Bibliography

Alesina, Alberto, and Lawrence H. Summers. "Central Bank Independence and Macroeconomic Performance: Some Comparative Evidence." *Journal of Money, Credit, and Banking* 25, no. 2 (May 1993): 151–162.

Archive: Some Thoughts on the Prospects for Asian Economic Cooperation. Speeches of Governor Buenaventura, presented at the First International Conference on Asian Political Parties, Manila Hotel, September 19, 2000. Available: http://www.bsp.gov.ph/archive/Speeches_2000/SomeThoughts.htm.

Barrons. Various issues.

Baumol, William. "The Transaction Demand for Cash: An Inventory Theoretic Approach. "*Quarterly Journal of Economics* 66, (November 1952): 545–556.

Blaug, Mark, Walter Eltis, Denis O'Brien, Don Patinkin, Robert Skidelsky, and Geoffrey E. Wood. *The Quantity Theory of Money: From Locke to Keynes and Friedman.* Brookfield, Vt.: Edward Elgar, 1995.

Bloomberg News Service Dedicated Terminal.

Board of Governors of the Federal Reserve System. *Banking Studies.* Washington, D.C., 1941.

Bordo, Michael, and Lars Jonung, *Lessons for EMU from the History of Monetary Unions.* London: iea Publications, 2000.

Bureau of the Census. *Historical Statistics of the United States: Colonial Times to 1970.* New York: Basic Books, 1976.

Bureau of Labor Statistics, *Employment and Earnings: January.* Washington, D.C.: Bureau of Labor Statistics, 1983–2001.

———. *Handbook of Labor Statistics: Bulletin 2070.* Washington, D.C.: U.S. Bureau of Labor Statistics, December 1980.

Carlino, G.A., and R. DeFina. "The Differential Regional Effects of Monetary Policy." *Review of Economics and Statistics* 80, (Cambridge: Nov. 1998): 572–587.

Clifford, Stephanie, and Matthew Maier. "Who's Who in Risk Management: Where to Find the Leading Risk Experts." *Business 2.0* (January 2002): Available: http://www.business2.com/articles/mag/0,1640,35900,FF.html..

Datastream Data Service available through Bloomberg News Service Dedicated Terminal.

Delaume, Georges R. "Economic Development and Sovereign Immunity." *American Journal International Law* 79, no. 319 (April 1985): 339.

de Soto, Hernando. *The Mystery of Capital: Why Capitalism Triumphs in the West and Fails Elsewhere.* New York: Basic Books, 2000.

Directorate General of the European Commission. "What Are the Main Economic Benefits of the Euro for Participating Member States?" in *Euro Essentials Changing over to the Euro: The Final Phase, Questions and Answers Using Quest.* Available: http://europa.eu.int/euro/quest/normal/frame.htm?language_nb=5.

Eichengreen, Barry. "One Money for Europe? Lessons of the US Currency Union." *Economic Policy* 10 (April 1990): 118–166.

———, with Tamim Bayoumi. "Is Asia an Optimum Currency Area? Can It Become One? Regional, Global and Historical Perspectives on Asian Monetary Relations," CIDER Working Paper C96–081, December 1996. Available from the CIDER website. Revised version published in Collignon, Stefan, Jean Pisani-Ferry, and Yung Chul Park, eds., *Exchange Rate Policies in Emerging Asian Countries.* London: Routledge, 1999.

European Central Bank Website: http://www.economagic.com/em-cgi/data.exe/ecb/t3–02–05+2.

Federal Reserve Bank of Philadelphia. *Money in Colonial Times.* Available: http://www.phil.frb.org/education/colonial.html.

Feldstein, Martin. "The Political Economy of the European Economic and Monetary Union: Political Sources of an Economic Liability." *Journal of Economic Perspectives* 11, no. 4 (Fall 1997): 40.

Felt, Joseph B. *A Historical Account of Massachusetts Currency.* Boston: Perkins and Marvin, 1839.

Frankel, J.A., and A.K. Rose. "The Endogeneity of the Optimum Currency Area Criteria." *The Economic Journal* 108 (July 1998): 1009–1025.

Galbraith, John Kenneth. *Money: Whence It Came and Where It Went.* Boston: Houghton Mifflin, 1975.

Haxby, James. *Standard Catalog of Obsolete United States Bank Notes, 1782–1866.* Iola, WI: Krause Publications, 1983.

Heilbroner, Robert L. *The Worldly Philosophers: The Lives, Times, and Ideas of the Great Economic Thinkers.* New York: Touchstone, 1999.

Hickson, William F. *Triumph of the Bankers: Money and Banking in the Eighteenth and Nineteenth Centuries.* London: Praeger, 1993.

Holtfrerich, Carl-Ludwig. "The Monetary Unification Process in Nineteenth-Century Germany: Relevance and Lessons for Europe Today." In *A European Central Bank? Perspectives on monetary unification after ten years EMS,*" ed. M. De Cecco and A. Giovani, 216–241. Cambridge: Cambridge University Press, 1989.

———. "Did Monetary Unification Precede or Follow Political Unification of Germany in the 19th Century?" *European Economic Review* 37 (1993): 518–524.

infoplease.com. *History:* http://www.infoplease.com/ce6/world/A0860964.html; *Austro–Prussian War:* http://www.infoplease.com/ce6/history/A0805396.html; *Franco–Prussian War:* http://www.encyclopedia.com/articles/04695Resultsof-theWar.html.

Ingrassia, Lawrence. "Exchequered Past, One Dollar is Worth One Dollar, but That Wasn't Always So." *Wall Street Journal,* 13 January, 1998, p. A1.

International Court of Justice. *The Court at a Glance.* Available: http://www.icj-cij.org/icjwww/igeneralinformation/icjgnnot.html. Accessed October 29, 2001.

International Monetary Fund. *International Financial Statistics.*

Investment Company Institute. *The Mutual Fund Factbook.* Available: http://www.ici.org.

Kenen, Peter B. "The Theory of Optimum Currency Areas: An Eclectic View." In *Monetary Problems of the International Economy,* ed. Robert A. Mundell and Alexander K. Swoboda, 41–60. Chicago: University of Chicago Press, 1969.

Kindleberger, C.P. *A Financial History of Western Europe.* London: George Allen and Unwin, 1981.

Kirgis, Frederic L. "Alien Tort Claims Act Proceeding against Robert Mugabe." *American Society of International Law* (September 2000). Available: http://www.asil.org/insights/insigh50.htm#N_1_.

Kouparitsas, Michael A. "Is the EMU a Viable Common Currency Area?" *Economic Perspectives of the Federal Reserve Bank of Chicago* IQ4 (1999): 2–20.

———. "Is the United States an Optimal Currency Area?" *Chicago Fed Letter* 146 (October 1999): 1–3.

Legal Tender Cases (Knox v. Lee; Parker v. Davis), 12 Wallace 457 (1871).

Lerner, E.M. "Inflation in the Confederacy, 1861–65." In *Studies in the Quantity Theory of Money,* ed. M. Friedman, 164–175. Chicago: University of Chicago Press, 1956.

McCallum, B.T. "Money and Prices in Colonial America: A New Test of Competing Theories." *Journal of Political Economy* 100 (1992): 143–161.

Mélitz, Jacques, and Fédéric Zumer. "Regional Redistribution and Stabilization by the Center in Canada, France, the UK, and the US." Discussion Paper 1829. Centre for Economic Policy Research, December 1998.

Merrill Lynch, *Global Index System* reported on Bloomberg News Service Dedicated Terminal.

Merrill Lynch/Cap Gemini Ernst & Young, *World Wealth Report 2001.* Available at: http://www.ir.ml.com/news/ML051401.pdf.

Mundell, Robert A. "A Theory of Optimum Currency Areas." *American Economic Review* (September 1961): 657–665.

Neely, Christopher J. *An Introduction to Capital Controls, Review—Federal Reserve Bank of St. Louis* (November/December 1999). Nashville, Tenn.: Van Hedge Funds Advisors International, 2001. Available: http://www.hedgefund.com/universe.htm.

Protocol on the Excessive Deficit Procedural the High Contracting Parties. *Treaty on European Union*. Article 1. Available: http://europa.eu.int/en/record/mt/protocol.html.

Sala-I-Martin, Xavier, and Jeffrey Sachs. "Fiscal Federalism and Optimum Currency Areas: Evidence for Europe and the United States. In *Establishing a Central Bank: Issues in Europe and Lessons from the United States*, ed. Matthew Canzoneri, Vittorio Grilli, and Paul Masson, 195–220. Cambridge: Cambridge University Press, 1992.

Schuler, Kurt, and Lawrence H. White. "Free Banking: History." In *The New Palgrave Dictionary of Money and Finance*, ed. Peter Newman, Murray Milgate, and John Eatwell, 198–199. London: Macmillan, 1992.

Singer, Brian D., and Kevin Terhaar. *Economic Foundations of Capital Market Returns*. Charlottesville, VA: AIMR Publications The Research Foundation of the institute of Chartered Financial Analysts, 1997.

Standard and Poor's Emerging Markets Data Base, 1995 Factbook. New York: Standard and Poor vs. Poors, 1996.

Sveriges Riksbank. *Sveriges Riksbank–The Swedish Central Bank*. Available: http://www.riksbank.com/upload/4990/riksbankeneng.pdf. Accessed April 19, 2001.

Symons, Edward L. Jr., and James J. White. *Banking Law*. 2nd ed. St Paul: West Wadsworth, 1984.

Treaty on European Union. Website: http://europa.eu.int/en/record/mt/protocol.html.

Van Hedge Funds Advisors International. Website: http://www.hedgefund.com/universe.

von Hayek, Friedrich A. *Denationalisation of Money: An Analysis of the Theory and Practice of Concurrent Currencies*. London: Institute of Economic Affairs, 1976.

von Waltershausen, Sartorius August. *Deutsche Wirtschaftsgeschichte 1815–1914*. Jena Stuttgart New York: G Fischer Verlag, 1923.

Waller, Steven A. *International Economics Links*. Available: http://www.flash.net/~stevew9/international.htm

World Bank. *World Development Report: 2000/2001, Attacking Poverty*. Washington, D.C.: International Bank for Reconstruction and Development and Oxford University Press, 2001.

———. *World Bank 2001 World Development Indicators*. Washington, D.C.: International Bank for Reconstruction and Development, 2002.

"World Stock Markets." *Standard and Poor's Emerging Stock Market Factbook, 2001*. New York: McGraw-Hill, 2001.

World Trade Organization. *International Trade Statistics 2001*. Available: http://www.wto.org/english/res_e/statis_e/its2001_e/stats2001_e.pdf.

Appendices

Appendix 1
Market Capitalization by Country and Region: 1988 & 1997

Region	Country	1988	Per Cent	1997	Per Cent
	Canada	951,092		1,099,320	
	United States	2,796,000		11,410,060	
North America		**3,747,092**	**34.60%**	**12,509,380**	**49.98%**
	Argentina	2,032		59,252	
	Bolivia	-		344	
	Brazil	62,060		508,200	
	Chile	6,969		72,046	
	Colombia	1,145		19,529	
	Costa Rica	-		820	
	Ecuador	-		2,146	
	El Salvador	-		499	
	Guatemala	-		139	
	Mexico	13,784		156,595	
	Panama	-		2,175	
	Paraguay	-		389	
	Peru	-		17,586	
	Uruguay	-		212	
	Venezuela	1,816		14,581	
Central/South America		**87,806**	**0.81%**	**854,513**	**3.41%**

	Country	1988	Per Cent	1997	Per Cent
	Barbados	-		1,141	
	Bermuda	-		47,870	
	Cayman Islands	-		44	
	Dominican Republic	-		140	
	Jamaica	796		2,206	
	Trinidad & Tobago	268		3,117	
Caribbean Islands		**1,064**		**54,518**	
Central/South America & Caribbean Islands		**88,870**	**0.82%**	**909,031**	**3.63%**
	Austria	8,862		35,724	
	Belgium	58,790		136,965	
	Denmark	30,178		93,766	
	Finland	30,615		73,322	
	France	244,833		678,960	
	Germany	251,777		825,233	
	Greece	4,299		36,100	
	Iceland	-		-	
	Ireland	9,288		25,900	
	Italy	135,763		344,665	
	Luxembourg	133,588		33,892	
	Netherlands	113,565		525,900	
	Norway	15,756		75,540	
	Portugal	7,172		38,954	

Region	Country	1988	Per Cent	1997	Per Cent
	Spain	91,118		574,340	
	Sweden	100,083		272,730	
	Switzerland	264,765		575,338	
	United Kingdom	771,206		2,073,680	
Western Europe		**2,271,658**	**20.98%**	**6,421,009**	**25.65%**
	Bulgaria	-		2	
	Croatia	-		4,246	
	Cyprus	-		2,011	
	Czech Republic	-		12,786	
	Estonia	-		1,008	
	Hungary	-		14,975	
	Latvia	-		337	
	Lithuania	-		2,550	
	Poland	-		13,340	
	Romania	-		2,137	
	Russia	-		128,207	
	Slovakia	-		1,826	
	Slovenia	-		2,400	
	Ukraine	-		3,667	
Central/Eastern Europe		**-**	**0.00%**	**189,492**	**0.76%**

Region	Country	1988	Per Cent	1997	Per Cent
	Armenia	-		16	
	Iran	-		15,123	
	Israel	5,458		46,350	
	Jordan	2,233		5,446	
	Kuwait	11,836		25,888	
	Lebanon	-		2,904	
	Oman	-		8,730	
	Palestine	-		662	
	Saudi Arabia	-		59,386	
	Turkey	1,668		61,090	
Middle East		**21,195**	**0.20%**	**225,595**	**0.90%**
	Australia	228,395		696,656	
	Bangladesh	430		1,522	
	China	-		206,366	
	Fiji	-		93	
	Hong Kong	74,407		413,323	
	India	23,845		139,420	
	Indonesia	253		29,105	
	Japan	3,906,680	36.07%	2,216,699	8.86%
	Malaysia	36,571		93,608	
	Mongolia	-		54	
	Nepal	-		200	
	New Zealand	14,529		90,483	
	Pakistan	2,460		10,966	
	Philippines	4,280		31,361	
	Singapore	53,392		196,290	

Region	Country	1988	Per Cent	1997	Per Cent
	South Korea	95,279		41,881	
	Sri Lanka	471		2,096	
	Taiwan	120,017		287,813	
	Thailand	8,811		23,538	
	Uzbekistan	-		465	
Asia w/o Japan		663,140	6.12%	2,265,240	9.05%
Asia		**4,569,820**	**42.20%**	**4,481,939**	**17.91%**
	Botswana	-		12,697	
	Egypt	1,760		20,830	
	Ghana	-		1,130	
	Ivory Coast	437		1,228	
	Kenya	474		1,811	
	Mauritius	-		1,663	
	Morocco	446		12,177	
	Namibia	-		689	
	Nigeria	960		3,646	
	South Africa	126,094		232,069	
	Swaziland	-		129	
	Tunisia	612		2,312	
	Zambia	-		705	
	Zimbabwe	774		1,969	
Africa		**131,557**	**1.21%**	**293,055**	**1.17%**
World		**10,830,192**	**1.0**	**25,029,501**	**1.0**

Sources:

• *Emerging Stock Markets Factbook 1998*, International Finance Corporation, Washington DC, May 1998, ISBN 0-8213-4200-2

• *The GT Guide to World Equity Markets 1989*, Euromoney Publications PLC and GT Management PLC, Euromoney Publications Plc, London, 1989, ISBN 1 870031 97 0

• *The Salomon Smith Barney Guide to World Equity Markets 1998*

International Federation of Stock Exchanges

Appendix 2
Market Capitalization of Leading International Stock Markets

1988–1997–Projected 2001

Region	1997 (actual)			2001 (forecast)		
	Market Capitalization	%	Growth 1988-97	Market Capitalization	%	Growth 1997-01
North America	12,509,380	50.0%	4.1%	14,730,750	51.8%	4.1%
Central/South America & Caribbean	909,031	3.6%	16.5%	1,760,731	6.2%	16.5%
Europe	6,610,501	26.4%	2.6%	7,323,393	25.8%	2.6%
Middle East	225,595	0.9%	17.0%	444,755	1.6%	17.0%
Japan	2,216,699	8.9%	-15.6%	1,187,497	4.2%	-15.6%
Asia without Japan	2,265,240	9.1%	4.3%	2,694,842	9.5%	4.3%
Africa	293,055	1.2%	-0.4%	288,301	1.0%	-0.4%
World	**25,029,501**	**100%**		**28,430,269**	**100%**	
Index	**231**			**263**		

Sources:
- *Emerging Stock Markets Factbook 1998*
- *The GT Guide to World Equity Markets 1989.*
- *The Salomon Smith Barney Guide to World Equity Markets 1998*
- *International Federation of Stock Exchanges*

Appendix 3 Backup Table

Market Capitalization of Leading International Markets

1988–1997–Projected 2001

Region	1988 (actual)			1997 (actual)			2001 (forecast Dec)		
	Market Cap	%	Market Cap	%	Growth	Market Cap	%	Growth	
North America	3,747,092	34.6%	12,509,380	50.0%	4.1%	14,730,750	51.8%	4.1%
Central/South America & Caribbean	88,870	0.8%	909,031	3.6%	16.5%	1,760,731	6.2%	16.5%
Europe	2,271,658	21.0%	6,610,501	26.4%	2.6%	7,323,393	25.8%	2.6%
Middle East	21,195	0.2%	225,595	0.9%	17.0%	444,755	1.6%	17.0%
Japan	3,906,680	36.1%	2,216,699	8.9%	-15.6%	1,187,497	4.2%	-15.6%
Asia without Japan	663,140	6.1%	2,265,240	9.1%	4.3%	2,694,842	9.5%	4.3%
Africa	131,557	1.2%	293,055	1.2%	-0.4%	288,301	1.0%	-0.4%
World	10,830,192	100%	25,029,501	100%		28,430,269	100%	
Index	100		231			263		

Sources:

• *Emerging Stock Markets Factbook 1998*, International Finance Corporation, Washington, DC, May 1998, ISBN 0-8213-4200-2

• *The GT Guide to World Equity Markets 1989*, Euromoney Publications PLC and GT Management PLC, Euromoney Publications Plc, London, 1989, ISBN 1 870031 97 0

• *The Salomon Smith Barney Guide to World Equity Markets 1998*

• *International Federation of Stock Exchanges*

Index

About the Authors

JOHN C. EDMUNDS is Director of the Stephen D. Cutler Investment Management Center at Babson College. He is also on the faculty of the Arthur D. Little School of Management in Chestnut Hill, Massachusetts. He was chairman of the finance faculty at Babson College from 1998 to 2000. Prior to 1993, he was Professor of Capital Markets at Instituto de Empresa in Madrid, where he was the first holder of a chair funded by Asesores Bursatiles, a leading Spanish securities firm. He has lived in six countries and spent 18 years abroad. He is fluent in Spanish and also speaks French. The author of *The Wealthy World* (2001), he is interested in capital markets, international finance, derivatives, and emerging markets.

JOHN E. MARTHINSEN is the Distinguished Chair in Swiss Economics of the Glavin Center for Global Entrepreneurial Leadership at Babson College. His main areas of interest are international finance, global macroeconomic analysis, and risk management. The winner of numerous distinguished teaching awards, he also served as Chairman of the Economics Division from 1992 to 1998. He has lived and worked extensively in Switzerland, and he has a wide range of consulting experience working for both domestic and international corporations, as well as in the public sector. He is the co-author of *Switzerland: A Guide to the Capital and Money Markets* (1996) and *Entrepreneurship, Productivity, and the Freedom of Information Act* (1984).